YOUR GARDEN WEEK BY WEEK

By the Same Author

PRACTICAL GARDENING
FOR AMATEURS.

YOUR NEW GARDEN.

SIMPLE ROSE
GROWING.

52 WEEK END JOBS
IN THE GARDEN.

"AMATEUR GARDENING"
POCKET GUIDE.

LONDON
W. H. & L. Collingridge, Ltd.
2-10 Tavistock Street, Covent Garden, W.C. 2

The entry to a
well-ordered garden.

YOUR GARDEN WEEK BY WEEK

by

A. G. L. HELLYER

ILLUSTRATED

LONDON
W. H. & L. COLLINGRIDGE, LTD.
2-10 TAVISTOCK ST., COVENT GARDEN, W.C. 2

Printed in Great Britain by
Billing and Sons Ltd., Guildford and Esher

FOREWORD

THE author of this book strides boldly and bravely into a field which many have endeavoured to cover but frequently with scant measure of satisfaction and sound benefit. The pursuit of horticulture fits uncomfortably into timetables and calendars. There is always so much in the variations of season and of locality or situation to upset one's programme that he who gardens entirely by the book will seldom escape more failures and disappointments than successes. Nevertheless, the novice who knows not when to sow and when to prune, when to plant and when to uplift must have something to guide him. Provided he will realise that the book is a guide and indicator and not an inflexible series of orders which must be obeyed literally by rule of calendar or clock but may, and should be treated with elasticity according to locality or seasonal variations and circumstances, he may be assured that he has in this volume sound teaching based upon practical experience of gardening in various parts of Britain.

The plan of the book is designed for ease and simplicity of reference and its whole make-up reveals a clear insight into the requirements of the novice gardener. Men who have had many years of experience may wonder why some extremely simple matters are dealt with so carefully, but from January to December the author had in mind those seekers after knowledge who, knowing not, need instructions in the elementary phases of gardening as well as the more intricate problems of advanced horticulture.

With the aid of the Index, in addition to the chronological sequence adopted throughout the whole scheme of the book, it will be the easiest of tasks to find whatever is wanted on any day in the year.

A. J. MACSELF.

CONTENTS

LIST OF PLATES

vii

LIST OF PLATES

viii

LIST OF ILLUSTRATIONS IN TEXT

LIST OF ILLUSTRATIONS IN TEXT

INTRODUCTORY

IN this book I have set out to provide something more than a mere calendar of operations. Week by week I have tried to show not only *what must be done* but also *the best way in which to do it*. The volume is intended primarily for beginners, and so I have not included stove plants and orchids, nor the more uncommon vegetables usually grown only by connoisseurs.

The plan of the book demands a few words of explanation. It is divided into twelve monthly sections each of which is further split into five sub-sections under the headings General Work, First Week, Second Week, Third Week, and Fourth Week. The first of these sub-sections contains all those tasks which cannot be referred to any particular week but must be spread more or less continuously throughout the month. In the other four sections the remaining work is more precisely allocated. The expert may feel that this is too arbitrary a scheme, contending that most garden tasks can be done over a longer period than I have indicated, but I would remind such that the book is intended for beginners and that these invariably desire precise guidance. As they gain in experience they will learn just what liberties they can take, but at first they will be more likely to get good results by following rather rigidly a definite calendar of operations than by trying to sort out a mass of vague information. The formalised scheme of four weeks per month will, I hope, simplify and not complicate the application of the information to each and every year. The odd days in the month must be tacked on at the end, or the beginning of the next as common-sense suggests.

The calendar is based mainly upon experience around London and may need a little adaptation for certain parts of the country. Differences, however, are likely to be most apparent in late winter and early spring and are of little account at other seasons. From February to April the extreme south-west may be anything from a fortnight to a month ahead, while very cold northern districts may be almost as much behind London and the Midlands, but, of course, these big differences are only applicable to outdoor work.

The lists of flowers, vegetables, and fruits in season are intended for reference when planning the garden in all its branches. They have been made as complete as possible and I make no apology for the strings of botanical names which they contain, for these provide the beginner with the only certain means of turning up further information and of explaining to the nurseryman exactly what he needs.

There are certain tasks which are " in season " from January to December, and to avoid monotony and save space I have not repeated them month by month. Here is a list of them.

DUTCH HOEING

This can be done whenever the surface of the soil is dry enough not to stick to the blade of the hoe. Its object is twofold: firstly to destroy weeds, and secondly to break up the surface soil and so prevent loss of water by evaporation. Always keep the blade of the hoe sharp, and work it backwards and forwards just beneath the surface so that weeds are severed from their roots, not pulled up and left lying on the surface to grow again.

WEED AND MOSS KILLING

Another method of killing weeds is by means of plant poisons, but it must be remembered that few of these are very selective in action, and so it is not safe to apply them to ground in which garden plants are growing. Sodium chlorate is one of the best and can be used in water in solutions varying from $\frac{1}{4}$ to 1 pound per gallon according to the " toughness " of the weeds that have to be killed. It is grand for watering on weedy paths and will kill nettles if sprayed on them a few times as they start to grow. Use a strength of $\frac{1}{2}$ pound per gallon for this. Solutions of sodium chlorate can also be used to clear vacant ground of weeds, so long as nothing is sown or planted until the chemical has been washed out again by rain. This may take anything from a fortnight to three months according to the rainfall and the nature of the ground. The effect of the poison will be lost more quickly in sand than in clay.

Several excellent proprietary preparations are made for killing moss on lawns, and these can be used at any season, so long as manufacturers' instructions regarding strength are not exceeded. Raking vigorously with a spring-toothed grass rake will remove a lot of the moss, but you must not overlook the possibility that the cause of the growth is poverty of soil or bad drainage—two conditions that must be rectified if you wish to effect a permanent cure.

DISBUDDING CARNATIONS

Perpetual-flowering carnations may be had in bloom at any time of the year and so may also need to be disbudded at any time. I have referred to this work in some detail in my notes for October, General Work, as that is the time at which young stock usually first requires disbudding. It should also be noted that this perpetual habit of flowering involves perpetual feeding while plants are forming buds. For this purpose it is best to use a carnation fertiliser prepared by a specialist.

GLASSHOUSE FUMIGATION

August is often a convenient time of the year at which to fumigate glasshouses, as during that month it is often possible to empty greenhouses completely and use fumigants that would hardly be safe if there were any plants about. But this must not be misinterpreted as implying that all fumigants are dangerous to vegetable growth. On the contrary, nicotine can be used safely at any time of the year and, indeed, is really only effective if the houses are stocked, as the pests which it kills are on the plants and would be carried out and in again on them. Naphthalene fumigation requires more care, while sulphur fumigation in stocked houses should only be attempted by the expert. Tetrachlorethane, sold for killing white fly, is harmless to tomatoes but harmful to chrysanthemums and some other plants. Manufacturers' instructions should always be followed.

LAWN MOWING AND ROLLING

There is a widespread but mistaken notion that the lawn mower and roller should be put away for the winter. Really good lawns cannot be produced in this way, for though it is true that winter mowing will be infrequent and that the roller must never be used on waterlogged soil, it is equally certain that complete neglect from October to April will result in coarse grasses ousting those of a finer nature. I have referred to this in the notes for April, General Work.

13

JANUARY

GENERAL

Dig All Available Ground

WHEN the ground is frozen so hard that it cannot be dug is the ideal time for wheeling out manure and placing it about in handy heaps for spreading and digging in as soon as conditions improve. It is not wise to dig soil immediately after a thaw nor during or immediately after a heavy fall of snow, for it is then too wet on the surface to break up properly. The clods will lie in the bottom of the trenches and gradually harden into brickbats, especially if the ground is of a clayey nature. But whenever the soil is soft enough to be dug, and yet not so wet that it sticks to the spade badly, digging can proceed—and it is an axiom of gardening that the early digger gets the crops.

Prick Over Bulb Beds

During the month tulips, daffodils, and hyacinths will appear through the soil. As soon as the green sprouts can be seen clearly, go over the beds carefully with a small border fork, pricking up the soil between the bulbs, but only to a depth of about an inch. This will improve aeration and kill moss, green, scummy growth, and weeds. At the same time give the soil a dusting of some good and properly blended chemical fertiliser. If you wish to make your own mixture, do so with seven parts superphosphate of lime, five parts sulphate of ammonia, two parts either sulphate or muriate of potash, and one part steamed bone-flour (all parts by weight). Use this at 4 ounces per square yard. Of course, you must choose a fine day for this work and one when the soil is neither very wet nor frozen.

Take Crysanthemum and Carnation Cuttings

A task which can be carried on as opportunity permits throughout January is that of taking late-flowering chrysanthemum cuttings. It is rather early yet to start on the outdoor flowering chrysanthemums, though even with these I would not hesitate to have a few cuttings of such a variety as old Roi des Blancs if there are any good ones showing, because this is notoriously shy in producing cuttings. Later on, when the proper time arrives, there may be no suitable shoots to be had—and a cutting in the pot is certainly worth a pair in the bush.

Nevertheless in the main it is the late-flowering kinds that are to be propagated in January and particularly the incurves and exhibition Japanese kinds. Full particulars are given in the notes for December, Third Week.

You should also propagate perpetual-flowering carnations as opportunity occurs. This task I have described in detail in the General Work notes for December.

Pot Rooted Carnation and Chrysanthemum Cuttings

During the month keep a careful watch on carnation cuttings taken during December, and if these are in pure sand get them potted up singly in 2-inch pots as soon as they are well rooted (which means that roots $\frac{1}{2}$ inch long have been formed). It is quite easy to tell when a cutting is rooted, because it will start to grow at once. Until then it will remain quite at a standstill. There is not the same urgency with carnation cuttings that are in soil and sand, nor with chrysanthemum cuttings, which are almost always rooted in soil and sand, but even with these it is a good plan to get them singly into pots before the roots get tangled together. Use 3-inch pots for the chrysanthemums, for these grow more rapidly. Propagating boxes must be ventilated freely as soon as cuttings commence to grow. Use a compost of three parts fibrous, rather heavy loam and one part equal proportions of wood ashes, old soot, mortar rubble, and sand for potting the carnations. The chrysanthemums will do well in a mixture of four parts medium loam, coarsely sifted, one part moss peat or leaf-mould, and two parts sharp sand with a sprinkling of fine bonemeal and ground chalk. Shade the plants from direct sunlight for a few days and then commence to harden them off by placing on a shelf near the glass and ventilating more freely.

General Greenhouse Management

The well-managed greenhouse should be full of plants during January, many of them in flower and all wanting careful watering. Greenhouse calceolarias are particularly susceptible to bad watering and may collapse quite suddenly if given too much; yet dryness is equally bad. Chinese primulas are apt to suffer severely if water is allowed to collect at the base of the leaves and in the heart of the plant. Do not forget the golden rule of all watering—namely, that when water is given it must be supplied in sufficient quantity to moisten the soil in pot or box right through. There is nothing worse than keeping the surface wet and letting the lower soil remain dry.

A POT OF CHRYSANTHEMUM CUTTINGS.

The leaves are still flagging—an indication that the cuttings are not yet rooted. As soon as growth recommences the cuttings should be potted individually.

Ventilation is also bound to be a tricky matter, especially in a small house or one that is not too well heated. The ideal is a constant circulation of air without draughts or sudden variations of temperature. Only the top ventilators will be needed during January, and even these must be closed at night. Open them a little during the day providing it is not freezing or foggy, but, if there is any choice in the matter, be sure to open them on the side away from the wind —and be equally sure to get them closed well before the sun goes down, for a little sun heat trapped late in the afternoon will go a long way towards keeping up the night temperature. Watch carefully for decaying leaves—a sure sign of a stuffy atmosphere (see November, General Work).

The ideal average temperature to be aimed at for the common winter-flowering plants such as primulas, cinerarias, calceolarias, and cyclamen is 55 to 60 degs. by day and 45 to 50 degs. at night. If winter-flowering begonias are grown, it will be all to the good

1. Pulling off a perpetual flowering carnation shoot from which a cutting will be prepared. 2. Inserting the carnation cutting after correct trimming. 3. Imported lily bulbs placed in damp fibre to plump up before being planted or potted. Sulphur is being dusted over them as a precaution against disease. 4. A stem-rooted lily correctly placed in its pot.

1. Removing a sucker shoot from an old chrysanthemum root. The shoot will make an ideal cutting. 2. Chrysanthemum cuttings rooting under cloches placed on the greenhouse staging. 3. Securing roots from which to prepare root cuttings (4). The plant is Morisia hypogæa. 5. Hippeastrums ready to be started into growth in the greenhouse. 6. Transferring hyacinths from the plunge bed to the greenhouse.

to have 5 or 10 degs. more, but most plants are able to stand quite a wide variation in temperature. A good deal of nonsense is talked upon this subject, and one is sometimes left with the impression that there are many plants which cannot be grown in anything but a thermostatically controlled atmosphere. A thermostat is certainly an immense help, but it is by no means a necessity. The great thing to avoid is any very sudden fluctuations, especially in the early morning or evening.

Bring Bulbs into the Greenhouse

Successive small batches of tulips, narcissi of all types, including trumpet daffodils, hyacinths, and Iris tingitana, should be brought into the greenhouse from plunge bed or frame to maintain a continuity of flowers later on (see November, First Week).

Force Seakale and Rhubarb

You should also bring in at least two batches of seakale and rhubarb to force in heat if you wish to maintain an unbroken succession. These, of course, are forced in complete darkness. (See November, Second Week.)

Pot and Plant Lilies

There is no doubt that early autumn is the best time to pot and plant most lilies, but it is sometimes impossible to get certain varieties then, especially if they have to be imported from the Far East. Such should be dealt with as soon as they are available, and this often adds quite appreciably to the extent of one's January tasks. In the case of bulbs that have travelled a long distance and have become rather soft or shrivelled, it is wise to plump them up before

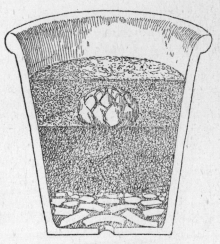

POTTING A LILY.

The pot is only partly filled with soil at first, room being left for top-dressings of soil and peat later on.

B

17

potting or planting them. This is done by placing them in seed trays, partly surrounding them with moist moss peat, and keeping this damp by daily syringing. As soon as the bulbs get plump and firm, plant or pot without further delay.

VENTILATE VIOLETS, ETC., IN FRAMES

Violets and other hardy or nearly hardy plants in frames, such as violas, pansies, anemones, pentstemons, bedding calceolarias, antirrhinums from late summer seeds and cuttings, sweet peas, cauliflowers, and bulbs, and alpines in pots, etc., must be ventilated just as freely as the weather permits. On all mild, sunny days remove the lights altogether for a few hours. If there is a cold wind blowing, tilt the lights with blocks of wood placed on the leeward side. At night the frames should be closed, and if the weather is very cold it is advisable to throw a few sacks over them into the bargain. An occasional stirring of the soil between the plants with a pointed stick does a lot of good.

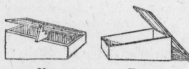

VENTILATION FOR FRAMES.

A block shaped like two or three steps (left) is useful for tilting the light on the side away from the wind. On fine, warm days the light can be slid off for a few hours.

TAKE ROOT CUTTINGS

Many plants can be raised more readily from root cuttings taken during January than in any other way. Well-known examples are Oriental poppies, perennial statices, anchusas, perennial verbascums, Romneya Coulteri, Phlox decussata, and gaillardias. The roots are cut up into pieces about 1 to 2 inches in length. In the case of all except the last three these cuttings are pushed vertically, right end up, into a sandy compost in well-drained pots. The tops of the cuttings should be just level with the soil. Romneya, phlox, and gaillardia cuttings are simply strewn thinly over the surface of the soil and covered with a further $\frac{1}{4}$ in. of compost. Place in a frame or greenhouse (slightly heated or unheated) and water moderately. Shoots will form slowly, and in late spring, after proper hardening off, the small plants can be established outdoors.

Protect Broccoli

The curds of broccoli will require protection as they commence to form. (See November, General Work.)

Sow Small Salads under Glass

Various small salads may be sown during the month in a slightly heated greenhouse or a frame placed on a hotbed. This latter is prepared by making a flat-topped mound of fresh horse manure or placing the manure in a wide, flat-bottomed hole. There should be at least 18 inches depth of manure well trodden down. This is covered with 5 or 6 inches of fine soil, and a frame is placed on top. When the first fierce heat of fermentation has died down, but the soil is nicely warm, seeds are sown in it and the lights are placed in position. Mustard and cress can be grown very readily in this manner or in shallow boxes in a warm greenhouse. Sow the mustard

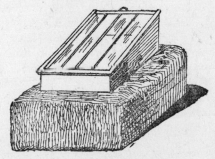

A Hotbed for Early Crops.

A frame is placed on a heap of fresh horse manure, which generates heat as it decomposes. An even better method is to dig a pit for the manure so that the frame is not perched up in such an exposed fashion.

every week and the cress about once a fortnight, as it lasts longer. A couple of small sowings of radishes and Tom Thumb lettuces made at fortnightly intervals under similar conditions in a frame or in deeper boxes or beds in the greenhouse will provide useful saladings later on.

Spray Fruit Trees with Tar Oil

When the weather is favourable spray all outdoor fruit trees and bushes with tar oil wash. The object of this is to kill any insect eggs which may be left in the crevices of the bark and to clean the trees of green, scummy growth, scale insects, etc. It is at this season of the year that really powerful insecticides can be used without fear of damaging the trees, and the gardener who neglects his opportunity must not be surprised if his trees in the summer are more freely attacked by pests and diseases than those of his more alert neighbour.

Tar oil washes are sold under many different trade names and can be purchased from any dealer in horticultural sundries. They are prepared by diluting with water, the usual strength being six parts of the neat tar oil to a hundred parts of water—*i.e.*, 6 gals. in 100 gals., 6 pints in 12½ gals. (100 pints), etc.—but instructions are always given on the tin, and you should consult these in case the purchased brand is not of standard strength.

The important thing in tar oil spraying is to employ a machine that will give a fine but driving spray capable of penetrating well down into the crevices of the bark. A powerful coarse spray is efficient but wasteful. It is also wasteful to attempt to spray trees when the weather is windy, and it is not effective to spray while it is freezing; so choose a calm and comparatively mild day for the work, and not one when it is raining, or the dilution will be upset.

COMPLETE FRUIT TREE PRUNING

Fruit tree pruning should really be done in November and December, but, if it is delayed then for one reason or another, it can be completed in January—but the sooner the better. Work on the peaches, nectarines, and apricots first, then do the plums, gooseberries, and currants, and leave the pears and apples till the last. Very soon sap will be on the move once more, and the wise gardener will always get his trees pruned while they are quite dormant.

COLLECT SCIONS FOR GRAFTING

This is a good time to collect suitable shoots for grafting if you intend to do any later on. Ordinary prunings do quite well. Select strong, well-ripened shoots formed the previous summer. Label them carefully and then heel them in in a trench about 4 inches deep prepared in a cool, shady place, preferably under a north wall or fence. The object is to keep them dormant until grafting-time (see March, Fourth Week). Old trees that are to be reworked should also be headed back now—*i.e.*, the main branches should be sawn off about a couple of feet from the trunk. Apples and pears stand this treatment best. Plums, cherries, and other stone fruits resent the hard cutting back.

Open Orchard House and Vinery

The orchard house and vinery should still be ventilated as freely as possible (see November, General Work), except in the case of early houses (see later). No heat must be used, and ventilators should be opened widely whenever it is not actually freezing hard. Light frost will do no harm, but rather good, preparing the trees for very rapid growth when the house is closed later on.

FIRST WEEK

Order Seeds and Seed Potatoes

The very first task for January should be to compile a complete list of all seeds that will be required during the following two or three months, and to get these ordered without delay. It is true that a good many of the seeds cannot be sown before March or even April, but later on seedsmen become inundated with orders and even with the best of organisations there may be delay in execution. There is no sense

A Sprouted "Set."
These sturdy sprouts can only be obtained by placing the seed potatoes in a light, dry, and frost-proof place.

Tray for Seed Potatoes.
This is a useful type of tray in which to set potatoes to sprout, as one tray can be stood on top of another, supported by the raised ends.

21

in risking that, because the seeds can be kept quite as well at home as in the seedsmen's store, and they will then be at hand the very moment that the most favourable opportunity arrives. Order seed potatoes at the same time, and as soon as they arrive set them up in shallow trays, eyed ends uppermost, and place them in a light but frostproof room, shed, or greenhouse to form sprouts. This is particularly important in the case of early varieties, but is worth doing with all kinds.

Bring Shrubs and Roses in Pots into Greenhouse

The first week in January is a good time to bring into the greenhouse the first batch of bush roses well established in pots. Give them a light, airy place, preferably on the staging, not too far from the glass. Water the soil moderately and syringe with slightly warm water every morning. Maintain a temperature of about 55 to 60 degs. All the roses must be pruned, previous year's growth being shortened to within an inch or so of the older wood. It is also a good plan to bring in a few deutzias, Indian azaleas, lilacs, viburnums, etc., to provide a succession to earlier batches (see November, First Week). A start may also be made with hydrangeas and astilbes, both of which require rather liberal watering once they have started into growth.

Prune Climbers in the Greenhouse

Several of the permanent climbers commonly grown in greenhouses should be pruned now. These include Plumbago capensis and the passion flower. The plumbago is pruned by cutting each of last year's growths back to 9 inches or thereabouts. This applies to fully developed specimens. In the case of young plants which have not yet filled their space, some shoots may be left unpruned. The passion flower is pruned by cutting out weak shoots altogether and reducing the remainder of the previous year's growths to about two buds each.

Sow Onions for Exhibition

If you aspire to great successes on the vegetable show bench later in the year, you must make a sowing of exhibition onions in a heated greenhouse. It is no use to sow onion seed as yet outdoors or in an unheated frame. But if sown thinly in loamy soil with plenty of sand and a little peat moss in well-drained seed trays and placed in a greenhouse with an average temperature of 55 to 60 degs., the seed will soon germinate and provide sturdy seedlings for transferring to the open ground in the spring. The best method is to sow the seeds singly 1 inch apart; then the seedlings need not be pricked off.

Sow Shorthorn Carrots on a Hotbed

If a hotbed is available, you can make a first sowing of shorthorn carrots. Sow these directly in the soil in the frame and not in boxes. The rows should be about 6 inches apart. If the seedlings are thinned to a couple of inches apart later on, there will be a nice supply of young roots in the early spring. An alternative method is to sow in a frame heated with hot-water pipes or special electrical soil-heating cables.

Start Early Peaches, Nectarines, and Apricots

With the aid of a heated orchard house it is possible to have ripe peaches, nectarines, and apricots at any time during the summer. If you wish to eat ripe fruits in June, this is the time to start the trees into growth. Close doors and ventilators and maintain an average temperature of 45 degs. at night, rising 5 or 10 degs. by day. Syringe the trees every morning with slightly warm water, and damp the floor of the house to maintain moisture in the atmosphere.

Start Early Vines into Growth

You may also start early vines such as Black Hamburg, Foster's Seedling, and Buckland's Sweetwater into growth, providing you have a heating apparatus installed in the vinery adequate to maintain a temperature of 55 degs. at night during February and March. Five degs. less than this, rising to 60 degs. by day, will do for the present, however. The higher temperature is only necessary when growth actually starts. Syringe the vines several times daily to keep the atmosphere moist, and give a little top ventilation by day whenever outside conditions permit this without lowering the temperature or causing cold draughts. Soak the border thoroughly with clear water and fill any evaporating trays over the pipes. Spread a 2-inch-thick layer of well-rotted stable manure all over the border to feed the roots.

Prune Late Vines

Late-fruiting vines such as Alicante and Gros Colmar should be pruned. Details of this are the same as for the pruning of early vines (see November, Fourth Week).

SECOND WEEK

Sow Exhibition Sweet Peas

This is the time for the exhibition grower to sow sweet peas in pots if this was not done in a frame in September. A warm greenhouse will be needed for germination, but a great amount of heat is not desirable; 50 to 55 degs. will be ample. Sow four or five seeds in each 3-inch pot. A fine compost for this purpose—and, indeed, for most seed sowing—is two parts medium loam, one part best moss peat, and one part sharp silver sand. To each bushel of this mixture should be added $\frac{3}{4}$ ounce of ground chalk and $1\frac{1}{2}$ ounces of superphosphate of lime. It is all to the good if the loam can be sterilised by steaming in a suitable apparatus. Several reliable soil sterilisers of moderate size are available which will enable you to do the work conveniently and well.

Start Begonia and Gloxinia Tubers

If you own a well-heated greenhouse, you may start tuberous-rooted begonias and gloxinias into growth. The begonias can be

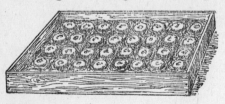

STARTING TUBEROUS-ROOTED BEGONIAS.
The tubers are set out in trays nearly filled with damp moss peat.

managed quite satisfactorily in a temperature of 55 degs., but a little more is advisable for the gloxinias. If the two have to be grown in the same house, the extra warmth will not do the begonias any harm. Prepare some rather deep seed trays with good drainage in the bottom and then a layer of moss peat. Set the tubers almost shoulder to shoulder in this and just cover them with more peat. Be careful to moisten the peat thoroughly some while before it is actually required. This is a tip that always applies when using moss peat. When it is quite dry it is very difficult to make it take up water, which runs off the granules instead of soaking into them, but once they have become moistened they go on soaking up water like a sponge. If the peat is well wetted a few days before the begonia and gloxinia tubers are to be boxed, no further watering will be needed at first, but do not let it dry out. Keep it just nicely moist until growth appears, and then give rather more water.

Sow Tomatoes for an Early Crop

Sow tomatoes now if you want a crop in June, but do not forget that this means plants 3 or 4 feet high by the beginning of May. They will take some accommodation, and the June crop may not be worth it if it means ruining your bedding plants. If you sow now, do so very thinly in well-drained seed boxes, using the compost referred to on page 24. Germinate in a temperature of 55 degs. or rather more. Tomatoes love warmth, and will get hard and blue in the cold, obstinately refusing to grow and becoming more miserable every week. Germination will be more rapid if each box is covered with a sheet of glass and brown paper. Keep the soil well moistened, but not sodden.

THIRD WEEK

Sow Begonias, Gloxinias, etc.

Sowings to be made now in the warm greenhouse are begonias, gloxinias, streptocarpus, cannas, verbenas, antirrhinums, and scarlet salvias. With the exception of cannas, all can be managed in an average temperature of 65 degs. The antirrhinums will even do with rather less, but for preference the gloxinias should have a little more, for they will then germinate more rapidly and grow more sturdily. Cannas need 75 degs., and even then germinate very irregularly. Do not forget that plants from these early sowings will be quite big by May, the time when many plants accommodated in the greenhouse during the winter can be put

25

out in the open once more. If your greenhouse is already rather full and you plan to sow half-hardy annuals later on (see February, Third Week) and take a lot of cuttings, it may be wise to omit these first sowings and be satisfied with smaller plants. But if space is not pinched there can be no gainsaying the advantage of an early start. It will be reflected in the abundance and quality of the flowers.

PLANT POTATOES IN FRAMES AND POTS

Potatoes in frames and pots are not difficult to grow, but they do take up a good deal of valuable space. However, if you want them, this is the time to start with one well-sprouted tuber in each 8-inch pot, or, if in a frame on a hotbed, tubers 9 inches apart in rows 1 foot apart. The layer of soil in the hotbed will need to be a good deal deeper than for seedlings—at least a foot instead of the 4 or 5 inches mentioned earlier (see Small Salads, General Work). A compost of equal parts turfy loam and sweet beech

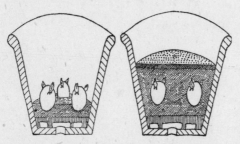

GROWING POTATOES IN POTS.

The potatoes are set low in the pot, and this is only half filled with soil at first. Later, as the haulm grows, more rich soil is added. The artist has shown three tubers in a 12-inch pot, but it is usually better to plant one in each 8-inch pot.

leaf-mould is ideal, with a sprinkling of any good potato fertiliser, but not more than 4 ounces per bushel.

MULCH ASPARAGUS BEDS

If possible, get some well-rotted manure (farmyard manure is best for the purpose, though stable manure will serve), break it up well, and spread it a couple of inches thick over the asparagus beds. This will have a marked effect upon the quality of the shoots later on, and the only condition under which this is inadvisable occurs when the soil is of a very heavy and cold nature and is already inclined to be waterlogged. Then a light dressing of hop manure will be more suitable.

Protect Fruit Trees from Birds

From now onwards birds are very liable to attack the buds of fruit trees, particularly plums and gooseberries. The best protection for small bush fruits is obviously a properly constructed fruit cage covering the whole plantation. Plum trees can be protected by passing black thread from twig to twig, but it is a laborious and troublesome proceeding. An easy and reasonably efficacious measure is to spray with a strong quassia wash. This makes the buds so bitter that the birds usually leave them alone.

FOURTH WEEK

Start Early Hippeastrums

You can start a first batch of hippeastrums by bringing the bulbs in the pots in which they flowered the previous year into a temperature of 60 degs. or thereabouts and giving them a gradually increasing quantity of water. If any of the bulbs that have been resting since October (see October, General Work) show any signs of starting, select these first in preference to those that are still quite dormant.

Pot on Greenhouse Calceolarias

It is time to give greenhouse calceolarias their final shift into the pots in which they will flower. These should be 7 or 8 inches in diameter. Use the compost referred to on page 43. Stand the plants in a light, airy place on the staging, water very carefully, and maintain an average temperature of 55 degs.

Force Rhubarb and Seakale Out of Doors

This is a good time to commence forcing rhubarb outdoors. There is not much point in starting earlier, as it will be well-nigh impossible to generate sufficient heat to start any growth. The essentials for successful forcing are complete darkness and a mild, even temperature. First of all, the roots must be covered with something : either special earthenware forcing pots, which are not unlike chimney pots with a lid on the top, or with old barrels or large boxes. Whatever you use, make some arrangement for having a removable lid on top so that the sticks of rhubarb can be gathered without having to move the whole contraption. Place the boxes, barrels, or pots in position and heap up dead leaves around them, the more the better so long as they are not completely covered. The leaves will keep the rhubarb crowns at a nice even temperature and encourage steady and early growth. Never attempt to force newly planted or semi-established crowns. Only really strong roots should be covered, preferably those three or four years old.

Seakale can also be forced outdoors where it is growing

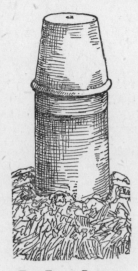

FOR EARLY RHUBARB.

Each strong root is covered with a large drainpipe, chimney pot, barrel or box, a lid of some kind is placed on top to keep out light, and strawy manure or leaves are heaped around to generate warmth.

FORCING SEAKALE.

The process is much the same as with rhubarb, but a much smaller covering is required. A large inverted flower pot is ideal.

by covering each strong crown with a large flower pot inverted and placing a piece of turf to block up the drainage hole in the bottom of the pot. Complete darkness is essential.

SOW LEEKS

This is a good time to make a first sowing of leeks if large stems are required. Sow the seeds singly 1 inch apart in well-drained seed boxes, using an ordinary compost (see p. 24). Germinate in a greenhouse or frame with an average temperature of 55 degs.

Sow French Beans for Forcing

You can obtain a May crop of French beans by sowing now—
five or six in each 8-inch pot filled to within a couple of inches
with good loamy soil with which a little sand and leaf-mould has
been mixed. Cover with a further inch of soil, water freely, and
place in the greenhouse in a temperature of 60 to 70 degs

FLOWERS, VEGETABLES, AND FRUITS IN SEASON DURING JANUARY

Hardy Herbaceous Plants.—Adonis *amurensis*, Helleborus *antiquorum*,
H. *colchicus*, H. *corsicus*, H. *fœtidus*, H. *niger*, H. *orientalis vars.*, Iris
unguicularis, Petasites *fragrans*, Pulmonaria *angustifolia azurea*, P. *rubra*,
P. *saccharata*, Saxifraga *ligulata*, S. *ciliata*.

Hardy Bulbs and Tubers.—Brodiæa *Leichtlini*, Bulbocodium *vernum*,
Colchicum *Decaisnei*, C. *hydrophyllum*, C. *libanoticum*, Crocus *alatavicus*,
C. *Billotti*, C. *Boryi*, C. *caspius*, C. *hyemalis*, C. *Imperati*, C. *Korolkowii*,
C. *Tommasinianus*, Cyclamen *coum*, Eranthis *hyemalis*, Galanthus *cilicicus*,
G. *plicatus*, Iris *Histrio*, I. *histrioides*, I. *reticulata and vars.*, Leucojum
vernum carpaticum, Sternbergia *lutea angustifolia*.

Rock Plants.—Polygala *Chamæbuxus*, Primula *juliana vars.*, P. *mega-
seæfolia*, P. *Winteri*, Saxifraga *Kellereri*.

Evergreen Shrubs.—Azara *integrifolia* (*shelter*), Berberis *japonica
hyemalis*, Daphne *Laureola*, D. *odora*, Erica *carnea and vars.*, E. *darleyensis*,
E. *lusitanica*, Garrya *elliptica*, Lonicera *fragrantissima*, Viburnum *Tinus
and vars.*

Deciduous Shrubs.—Chimonanthus *fragrans*, Corylus *Avellana and vars.*,
Daphne *Mezereum grandiflora*, Hamamelis *japonica*, H. *mollis*, H. *vernalis*,
Lonicera *Standishii*, Nuttalia *cerasiformis*, Rhododendron *mucronulatum*,
Viburnum *fragrans*.

Deciduous Trees.—Cratægus *monogyna præcox*, Prunus *Davidiana*, P.
subhirtella autumnalis.

Hardy Climbing Plants.—Clematis *calycina*, C. *cirrhosa*, Jasminum
nudiflorum.

Greenhouse Plants.—Arum lilies, azaleas (*Indian, in variety*), Begonia
fuchsioides, B. *manicata*, B. *socotrana*, hybrid begonias of the Optima and
Gloire de Lorraine types, Boronia *heterophylla*, B. *megastigma*, bouvardias,
Browallia *speciosa major*, camellias, carnations (*perpetual-flowering*),
cinerarias (*hybrids*), Coleus *thyrsoideus*, cyclamens (*Persian*), Daphne *indica*,
Erica *gracilis*, E. *melanthera*, epacris, Euphorbia *fulgens*, freesias, gardenias,
hyacinths (*Roman and large-flowered*), Iris *tingitana*, I. *reticulata*, Jasminum
primulinum, lachenalias, narcissi (*Paper White, Soleil d'Or, Christmas
Cheer, etc.*), poinsettias, Primula *kewensis*, P. *malacoides*, P. *obconica*, P.
sinensis and vars., Sparmannia *africana*, tulips (*Duc van Tholl*).

29

YOUR GARDEN WEEK BY WEEK

PLANTS IN FRAMES.—Anemone *coronaria vars.* (*St. Brigid and du Caen anemones*), Helleborus *niger vars.* (*Christmas roses*), violets (*double and single*).

VEGETABLES IN STORE.—Jerusalem artichokes, beetroots, carrots, onions, parsnips, potatoes, turnips, shallots.

VEGETABLES IN GARDEN.—Jerusalem artichokes, broccoli (maincrop), broccoli (sprouting), Brussels sprouts, celery, coleworts, endive, kales, leeks, lettuces, parsnips, savoys, spinach (sown August), turnips.

VEGETABLES UNDER GLASS.—Endive, lettuce, mushrooms, mustard and cress, radishes, rhubarb, seakale.

FRUITS IN STORE.—Apples : *Adams' Pearmain* (*D*), *Annie Elizabeth* (*C*), *Baumann's Red Winter Reinette* (*CD*), *Barnack Beauty* (*CD*), *Beauty of Kent* (*C*), *Beauty of Stoke* (*CD*), *Belle de Boskoop* (*CD*), *Bismarck* (*C*), *Blenheim Orange* (*D*), *Bramley's Seedling* (*C*), *Brownlees' Russet* (*D*), *Christmas Pearmain* (*D*), *Claygate Pearmain* (*D*), *Cornish Gillyflower* (*D*), *Court Pendu Plat* (*D*), *Cox's Orange Pippin* (*D*), *Cutler Grieve* (*D*), *Edward VII.* (*C*), *Gascoyne's Scarlet* (*D*), *Houblon* (*D*), *Imperial* (*D*), *John Standish* (*D*), *King of Tompkin's County* (*D*), *King's Acre Pippin* (*D*), *Lane's Prince Albert* (*C*), *Laxton's Pearmain* (*D*), *Lord Hindlip* (*D*), *Madresfield Court* (*D*), *Margil* (*D*), *May Queen* (*D*), *Monarch* (*C*), *Newton Wonder* (*C*), *Norfolk Royal* (*D*), *Orlean's Reinette* (*C*), *Reinette du Canada* (*D*), *Ribston Pippin* (*D*), *Rosemary Russet* (*D*), *Roundway Magnum Bonum* (*D*), *Royalty* (*D*), *Saltcote Pippin* (*D*), *St. Cecilia* (*D*), *Superb* (*D*), *Triumph* (*D*), *Wellington* (*C*), *Wyken Pippin* (*D*). Grapes : *Alicante, Appley Towers, Canon Hall Muscat, Golden Queen, Gros Colmar, Gros Guillaume, Lady Downe's Seedling, Lady Hutt, Mrs. Pearson, Mrs. Pince, Muscat of Alexandria, and Prince of Wales.* Pears : *Bellissime d'Hiver* (*C*), *Beurre Easter* (*D*), *Blickling* (*D*), *Catillac* (*C*), *Forelle* (*D*), *Glou Morceau* (*D*), *Josephine de Malines* (*D*), *Le Lectier* (*D*), *Uvedale's St. Germain* (*C*), *Vicar of Winkfield* (*CD*), *Winter Nelis* (*D*),

NUTS IN STORE.—Cobnuts, filberts, walnuts.

GALANTHUS CILICICUS.

FEBRUARY

GENERAL

FINISH PLANTING TREES AND SHRUBS

THERE is still just time to plant fruit trees, and also deciduous ornamental trees and shrubs, including roses, but the earlier this can be done in February the better, providing soil conditions are good. There is considerable controversy about the pruning of fruit trees transplanted as late as this, some experts urging that it is unwise to give the tree two shocks at once, root disturbance and a curtailment of branches. This group argues that it is better to leave the late-planted trees unpruned until the following November and then, if they have not made much new growth, to cut them hard back into the older wood; in other words, to prune them to just about the point where they would have been cut had the work been done at planting time. My own view is that this is a waste of time, and that in any case the idea that proper pruning is a shock is a fallacy. I would not hesitate to prune late-planted fruit trees immediately before planting. Ornamental shrubs and trees should certainly be cut back fairly drastically to encourage vigorous growth later on. February-planted roses are better left unpruned until the end of March.

COMPLETE DIGGING AND BREAK DOWN SOIL

The good gardener will certainly have completed all his digging and trenching by this time, but sluggards may still have some work to do. The quicker it is finished the better. Ground that was turned over earlier in the winter and left rough should be broken down to a fine surface some time during February. It is essential to choose a day when the surface is fairly dry. You will do more harm than good if you walk about on beds that are soaking wet. Still, the right day often turns up several times during this month, and may be looked for after a period of steady east winds. Lawn sites that are to be sown or turfed later should also be prepared now.

31

COMPLETE PLANTING OF LILIES

There is still time to plant lilies outdoors and also to transplant established lilies from one part of the garden to another. The latter will be in growth and must be handled in the same way as herbaceous plants—that is to say, they must be lifted carefully and with a good body of soil, which should be kept around the roots while replanting.

CONTINUE TO POT ROOTED CUTTINGS

Throughout the month you must keep a sharp eye on chrysanthemum and perpetual-flowering carnation cuttings, and pot them singly as soon as they start to grow freely (see January, General Work).

TAKE CHRYSANTHEMUM AND CARNATION CUTTINGS

As opportunity occurs during the month continue to take chrysanthemum and perpetual carnation cuttings. It is getting late for exhibition Japanese chrysanthemums in full-size pots, but decorative varieties can still be propagated with advantage, and February is the ideal month to start on the hardy border varieties.

GENERAL GREENHOUSE MANAGEMENT

WATERING BY PARTIAL IMMERSION.

Each pot or pan is held almost to its rim in a tub until the rising water darkens the surface of the soil.

Plants in flower or coming into flower in the greenhouse are very much the same as those for January, and for general management I refer you to notes in that month (see January, General Work). If there are any bright, warm days, seize the opportunity to give more top ventilation, but beware of cold winds. An occasional thorough airing, so long as it does not involve a drop in temperature or cold draughts, does the greenhouse a lot of good. Most plants will require

1. Removing an apple shoot from which grafts may be prepared. 2. Heeling in fruit shoots for grafting. 3. Tying in the young laterals on a fan-trained peach tree. 4. A soft fruit plantation completely covered with a permanent wire-netting cage as a protection against birds.

1. Dusting air-slaked lime around seakale crowns before forcing outdoors.
2. The seakale crowns are then covered with inverted flower pots, and the drainage holes in these are covered with pieces of turf to exclude light.
3. Staking freesias. 4. Tuberous-rooted begonias started into growth in boxes and ready for potting singly. 7. Hippeastrums started in a warm greenhouse and already showing flower spikes.

rather more water, but begonais of the Optima type should have less.

Seedlings from January sowings of begonias, tomatoes, leeks, onions, etc., should now be appearing. At any rate, it is essential to examine the seed trays and boxes very carefully every day so that covering materials can be removed before seedlings get thin and drawn. Give water if the soil appears to be dry. The best method is to hold each receptacle almost to its rim in a pail of water for a few moments and let the water soak up from below, but if there are a number to be done and this method takes too long, water from an ordinary watering-pot fitted with a very fine rose. Be sure to go over the surface several times, because the fine spray of water tends to collect on the top and not soak in immediately.

Ventilate Frames According to the Weather

There is little to add to my remarks on this subject in the General Work for January. As the days get a little longer you will be able to ventilate more freely, but run no unnecessary risks with frost.

Continue to protect Broccoli

The curds are still liable to be damaged by frost, and must be protected as they form (see November, General Work).

Sow Small Salads for Succession

To maintain a supply of mustard and cress and radishes, make further small sowings as advised in the notes for January, General Work.

Harden Off Autumn-sown Cauliflowers

Cauliflower seedlings growing in frames from late summer sowings must be gradually hardened off during February in readiness for planting out next month. Take the lights right off during the daytime if the weather is not frosty and the wind is not very cold. Even at night a little ventilation can be given on the leeward side if weather conditions are at all reasonable.

c

Continue to force Seakale

Continue to pot and force seakale roots for succession (see November, General Work). There is not much point in bringing in any further supplies of rhubarb, however, as successional supplies will be obtained from the roots covered outdoors (see January, Fourth Week).

Pollinate and Disbud Early Peaches, Nectarines, etc.

Peaches, nectarines, and apricots in the early orchard house will be in flower during the month, and as there will certainly not be enough insects about to effect pollination it is necessary to do this by hand. The best method is to have a camel-hair brush and scatter the dry pollen from bloom to bloom with this, the most favourable time being towards midday when the sun is shining. While the fruit trees are in bloom it is necessary to discontinue syringing and to raise the temperature by about 10 degs. night and day and keep the atmosphere dry by judicious ventilation (see January, First Week). When the fruit is set syringe the trees freely again once every morning.

DISBUDDING A PEACH.

Left: a typical fruiting lateral before disbudding. Right: the same lateral at a later stage. Two young shoots have been retained near the base, but these may be reduced to one later.

As shoots grow you must in the case of peaches and nectarines commence the process known as disbudding. The small side shoots that form on the fruiting laterals are gradually pinched off, a few at a time, until only two are left to each lateral, one at its base and the other at its extremity. Then in the winter the old fruiting lateral is cut right out and the young basal shoot is trained in its place. The object of leaving the terminal shoot is simply to encourage the flow of sap through the branch and so help the fruits to swell. This method of disbudding is only fully practised on established trees that have filled their space. Small young trees may be allowed to form new laterals wherever there is room for these to be trained in as branches. Apricots bear on old as well as new wood, and with these only shoots that are awkwardly placed are removed. Other side growths are cut back to four or five well-developed leaves each as soon as they commence to get hard and woody at the base.

Pollinate and Train Early Vines

Vines started into growth last month (see January, First Week) will also come into flower during February and will need hand-pollination just like the peaches. The young laterals must be pulled down little by little until they lie along the training wires. If more than one lateral forms at each spur, pinch out the growing point of the weaker at the earliest opportunity. The points of the flower-bearing laterals must also be pinched just beyond the second leaf formed after the truss. If any secondary laterals form, pinch these just beyond the first leaf. While the vines are in flower, raise the temperature to 65 degs. at night, rising about 10 degs. by day. From this stage onwards you should soak the border occasionally with very weak liquid manure. Give sufficient to wet the soil to a depth of a couple of feet, and repeat as soon as the soil looks at all dry an inch or two below the surface.

FIRST WEEK

Prune Flowering Shrubs and Clematises

Flowering shrubs which should be pruned now include Hydrangea paniculata; Spiræas japonica (and varieties such as Anthony Waterer), Douglasi, Menziesi, bullata, salicifolia, ariæfolia, Aitchisoni, arborea, Lindleyana, and sorbifolia; Tamarix pentandra; Hypericum moserianum; all kinds of willows, unless grown principally for bark effects (see April, First Week); also Cornus alba and its varieties. In all cases stems made last year should be cut hard back to within one or two joints of the older wood. In the case of the bigger shrubs you can, if you wish, allow some strong branches to remain at three-quarter length to build up a main framework of growth and so lay the foundation of larger specimens than could be obtained by constant hard pruning.

This is also the time to prune all clematises of the lanuginosæ type. Cut out all weakly or imperfectly ripened and consequently soft vines to make room for the sturdier growths, which should be retained at full length.

Pot Annuals for the Greenhouse

If you were able to sow various annuals in September (see September, First Week) for flowering in the greenhouse during the spring, you should get the plants potted singly into 5- or 6-inch pots, according to the growth they have made. Use a rather light compost, about two parts loam, one part leaf-mould, and one part really coarse sand. Stand on the staging or a shelf quite close to the glass to encourage sturdy growth. Schizanthus sown in August (see August, Third Week) must also be potted on in the same way. If you want very bushy plants pinch out the tips of the shoots.

Force Roses, Flowering Shrubs, etc.

Bring further batches of bush roses, azaleas, deutzias, lilacs, astilbes, etc., well established in pots, into the greenhouse to provide a succession of flowers after those introduced in January (see January, First Week).

Start Achimenes

Place achimene tubers thinly in shallow boxes half-filled with a light sandy compost and just cover them with the same mixture. Water very moderately and place on the staging in a temperature of about 60 degs. Very soon shoots will appear, and when these are a couple of inches in length the plants should be transferred to pots or pans. Five or six roots can be grown in a pot 5 inches in diameter. An alternative method is to grow them in hanging baskets, but in any case the initial starting process is the same. Do not start all the tubers at once. Successional starting will give a longer display.

Sow Broad Beans under Glass

You can make a sowing of broad beans in boxes or pots during this week. Do not scatter the seeds haphazard, but set them out at regular intervals 2 inches apart each way, and cover them with about ¾ inch of soil. Germinate in a slightly heated greenhouse or even a frame, providing the latter is well covered with sacks or mats on frosty nights. This method of sowing early in boxes gives far more reliable results, at any rate on all save the lightest of soils, than the old-fashioned scheme of sowing out of doors in the autumn.

Sow Lettuces, Culinary Peas and Cauliflowers

If you want a really early outdoor supply of lettuces make a small sowing of a cabbage variety in seed boxes and place in a warm greenhouse to germinate. An average temperature of 55 degs. will be sufficient to ensure this. Seedlings from this indoor sowing will be planted out later, after proper hardening.

It is also an excellent plan to make a sowing of an early culinary pea in boxes and germinate in the same way as the lettuces. These seedlings will also be planted outdoors later. If you happen to live in a very mild part of the country or have an unusually sheltered garden, you may even make an outside sowing of peas on a border with a southerly aspect, but you must certainly choose a really hardy variety, such as Meteor or Peter Pan.

Cauliflowers require a long and steady season of growth if they are to be a real success, and if you have a warm greenhouse you should certainly make a first sowing now. A temperature of 55 to 60 degs. will be quite adequate for germination. It is even possible to germinate them satisfactorily on a good hotbed made up as described for carrots (see January, General Work). Sow the seeds as thinly as possible, either in deep seed trays or, if in a frame on a hotbed, directly in the soil in shallow drills.

Sow Cucumbers for an Early Crop

Sow a few cucumber seeds for an early crop if you have a well-heated greenhouse. Place the seeds singly in 3-inch pots filled with a compost of loam, leaf-mould, and sand in about equal parts and germinate in a temperature of 75 degs. in a close frame, preferably with bottom heat. It is an excellent plan to half-fill the frame with moss peat or coconut fibre and plunge the pots

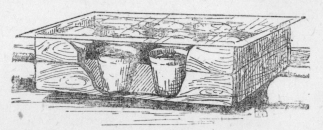

RAISING EARLY CUCUMBERS.

The seeds are sown in pots, which are then plunged in fibre in a box placed on the hot-water pipes. A pane of glass across the top of the box converts it into a close frame.

to their rims in this. Cucumbers need more warmth than tomatoes in the early stages, as they must be kept in rapid growth.

PLANT JERUSALEM ARTICHOKES

Plant Jerusalem artichokes at the earliest opportunity. These are amongst the hardiest of all vegetables, and as they make a lot of tall, sunflower-like growth they may well be used as a wind-break in exposed gardens. They will grow almost anywhere, and good crops are to be had from soil that would be far too poor to produce potatoes. Simply plant the tubers 15 inches apart in rows 3 feet apart. Cover with 3 inches of soil.

PRUNE AUTUMN-FRUITING RASPBERRIES

Autumn-fruiting raspberries such as Hailsham and November Abundance must now be cut right back to within 6 inches of the ground. These varieties fruit on the young growth produced after pruning. The variety Lloyd George can also be pruned in this way for autumn fruiting, but is really more profitable as a summer variety, in which case it is pruned in August (see August, Second Week).

START SECOND EARLY VINES INTO GROWTH

If you have more than one vinery and wish to have a succession of ripe grapes, or if you were afraid to start vines in January owing to lack of artificial heat you may do so now. It is still necessary to maintain the same temperatures as before (see January, First Week), but with lengthening days and more sun heat this is not so difficult.

SECOND WEEK

PLANT ANEMONES AND RANUNCULUSES

This is an excellent time to make a good planting of anemones of the St. Brigid, Du Caen, and fulgens types, and also of Turban ranunculuses for a summer display. The anemones should be $2\frac{1}{2}$ to 3 inches deep and the ranunculuses about 1 inch less. The latter are queer-looking things, like dried-up claws, and the claws should be planted downwards. Space both subjects about 6 inches apart each way.

PRUNE AND START GREENHOUSE PLANTS

Several well-known greenhouse plants require pruning now. Bougainvilleas should have last year's growth cut hard back unless you wish to retain some growths for extension. Bouvardias, gardenias, fuchsias, zonal and ivy-leaved pelargoniums, and Diplacus glutinosus should be cut sufficiently to give them a solid foundation for the coming season's growth and so prevent the least suspicion of untidiness. You can give all these plants water in gradually increasing quantity from now onwards as growth commences. A slightly higher temperature will also be all to the good, though it is not essential. All need as much light as they can get.

SOW PARSNIPS

If the weather is at all favourable do not hesitate to sow parsnips out of doors, for the longer and more steadily they can grow the better. However, there is no sense in sowing if the ground is sodden or frozen. Better wait two or three weeks than have all the seeds rot away. Sow in drills 1 inch deep and about 18 inches apart, scattering the seeds as thinly as possible, for later on the seedlings must be thinned to at least 9 inches apart in the rows. Those who grow for exhibition very often make a hole

39

for each parsnip with a large iron crowbar. This is driven in to a depth of about 2 feet, the hole is then almost filled with fine potting soil, two seeds are sown, and a little more fine soil placed on top. The object of this is to encourage the tap root to grow straight down into the soft potting soil, and so obtain specimens of perfect shape. If both seeds germinate the weaker seedling is pulled out.

LIFT AND STORE PARSNIPS

Parsnips that have been left in the ground all the winter will soon be starting to grow again, and it is best to lift them without delay and store in some cold place. A position beneath a north wall will do very well. It is only necessary to place the roots in a heap and cover them with a little soil; they are quite hardy and will not be injured by frost.

PLANT SHALLOTS AND POTATO ONIONS

There used to be an old-time idea that shallots should be planted on the shortest day of the year. There are, no doubt, some gardeners who follow this out still, but my own opinion is that, at any rate around London and on heavy soils generally, it is much better to wait until the second week in February. Indeed, even then, I would not plant unless the surface of the bed can be broken down reasonably fine. Better wait than plant in mud. The method of planting is simply to push good bulbs firmly into the soil until only the top third can be seen. Plant 9 inches apart in rows 1 foot apart. Potato onions, which are very much like shallots, are planted in exactly the same way and at the same time. Choose an open position and, for preference, ground that is well drained and has been adequately manured earlier in the winter.

PLANT OUT SPRING CABBAGES

Cabbages for a spring supply are sown in July or August and are usually planted out in the early autumn in the beds in which they are to mature. But sometimes one cannot find sufficient room for all the seedlings, and if there are some still left in the seed beds, now is the time to get them planted, always providing the weather is reasonably good. If it is not, seize the first favourable opportunity. These late plants are not likely to make such big hearts as the earlier ones, so it will be sufficient to plant them 10 inches to 1 foot apart in rows 18 inches apart.

THIRD WEEK

Sow Half-hardy Annuals and Greenhouse Plants

I usually make this week a busy one in the greenhouse, reserving it for sowing a great number of half-hardy annuals, greenhouse plants, etc. The half-hardy annuals are principally required for summer bedding, but some of them may also come in useful for potting later on and growing as greenhouse plants during the summer (see my notes on hardy annuals in the greenhouse, March, First Week).

The principal half-hardy annuals to be sown now are ageratum, amaranthus, anagallis, antirrhinums, Begonia semperflorens, brachycome, cobæa, cosmeas, Dianthus Heddewigi, eccremocarpus, kochia, limonium (statice), lobelias, marigolds of both French and African types, marguerite carnations, nicotianas, nemesias, Phlox Drummondi, petunias, scarlet salvias, salpiglossis, schizanthus, ten-week stocks, and verbenas. The greenhouse plants include balsams, begonias, celosias (including cockscombs), celsias, Clerodendron fallax, gloxinias, Impatiens Sultani, and I. Holsti, mimulus, Rehmannia angulata, streptocarpus, and trachelium. You may have sown some of these already (see January, Third Week), but even so plants from this later sowing will prove very useful for succession. Dahlias also come very well from a sowing made at this time, and make good strong plants for putting out early in June. All will germinate in a temperature of 55 to 60 degs.

In all cases use the compost of two parts rather light but fibrous loam (preferably steam sterilised), one part moss peat, and one part coarse silver sand that I have already recommended, and do not forget to add 1½ ounces of superphosphate and ¾ ounce of ground chalk to each bushel of the mixture. Seed boxes will do for all seeds, though perhaps it is a little better to have the really choice greenhouse seeds, such as celosias, begonias, and streptocarpus, in earthenware seed pans. Whichever you use be sure to make them thoroughly clean by scrubbing them out with a stiff brush, and then provide plenty of drainage material, first of all with a layer of

41

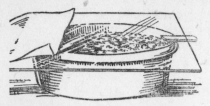

VENTILATION FOR SEED PANS.

Most seeds germinate more quickly if the seed pans are covered with glass and paper, but the latter must be removed as soon as the seedlings appear and the glass should be tilted a little. After a few days it can be removed.

broken pots and then with a thin scattering of either rough leaf-mould or sphagnum moss. Prepare the boxes a day before you actually intend to sow the seeds and give the soil a thorough watering. Then stand the boxes on the staging to drain. Never fill a seed receptacle right to the rim; leave at least $\frac{1}{2}$ inch for watering. The day after watering sow the seeds very thinly and evenly, cover lightly with soil (a good general rule is to cover a seed with twice its own depth of soil), and then place a sheet of glass over each pan or box and a large piece of brown paper over the lot. Any more water that may be needed must be given either from a can fitted with a very fine rose or else by holding the pan or box almost to its rim in a tub of water.

START DAHLIA TUBERS FOR CUTTINGS

If you wish to increase your stock of dahlias considerably, get the old dahlia tubers out of store and place them in boxes in the greenhouse to start into growth. Old apple boxes serve very well for this purpose, or orange cases can be used—indeed, anything that is deep enough to take a dahlia tuber. Any old potting compost can be utilised. Place a little in the bottom of the box, then stand the tubers on it, as many in a box as can be accommodated comfortably, and place more soil around them until the fleshy tubers themselves are just covered, but the stumps of last year's stems are ex-

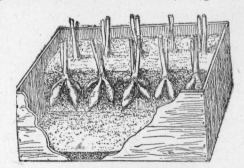

STARTING DAHLIA TUBERS.

The old roots are arranged in boxes and surrounded with light soil. Then they are placed in a warm greenhouse and watered moderately.

posed. Give a moderate watering and place in any light or semi-light place. They can go under the greenhouse staging for the time being, but as soon as growth starts they must be brought out into full light or the shoots will be blanched and useless. Give more water as necessary, sparingly at first but much more freely when growth appears. Any temperature over 55 degs. will be sufficient to start growth.

Pot Early Begonias and Gloxinia Tubers

If you were able to start begonia and gloxinia tubers into growth during January they will almost certainly need potting up by this time. It is not wise to leave them until their roots become matted together in the trays. Get them out when they have two or three leaves each and place them separately in the smallest sized pots that will accommodate them comfortably. A good compost for this purpose is seven parts medium loam, three parts moss peat, two parts coarse sand with $1\frac{1}{2}$ ounces of hoof and horn meal, $1\frac{1}{2}$ ounces of superphosphate, $\frac{3}{4}$ ounce of sulphate of potash, and $\frac{3}{4}$ ounce of ground chalk added to each bushel. This, incidentally, will be found a very good standard compost for most potting. The tubers should only just be covered with soil. Make them moderately firm, give them a thorough watering, and stand them at the warmest end of the house. A temperature of 60 to 65 degs. will not be too much for a few days. Syringe every morning with slightly warm water to prevent flagging, and shade for a few days from strong direct sunshine.

Start Begonias, Gloxinias, and Hippeastrums

A further batch of begonias, gloxinias, and hippeastrums may be started into growth to provide a succession after those started in January (see January, Second and Fourth Weeks). Even if you were unable to start any then you may be safe in doing so now, for it will be easier to maintain the requisite temperatures.

Start Clivias and Vallotas

These plants may also be arranged to make growth now, but as they are never dried off to the extent of hippeastrums this simply means increasing the water supply a little and standing in a warmer part of the house. A temperature of from 55 to 60 degs. will be ample unless very early flowers are required.

43

Sow Early Celery

This is the time to make the earliest sowing of celery to give fully blanched stems by the end of August. I do not advise you to attempt this first sowing unless you have plenty of frame space available and are fairly accustomed to handling plants under glass. It is much easier to grow celery from a March sowing, and from this you should have good sticks by Michaelmas. However, if you intend to enter in some August shows a few sticks of celery may make all the difference. A temperature of from 60 to 65 degs. will be necessary for germination. The seeds should be sown as thinly as possible in the usual seed compost (see p. 24). It is an advantage to cover each box with a sheet of glass and another of brown paper. Of course, an early variety should be chosen.

Sow Maincrop Tomatoes

A second sowing of tomatoes (see January, Second Week) will provide you with good sturdy plants for planting in the greenhouse in May as soon as you have cleared it of bedding plants, early-flowering plants, etc. Details of sowing are as before.

Pot Tomato Seedlings

Tomato seedlings from the January sowing should be potted separately in 3-inch pots as soon as they have made two or three rough leaves each beyond the first pair of plain seed leaves. Transfer them carefully to these pots, using the same kind of compost as that advised for the seed boxes (see January, Second Week). Water freely and keep shaded from direct sunshine for a day or so until they get over the shift. Later sowings may be pricked off into deeper boxes before potting, but I find that for the earliest crop it is better to pot separately as soon as possible.

Sow Turnips

Make a first sowing of turnips outdoors in a warm, sheltered place. Sow the seeds thinly in drills $\frac{1}{2}$ inch deep and 10 inches apart. You should only sow a few seeds now and subsequently make small successional sowings every fortnight or so until the end of July, as by this method you will have a constant supply of young roots instead of a lot of old, tough, and strongly flavoured ones.

START THE UNHEATED ORCHARD HOUSE

Give considerably less ventilation to the unheated orchard house containing peaches, nectarines, etc. By day the top ventilators may be opened a little if the weather is fine, but early in the afternoon the house should be closed completely. This will encourage the trees to start into growth.

FOURTH WEEK

PRICK OFF EARLY SEEDLINGS

It should now be possible to prick off some of the early seedlings such as begonias, gloxinias, streptocarpus, etc., sown in January (see January, Third Week). They will be very small

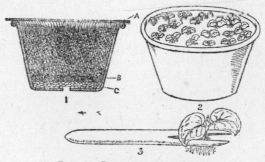

RAISING BEGONIAS FROM SEED.

The seed pans must be covered with glass (1) until the seeds germinate, but then air must be admitted in increasing quantity until, after a few days, the glass can be removed altogether. When the seedlings have made two true leaves each they must be transferred to other pans or boxes (2). It is very difficult to hold these tiny seedlings in one's fingers, and a forked stick (3) often proves very useful.

and it may be necessary to use a small forked stick to lift them, but early pricking out before roots become matted together is amply repaid. Fill rather deep seed trays or big earthenware pans with the same kind of compost as that used for seed raising, and dibble the seedlings in about 2 inches apart each way. Water freely and keep rather warm and shaded for a few days until they recover from the shift, after which they may be placed on the ordinary greenhouse staging in a temperature of about 60 degs.

45

Plant Chives

Chives are not a very important vegetable crop, but a small bed comes in very useful for flavourings. This is the time of year to plant it or to divide old clumps that have got overcrowded. Simply lift the plants and pull them apart, replanting small tufts about 9 or 10 inches apart in rows 1 foot apart. Any ordinary soil and reasonably open position will do.

Plant Potatoes in a Sheltered Border

If you have a very sheltered border, preferably one with a south aspect, and you are not afraid to take a small risk, you can now make a first planting of early potatoes. They will need watching later on and you will probably have to protect the young shoots with dry straw or bracken, but if you are successful there is no reason why you should not be digging new potatoes early in June. Of course, for this first planting it is essential to choose a quick-growing variety such as Arran Pilot or Sharpe's Express. Also you should use only well-sprouted sets. Reduce the number of sprouts to two or three sturdy ones on each tuber. Plant in trenches about 5 inches deep and 2 feet apart, setting the tubers 9 inches apart with the eyes pointing upwards. Surround each tuber with a couple of handfuls of leaf-mould or moss peat and sprinkle a little potato fertiliser in the bottom of each trench (about 2 ounces per yard run). Then refill the trenches but do not firm the soil much. Plenty of good potato fertilisers can be bought ready to use, but if you prefer you can make your own with eight parts superphosphate of lime, five parts sulphate of ammonia, and three parts sulphate of potash. This mixture will keep for quite a long time in a dry place. If it sets hard after a few days, break it up thoroughly with the back of a spade.

Plant Out Autumn-sown Onions

Directly the soil is in good condition—that is to say, as soon as you can walk on it without it sticking to your boots—plant out seedling onions from the August sowing. The method is to plant with a small dibber, just dropping the seedlings into holes about 2 inches deep. Plant 9 inches apart in rows 15 inches apart. Incidentally, the position chosen should be fully open and the soil must have been well cultivated earlier in the winter—plenty of manure in the bottom spit and any quantity of wood ashes mixed with the surface soil. Onions growing in rough, hard soil are almost certain to be misshapen.

PRICK OFF LETTUCE AND CAULIFLOWER SEEDLINGS

These seedlings from the sowings made three weeks ago should now be ready for pricking off into deeper seed boxes filled with the same kind of compost as that used in the seed trays. Lift the seedlings very carefully with a sharpened wood tally and dibble them in 2 inches apart each way. Water freely and keep shaded for a day or so until they start to grow again.

SOW PARSLEY IN A SHELTERED PLACE

Make a small sowing of parsley in a warm, sheltered place. It is much too early yet for the main sowing, but plants raised now will be useful in early summer before the main crop is ready. Parsley seed is quite cheap, so there is no great loss even if the sowing does not prove a success.

SOW FRENCH BEANS FOR SUCCESSION

Sow some more French beans in 8-inch pots if you wish to keep up a successional supply under glass during the spring (see January, Fourth Week).

SOW MELONS IN A HEATED GREENHOUSE

This is a good time to sow melon seeds. Sow them singly, $\frac{1}{2}$ inch deep, in small pots (those $2\frac{1}{2}$ inches in diameter will be admirable), and start them into growth in a temperature of 60 to 70 degs. It is a good plan to plunge the pots to their rims in moss peat or coconut fibre in a propagating box placed over the heating apparatus (see p. 38).

PRUNE COBNUTS AND FILBERTS

Cobnuts and filberts must be pruned as soon as the small red female flowers can be seen. These, by the way, are rather insignificant and you must look closely to find them. It is the male catkins that make the show. The leading shoots of established bushes which fill their space are shortened to a couple of buds each. If there is still room for the bushes to extend there is no need to prune these leaders at all, or at the most only to remove

47

their tips. Side shoots are cut back to the first catkin, reckoning from the tip, or, if there are no catkins, to the first female flower. Some shoots may have catkins only. These should be left un-pruned until the catkins fade and then be cut right back to two

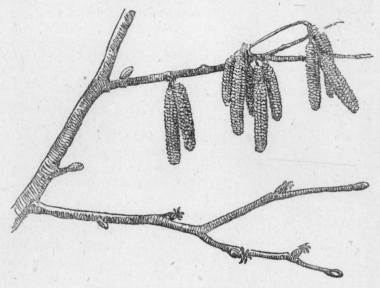

TYPICAL SHOOTS OF COBNUT IN FLOWER.

The upper shoot is bearing catkins only, while the lower forked stem has four female flowers. Pruning consists in shortening the lower shoot to the two flowers nearest its extremities. Later, when the catkins have faded, the upper shoot must be shortened to two buds or leaves.

buds. There is no point in keeping them, as they will not produce any nuts. Badly placed branches which crowd up the centre of the bush should be removed altogether, even if this means using a saw. The ideal nut bush is roughly in the form of a goblet, with a short main trunk and branches radiating from it at regular intervals.

SPRAY PEACHES AND NECTARINES OUTDOORS

If your outdoor peaches or nectarines were attacked by red spider the previous summer, spray them now with lime-sulphur wash at the usual winter strength advised by the manufacturers. This treatment will also check the leaf-curl disease.

48

1. Pot-grown roses hard pruned and starting into growth in the greenhouse.
2. A shrubby spiræa after winter thinning out and shortening of growth.
2. Chrysanthemum cuttings rooted and ready for potting singly. 4. Perpetual
carnation cuttings rooted in a propagating box and now being accustomed
to the ordinary atmosphere of the greenhouse. 5. Vine rods lowered to
check a sudden uprush of sap and so encourage even growth from all the
spurs. 6. Tying down a young vine lateral. 6. Pinching out the tip of a
vine lateral a leaf beyond the flower truss.

1. Pollinating peach bloom with a camel-hair brush.   2. An improvised close frame for seed raising.   It is made from a deep box stood over the hot-water pipes and covered with sheets of glass and brown paper. 3. Lifting a tomato plant from the seed box.   4. Pricking off the tomato seedling into another box.

FLOWERS, VEGETABLES, AND FRUITS IN SEASON DURING FEBRUARY

HARDY HERBACEOUS PLANTS.—Adonis *amurensis*, Arisarum *proboscideum*, Euphorbia *biglandulosa*, Helleborus *abschasicus*, H. *antiquorum*, H. *caucasicus*, H. *colchicus*, H. *corsicus*, H. *fœtidus*, H. *guttatus*, H. *odorus*, H. *olympicus*, H. *orientalis vars.*, H. *viridus*, Iris *unguicularis and vars.*, Petasites *fragrans*, Pulmonaria *angustifolia*, P. *rubra*, P. *saccharata*, Ranunculus *Ficaria vars.*, Saxifraga *ciliata*, S. *ligulata*, S. *Stracheyi*.

HARDY BULBS AND TUBERS.—Chionodoxa *Luciliæ*, Colchicum *crociflorum*, C. *hydrophilum*, C. *libanoticum*, C. *montanum*, Crocus *ærius*, C. *alatavicus*, C. *ancyrensis*, C. *aureus and vars.*, C. *Balansæ*, C. *banaticus*, C. *biflorus and vars.*, C. *candidus*, C. *carpetanus*, C. *chrysanthus and vars.*, C. *corsicus*, C. *dalmaticus*, C. *etruscus*, C. *Fleischeri*, C. *gargaricus*, C. *Imperati*, C. *Korolkowii*, C. *Olivieri*, C. *sativus and vars.*, C. *Sieberi*, C. *stellaris*, C. *Tommasinianus*, Cyclamen *coum*, C. *ibericum*, Erythronium *Dens-canis*, Eranthis *hyemalis*, Galanthus *byzantinus*, G. *Elwesii*, G. *latifolius*, G. *nivalis in var.*, G. *plicatus*, Hyacinthus *azureus*, Iris *bukeriana*, I. *Danfordiæ*, I. *histrioides*, I. *persica*, I. *reticulata*, I. *sindjarensis*, I. *rosenbachiana*, Leucojum *vernum carpaticum*, Merendera *caucasica*, Narcissus *Bulbocodium and vars.*, N. *minor and vars.*, N. *Pseudo-narcissus pallida præcox*, Scilla *amœna*, S. *bifolia and vars.*, S. *sibirica*, Tulipa *biflora*, T. *saxatilis*.

HARDY ROCK PLANTS.—Anemone *angulosa*, A. *blanda*, Cardamine *diphylla*, C. *polyphylla*, Corydalis *angustifolia*, C. *bracteata*, C. *tuberosa*, Doronicum *caucasicum*, Draba *pyrenaica*, Lithospermum *rosmarinifolium* (*shelter*), Omphalodes *verna*, Polygala *Chamæbuxus*, Primula *Allioni*, P. *megaseœfolia*, P. *juliana vars.*, P. *Winteri*, Saxifraga *apiculata*, S. *Borisii*, S. *burseriana and vars.*, S. *Elizabethæ*, S. *Haagii*, S. *Irvingii*, S. *Jenkinsii*, S. *juniperifolia*, S. *Kellereri*, S. *kewensis*, S. *megasæflora*, S. *oppositifolia and vars.*, S. *Paulinæ*, S. *scardica and vars.*, Sisyrinchium *grandiflorum*, Synthyris *reniformis*, Viola *florariensis*.

EVERGREEN SHRUBS.—Azara *integrifolia*, A. *microphylla*, Berberis *aquifolium*, B. *japonica and vars.*, Camellia *reticulata* (*shelter*), Daphne *Laureola*, D. *odora*, Erica *arborea and vars.*, E. *carnea and vars.*, E. *darleyensis*, E. *lusitanica*, E. *mediterranea*, Garrya *elliptica*, Lonicera *fragrantissima*, Pieris *japonica*, Ribes *laurifolium*, Sarcococca *humilis*, Ulex *europæus vars.*, Viburnum *Tinus and vars.*

DECIDUOUS SHRUBS.—Chimonanthus *fragrans*, Cornus *Mas*, Corylopsis *Griffithii* (*shelter*), Corylus *Avellana and vars.*, C. *maxima and vars.*, Cydonia *japonica and vars.*, Daphne *Mezereum*, Edgeworthia *papyrifera*, Hamamelis *mollis*, H. *japonica and vars.*, H. *vernalis*, Lonicera *Standishii*, Nuttalia *cerasiformis*, Stachyurus *præcox*, Viburnum *fœtens*, V. *fragrans*, V. *grandiflorum*.

DECIDUOUS TREES.—Alnus *incana vars.*, A. *japonica*, A. *oregona*, Corylus *Colurna*, Prunus *cantabrigiensis*, P. *Davidiana*, P. *subhirtella autumnalis*, P. *Conradinæ*.

HARDY CLIMBING PLANTS.—Clematis *calycina*, C. *cirrhosa*, Jasminum *nudiflorum*.

D

GREENHOUSE PLANTS.—Arum lilies, Acacia *armata*, A. *baileyana*, A. *dealbata*, azaleas (*Indian and Mollis*), camellias, begonias (as Jan., except Optima type), Boronia *heterophylla*, B. *megastigma*, Browallia *speciosa major*, camellias, carnations (*perpetual*), cinerarias (*hybrids*), Coleus *thyrsoideus*, Coronilla *glauca*, correas, cyclamen (*Persian*), Daphne *indica*, Eupatorium *vernale*, freesias, gardenias, hyacinths, bulbous irises (*tingitana*, *Spanish*, etc.), Jasminum *primulinum*, lachenalias, narcissi (*including Golden Spur*, *Præcox*, etc.), primulas (*as Jan.*), Sparmannia *africana*, tulips (*early-flowering*

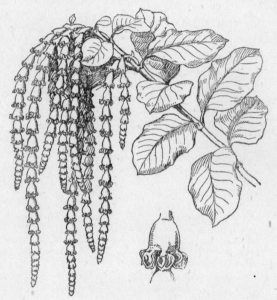

GARRYA ELLIPTICA.

vars.), also forced shrubs such as deutzias, cherries, almonds, peaches, viburnums, etc.

PLANTS IN FRAMES.—Anemone *coronaria vars*. (*St. Brigid and du Caen anemones*), Helleborus *niger vars.* (*Christmas roses*), violets (*double and single*).

VEGETABLES IN STORE.—Jerusalem artichokes, beetroots, carrots, onions, parsnips, potatoes, turnips, shallots.

VEGETABLES IN GARDEN.—Jerusalem artichokes, broccoli, sprouting broccoli, Brussels sprouts, coleworts, celery, endive, kales, lettuces, leeks, spring onions, parsnips, savoys, spinach, turnip tops.

VEGETABLES UNDER GLASS.—Endive, lettuces, mustard and cress, mushrooms, radishes, rhubarb, seakale.

FRUITS IN STORE.—Apples : *Adams' Pearmain* (D), *Annie Elizabeth* (C), *Barnack Beauty* (CD), *Beauty of Kent* (C), *Beauty of Stoke* (CD), *Belle de Boskoop* (CD), *Brownlees' Russet* (D), *Cornish Gillyflower* (D), *Court*

Pendu Plat (D), Cox's Orange Pippin (D), Duke of Devonshire (D) Edward VII. (C), John Standish (D), King's Acre Pippin (D), Lane's Prince Albert (C), Laxton's Pearmain (D), Lord Burghley (D), Lord Hindlip (D), May Queen (D), Monarch (C), Newton Wonder (C), Norfolk Royal (D), Reinette du Canada (D), Rosemary Russet (D), Roundway Magnum Bonum (D), Superb (D), Wellington (C), Wyken Pippin (D). Grapes : Alicante, Gros Guillaume, Lady Downe's Seedling, Mrs. Pearson, Mrs. Pince, Muscat of Alexandria, and Prince of Wales. Pears : Bellissime d'Hiver (C), Bergamotte d'Esperen (D), Beurre Easter (D), Catillac (C), Josephine de Malines (D), Olivier de Serres (D), Uvedale's St. Germain (C), Verulam (C), Winter Orange (C).

Nuts in Store.—Cobnuts, filberts, walnuts.

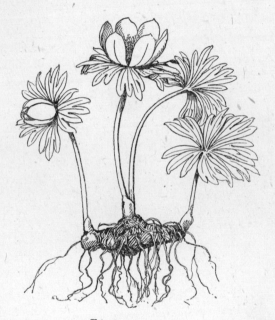

Eranthis hyemalis.

MARCH

GENERAL

Transplant and Divide Herbaceous Perennials

MARCH is usually the best month of the whole twelve during which to transplant the majority of herbaceous plants. There are a few exceptions, but they are not very important. German irises are usually planted by experts at the end of June because they will then give a full display of flowers the following year, but they can be transplanted with equal safety in March, the only drawback being that there will be few flowers the following summer. Similar remarks apply to pyrethrums, which are also moved by experts immediately after flowering. Pæonies and eremuri are often quoted as examples of plants that benefit greatly by autumn transplanting. My own opinion is that this is well enough on

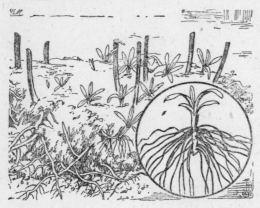

PHLOX CLUMP AND DIVISIONS.

The young rooted piece shown in the inset will make a far better plant than old woody portions from the centre of the clump.

properly drained soil, but that even with these plants it is better to wait until March if one has to contend with heavy clay. The actual moment during the month chosen for planting may be decided to some extent by opportunity and pressure of other work, but do not fail to seize any really good days early in the month or you may find that later on persistent rain holds you up.

When transplanting old clumps always break them up into smaller pieces, and if you have plenty of stock throw away the hard central portions of the clumps and keep only the young outside pieces. This is particularly important in the case of vigorous spreading things like Michaelmas daisies, heleniums, rudbeckias, and soli-

dagos. Split up by hand where possible, and for very tough clumps use a couple of small border forks thrust back to back through the middle of the mass and then levered apart. Only use a knife with plants that make a solid crown—*e.g.*, pæonies, delphiniums, and Caucasian scabious—and even then be careful only to cut the crowns and not the roots; pull these apart.

How to Divide a Plant by Hand.

Pull the clumps apart carefully without breaking the crowns away from the roots to which they are attached.

Always replant with a spade or trowel and not a dibber. Prepare good wide holes, spread roots out well, work some fine dry soil around them (it is an excellent plan to prepare a barrow-load of this in advance), and make thoroughly firm.

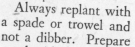

Lay Turves

This is a good month for turf-laying, and also for repairing bare places in lawns. So, if you have any of this work to do, choose any day during March when the surface is dry enough to be walked on without sticking to your boots and it can be broken down reasonably well with the fork or rake. Beat the turves down on to the soil with a special wooden turf beater or roll them with a light roller, first in one direction and then transversely.

General Greenhouse Management

The greenhouse will now be filling with many more seedlings and young rooted cuttings than before. These must have plenty

53

joint and then insert them in well-drained boxes or 4-inch pots filled with a sandy compost, dropping them in just sufficiently deep to keep them erect. They can be rooted on the greenhouse staging if they are shaded during the day, but better results with all except geraniums are obtained by placing them in a propagating box, especially if this is over the hot-water pipes or other heating apparatus. It is quite a simple matter to fix up a temporary propagating case from a deep box half-filled with coconut fibre or moss peat and covered with a few large panes of glass.

You can propagate quite a number of popular greenhouse plants in precisely the same way. It is worth trying a few shoots of any perennial that is just making new growth. A few examples are abutilons, bouvardia, brugmansia (datura), coleus, eupatoriums, gardenia, justicia, lantana, libonia, berried solanums, the double-flowered tropæolums, and petunias. All these should be kept as close as possible in a frame warmed from below until they are rooted. Winter-flowering begonias of the Gloire de Lorraine type make basal growths at this time of the year, and these can be secured as cuttings when a couple of inches in length.

STOP EARLY CARNATIONS

Complete the propagation of perpetual-flowering carnations from cuttings as soon as possible. Cuttings that were rooted in December and January will be ready for stopping some time during the month. This simply means that the top of each cutting is broken off with a sideways movement. The effect of this is to make the plants produce side shoots. The right stage of growth for stopping is when the plant has made about seven joints. One complete joint is broken out.

POT CHRYSANTHEMUM AND CARNATION CUTTINGS

You must continue to pot chrysanthemum and perpetual-flowering carnation cuttings as soon as they are well-rooted (see January, General Work).

Perpetual-flowering carnations that were potted into 2-inch pots in January and early February will also need a move on into 3- or 3½-inch pots some time during the month. Use the same compost as before, but rather coarser in texture. Do not place the plants in a frame like the chrysanthemums, but stand them

56

on staging or a shelf in the greenhouse with an average temperature of 55 degs., and as much ventilation as possible without cold draughts.

Chrysanthemum cuttings that were rooted during December and January should be ready for the second potting into 5-inch pots quite early in the month. Use a rather coarser compost than before and pot a little more firmly. A good mixture is eight parts good loam, one part sweet leaf-mould or moss peat, one part well-rotted cow or horse manure, one part coarse sand,

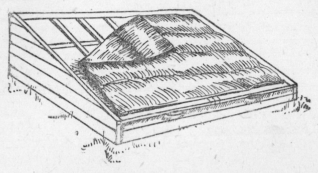

A POSSIBLE DANGER WITH FRAMES.

When protecting frames with mats or sacking on frosty nights make certain that the covering is well fastened down, or it may blow back and expose some of the plants.

and one part old mortar rubble. Add a 5-inch potful of bone-meal to each bushel of this mixture. After potting place the plants in a frame but keep the lights on at first and have plenty of thick sacks or mats at hand to cover them on cold nights.

This is also a good time to purchase rooted cuttings of all kinds of chrysanthemums. Pot the cuttings up singly directly they arrive, and place them in the greenhouse, keeping them shaded from direct sunshine for a few days and syringing with slightly warm water every morning.

TAKE CHRYSANTHEMUM CUTTINGS AND SPLIT BORDER KINDS

The best way to grow outdoor chrysanthemums is from cuttings, and you can continue to take these throughout March. Instructions are as for indoor kinds (see December, Third Week). However, if you have no facilities for handling cuttings you can still get quite good results by treating the border chrysanthemums like ordinary herbaceous perennials, lifting the roots now and splitting them up into small pieces. Throw away the hard, woody stumps of last year's growth and keep only the young outer shoots. Plant these 18 inches apart in the border or, if in rows, 1 foot apart in lines 2 to 3 feet apart. Propagation of the main stock of late-flowering chrysanthemums should now be almost completed, but towards the end of the month you may take a few more cuttings to be flowered in 6-inch pots.

Make Successional Sowings

Several vegetables that you have already sown will need to be resown during the month to provide a succession. You will need two or three more sowings of radishes as described in the notes for February, General Work. For the first three weeks of the month these should be made in a frame unless you are in an exceptionally favourable district, for radishes must grow rapidly to be of any use. At the end of the month you can make a sowing outdoors in a warm, sheltered border. One or two small sowings of turnips (see February, Third Week) will ensure a constant supply in early summer. Mustard and cress may be sown quite frequently in a warm frame or greenhouse (see January, General Work). Make another sowing of lettuces in the greenhouse early in the month (see February, First Week). At the end of the month it will be safe to sow outdoors (see Fourth Week).

Prick off Seedlings

During the month many seedlings raised in the warm greenhouse or frame last month will be ready for pricking out. In most cases the ideal time is when the seedlings have made two true leaves each in addition to the first seed leaves (these are quite different in character from the true leaves and can be distinguished quite easily). Monocotyledons, such as onions and leeks, only make one seed leaf and are pricked off as soon as they can be handled conveniently. However, if you followed my advice (see January, First and Fourth Weeks) and spaced the seeds singly, no pricking off will be necessary as the tiny plants will have plenty of room.

For general pricking off use the same compost as that advised for the seed trays (see p. 24). Lift the seedlings with as little root

58

injury as possible and dibble them in 2 inches apart each way, making the soil firm around their roots. Water freely and shade for a few days while the tiny plants are recovering from the check of the move. You can either prick off into other boxes like those used for the seeds but preferably a little deeper, or else, if in frames, directly into a bed of fine soil. Amongst the seedlings needing this attention will be cauliflowers and lettuces sown under glass for

A USEFUL TYPE OF PRICKING-OFF TRAY.

One side is held by two screws only and so is quickly removable. When planting time comes it is a simple matter to shovel the plants out with a trowel.

planting out, tomatoes (unless you can pot them singly straight away to save time as I described in my notes for February, Third Week), and many half-hardy annuals and greenhouse plants.

TREAT PEACHES, ETC., ACCORDING TO GROWTH

Peaches, nectarines, and apricots in the unheated orchard house will come into bloom early in the month and will require hand-fertilisation exactly as described in the notes for February, General Work. Later they must be disbudded little by little, as described in the same place.

Peaches and nectarines which were started in January should now have fruit well set, and you can commence to thin these; but do not complete the work as yet, because there is often a heavy natural fall during the stoning period (see April, General Work). Simply content yourself so far with reducing the number of fruits per cluster so that they have room to swell.

COMMENCE TO THIN THE EARLIEST GRAPES

Some time during the month bunches of grapes in the earliest vinery will be ready for their first thinning. The ideal time to

59

THINNING A BUNCH OF GRAPES.

This work must be done at an early stage and with the utmost care. Use a pair of pointed scissors and do not touch the bunch with the fingers.

start is about a fort-night after the grapes first set. Use a special pair of grape scissors with pointed blades and commence thin-ning at the bottom of the bunch. Leave the extreme point of the bunch, but remove all the berries that are within $\frac{3}{4}$ inch above it. Berries at the top of the bunch can be left almost twice as thick as this, those be-tween being given an intermediate amount of room. Do not touch the berries by hand, but use a small forked stick to turn them if necessary.

Vines started into growth in February will be in need of pollin-ation, training, and stopping exactly as I described for the earliest vines (see February, General Work).

FIRST WEEK

Sow Sweet Peas Outdoors

If you were unable to sow sweet peas in the autumn or in January under glass you should certainly make an outdoor sow-ing at the earliest possible moment now. Some growers are successful from sowings made in the open as early as the second week in February, but my opinion is that little is gained in this way, and that the soil is much more likely to be in the right condition during March. Sow the seeds 2 inches deep and 4 inches apart in rows 10 inches apart, with an alleyway at least 5 ft. wide between each pair of rows.

This is also the time to pinch out the tips of sweet peas sown in January, a task which must be done even if the peas are to be grown on the single stem (cordon) system. Side growths produce better flowers than the main stems.

BED OUT WALLFLOWERS, FORGET-ME-NOTS, ETC.

If it was not possible to complete the planting of wallflowers, forget-me-nots, Canterbury bells, polyanthuses, and double daisies in October, now is the time to get the plants into their flowering quarters. Do not delay if weather and soil conditions are right. (See October, General Work, for particulars.)

SOW ANNUALS FOR THE GREENHOUSE

A great many of the familiar hardy annuals that are grown for flowering in summer beds also make good greenhouse pot plants. Included under this heading are annual anchusa, calendula, annual chrysanthemum, clarkia, eschscholtzia, godetia, gypsophila, heliophila, ipomæa, larkspur, Mesembryanthemum criniflorum, mignonette, nasturtium, nemophila, phacelia, salpiglossis, sweet scabious, annual statice, ursinia, and viscaria. Sow seed now in well-drained seed trays and germinate in the greenhouse in a temperature of 55 to 60 degs. You will then have good strong plants commencing to flower at the end of May, just when your greenhouse has been cleared of most of the winter and spring subjects. Prick off the seedlings 2 inches apart each way into similar soil and boxes as soon as they have made two true leaves each.

REPOT FOLIAGE PLANTS, FERNS, ETC.

Early March is a great time for potting, at any rate so far as summer and autumn-flowering plants are concerned, and also all plants that are grown principally for their foliage. Winter-flowering plants are a different matter, and are generally best repotted as soon as they have finished blooming. Now is the time to deal with palms, aspidistras, ferns of all kinds, including the so-called asparagus fern and Asparagus Sprengeri, smilax, coleus, crotons, cacti and succulents generally, dracœnas, marguerites, fuchsias, pelargoniums (this genus includes the familiar bedding geranium), and heliotropes. It is usually advisable to give plants that are to be repotted a shift into a pot one size larger than that which they occupied before. If for any reason it is essential that the plants should be kept in the same size pot you must first reduce

61

the size of the ball of soil around the roots. The way to do this is to tap the plant out of its old pot by rapping the rim of this upside down on the edge of the potting bench and holding one hand close up to the ball of soil to support it as it comes away. If there is any difficulty push a stick through the drainage hole in the bottom of the pot. Then get a pointed stick and carefully loosen the soil around the edge of the ball without injuring the roots. If the compost is neither too wet nor too dry it can be done fairly readily. Do not remove all soil, but just sufficient to get a reasonable quantity of new compost into the new pot. Even when potting for a size larger receptable it is advisable to loosen roots a little in this way. After potting always give the

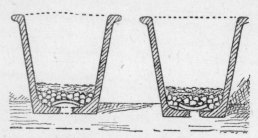

PREPARING POTS FOR POTTING.

The correct method is shown on the left. The large piece of broken pot used to keep the finer rubble from passing through the drainage hole has been placed the right way up. On the right it is the wrong way, blocking up the hole and doing more harm than good.

plants a thorough soaking with water at the same temperature as that of the house and then transfer them to a slightly warmer temperature than that in which they were growing previously. In a small house this can usually be done by moving them to the boiler end. Syringe every morning with tepid water, and

shade from direct sunshine. These special precautions need only be maintained for a week or ten days, after which normal conditions should be resumed. The idea is to prevent the leaves from flagging during such time as new roots are being formed, and to encourage rooting as much as possible.

A good general compost for most of this potting consists of seven parts good quality loam, preferably steam-sterilised (see p. 24), three parts moss peat, and two parts coarse sand, with $1\frac{1}{2}$ ounces hoof and horn meal, $1\frac{1}{2}$ ounces superphosphate of lime, $\frac{3}{4}$ ounce sulphate of potash, and $\frac{3}{4}$ ounce ground chalk added to each bushel of the compost. Add one part of leaf-mould for all ferns.

Pot Rooted Cuttings

Another kind of potting which you should do at the earliest opportunity is that of late summer and early autumn rooted cuttings of tender bedding plants, including marguerites, geraniums, heliotropes, and fuchsias. These will be just starting into growth, and if you transfer them singly to 3-inch or 3½-inch pots in the compost just mentioned they will soon grow into sturdy specimens. After potting, shade the plants for a few days, but stand them on the greenhouse staging in a light place as soon as growth recommences.

Start Achimenes for Succession

You should now start another batch of achimenes to provide a succession of flowers to those started in February (see February, First Week).

Sow Cauliflower, Broccoli, etc., in a Frame

If you were not able to sow cauliflowers in the greenhouse (see February, First Week) you should now sow seeds in a frame. It is even worth making this sowing as an addition to the greenhouse one if you choose a rather later variety than that sown before, because you will then prevent any chance of a break in the supply of curds in the autumn. Sow thinly, as advised for cabbages above. Also sow a few seeds of an early broccoli, such as Veitch's Self-protecting or Sandringham

A Handy Frame for Seedlings.

Drills have been prepared in readiness for the seeds by pressing a length of broom-handle into the soil.

Winter White, for these are hardier than the cauliflowers and may stand you in good stead if hard frost comes early in the autumn.

Brussels sprouts must have a long and steady season of growth if they are to be really successful. Sow now in boxes and germinate in a frame (preferably on a mild hotbed) or in a slightly heated greenhouse. If you also want a supply of cabbages in midsummer, sow an early variety now under exactly the same conditions as the Brussels sprouts.

SOW ONIONS

A most important sowing for this first week in March, if the weather is reasonably kind, is that of maincrop onions. Sow in drills ½ inch deep. The drills themselves should be 9 inches to 1 foot apart, the latter if you are after big bulbs for exhibition. As I have already remarked, it is almost impossible to make the surface of the onion bed too fine and light, but there should be plenty of richness in the way of animal manure below. With the top 4 inches mix only wood ashes and similar lightening things so that the bulbs can swell without restriction.

SOW SPINACH IN A SHELTERED PLACE

A first sowing of summer spinach can be made in a sheltered border—preferably one with a southern aspect. Sow thinly in drills nearly 1 inch deep and 1 foot apart. Other successional sowings will be made later, so this first sowing need only be a small one.

SOW BROAD BEANS AND CELERY

Make another sowing of broad beans in boxes for planting out (see February, First Week). If you were unable to make the first sowing through lack of heat you may yet manage this one, for it is possible to germinate the seeds now in a practically unheated house or in a frame on a mild hotbed.

This is the time to make the main sowing of celery for a supply from October on through the winter. Treat the seeds exactly as described for the earlier sowing (see February, Third Week).

PLANT PICKLING CABBAGE

Red pickling cabbage, sown in August and pricked off in September (see September, Third Week), must now be planted where it is to mature. Choose an open position and rather good ground, and plant the cabbages 2 feet apart each way.

1. Removing a young lupin shoot from which a cutting may be prepared.
2. An old lupin root lifted for division. 3. Healthy pieces cut from the old
lupin root. 4. Cuttings of hardy perennials rooting in boxes in an unheated
frame. 5. Dividing a fibrous-rooted perennial with the aid of a pointed
stick. 6: Dividing a hardy fern with two hand forks levered apart.

1. A pot-bound fern tapped out of its old pot.   2. Loosening the mass of roots and soil with a pointed stick.   3. The fern after division into three pieces, each of which will be potted separately.   4. Pinching or "stopping" chrysanthemums for the first time.   5. Stopping as applied to perpetual flowering carnations.

PLANT RHUBARB, HORSE-RADISH, AND SEAKALE

You can make a new rhubarb plantation if you wish now, or transplant old roots from one part of the garden to another. Be certain to dig out a hole big enough to take all the roots and allow the crowns to be just level with the surface of the ground. It is a spade job and not one that can be done with a trowel. The ground should have been well manured first and the position may be open or slightly shaded, but preferably the former.

A small plantation of horse-radish is always useful, but you should be certain to make it in an out-of-the-way part of the garden and one where it can be more or less permanent, because once established it is extremely difficult to get rid of. The roots are planted with a

CUCUMBERS PLANTED ON STAGING.

This is the best method of making up the beds in a greenhouse with deep wooden or brick walls. Note the arrangement of training wires.

dibber 1 foot apart each way, and are dropped right into the soil so that the crowns are 4 inches beneath the surface. The only further cultivation that is necessary is an occasional hoeing to keep down weeds.

The seakale thongs that were removed earlier from the planting crowns and tied up in bundles (see November, Second Week) can also be planted outdoors to form new beds. Cut the roots into pieces about 6 inches long and make a nick or sloping cut at the bottom end of each so that you may be certain to plant them the

E

right way up. Plant with a dibber, making holes 6 inches deep so that the cuttings are just level with the soil. Plant them 1 foot apart in rows 18 inches apart.

New stocks can be obtained by sowing seeds outdoors now. Sow in drills 1 foot apart and ½ inch deep.

PLANT EARLY CUCUMBERS

Cucumbers raised last month (see February, First Week) will now be ready for planting. Prepare the bed in a greenhouse or forcing pit in which you can maintain a temperature of 60 degs. minimum. The bed can be on the ground or on staging, but should not be more than a couple of feet from the glass. Slates or sheets of corrugated iron make a good base. On this spread some old clinkers or straw for drainage and then spread a 6-inch layer of rough turfy loam mixed with about one-third its own bulk of well-rotted stable manure and a good sprinkling of bone-meal and wood ashes. At intervals of 3 feet make low mounds, each consisting of about 1 bushel of the same compost, and plant a cucumber on the summit of each. Place a stake to each plant and make it secure to this. Train the main stem, as it grows, towards the apex of the house and tie laterals to horizontal wires stretched 15 inches apart 9 inches below the glass. Water the plants freely and syringe them twice daily with tepid water to keep the atmosphere moist. Little air will be needed at first, but open the top ventilators when the temperature reaches 75 degs.

SOW CUCUMBERS

Cucumbers may be sown at almost any time of the year for successional cropping, but the average amateur will find that a sowing made now will prove most useful for his general needs.

SOWING CUCUMBERS.

One seed is placed in each small pot and covered with about ½ inch of soil.

It will provide him with plants just commencing to fruit well in June and these will continue for the greater part of the summer if well top-dressed and not allowed to carry too many fruits at one time. Sow the seeds singly in pots and germinate in warmth exactly as I described for an early crop (see February, First Week).

PLANT STRAWBERRIES

The best time for planting strawberries is at the end of August or early September, but if for some reason it is not possible to complete planting then, the work may be finished in March. Do not allow these late-planted strawberries to bear any fruit the first year. Cut off all flower trusses that may form.

SECOND WEEK

Sow Herbaceous Perennials and Alpines

A great many herbaceous perennials and rock plants can be raised easily from seeds sown at this time of the year in either a frame or an unheated greenhouse. These include delphiniums, lupins, perennial gypsophilas, perennial statices, thalictrums, coloured primroses and polyanthuses, violas and pansies, campanulas, hypericums, meconopses, aquilegias, dianthuses, etc. I make no attempt to give a full list because it is really worth while trying anything of which you can obtain seed. The method is to sow thinly in well-drained boxes or pans (the latter are better in some ways, especially if the seeds happen to be slow in germinating) filled with the compost mentioned on page 24. Cover the seeds to twice their own depth with very fine soil and then place them in the frame or greenhouse and shade from direct sunlight. Remove the shading as soon as the seedlings can be seen.

Auriculas may also be sown now, but are best in well-drained seed pans, as the seeds are slow and irregular in germination. Place the pans in a frame or greenhouse and water as necessary by partial immersion rather than from a watering-pot. Sow very thinly so that seedlings can be pricked off as they appear.

Sow Roses, Trees, and Shrubs

This is also a good time to sow seed of roses and any other shrubs and trees that may be available. It is not worth sowing rose seed saved haphazard, but if you or any of your friends have made some special crosses, it is quite possible that they may yield good results. Do not expect too much, however. One really worth-while rose out of a hundred seedlings is quite good going. All these seeds should be sown outdoors in a sheltered border of finely prepared soil without any manure, or at most a sprinkling of bonemeal. If the seed has been stratified (see November, General Work) rub the mass of sand, pulp, and seed through the hands to separate the seeds roughly. Then everything can be scattered in the seed drills as evenly as possible. Sow in drills about ½ inch deep and press the soil down fairly firmly on top of the seeds, but not so hard as to make it puddle. Many of the seeds may not germinate the first year, so be certain to sow in a place where you can leave them undisturbed if necessary.

Sow Cacti, Fuchsias, and Geraniums

This is a good time to sow seeds of cacti and succulents, and also fuchsias and geraniums. Sow the seeds very thinly in well-drained pots, using a light, sandy compost. Germinate in a greenhouse in a temperature of about 60 degs. The pots containing the fuchsia and geranium seeds can be covered with glass or brown paper, but the cactus and succulent seeds should only be covered with glass; they germinate better in the light.

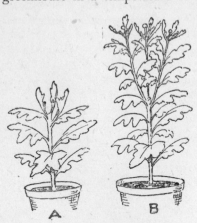

STOPPING A CHRYSANTHEMUM.
A. *The young plant shortly after the first stopping.* B. *The same plant later; the side shoots, just visible in A, have grown into sturdy stems, each terminated by a flower bud, technically known as a "first crown bud."*

Stop Chrysanthemums

Well-known Japanese chrysanthemums which should be stopped now are Franconia, Louisa Pockett, Mrs. Alex Aikman, Mrs. F. Woodward, T. W. Pockett, Romulus, and The Melba. Stopping simply means pinching the growing tip out of each plant with the object of making it produce side shoots. If your desire is to have very large blooms for exhibition each plant must be kept to one stem and this must not be allowed to carry more than one flower. In this case you must only keep the uppermost of the side shoots that form after stopping. Rub the others out at the earliest opportunity. If your object is to have several smaller flowers per plant, you may retain about three of the best side shoots after this first stopping.

Sow Herbs

Sundry herbs, including thyme, sage, and marjoram, can be raised from seed sown in a frame or practically unheated greenhouse and treated in exactly the same way as the seed of rock plants or herbaceous perennials.

Sow Culinary Peas Outdoors

Make a first sowing of an early culinary pea outdoors where the plants are to grow. I find the best method is to scoop out a trench with a spade. It should be just the width of the spade (about 9 inches) and not more than 3 inches deep. Place the peas singly in this trench in two lines, one at each side, the peas themselves being about 3 inches apart in the lines, and staggered on opposite sides of the trench. Then cover with an inch of soil. The depression left will provide the tiny seedlings with some protection and will make watering a simple matter. Do not sow all your early peas at once, or they will all mature at once. Practise successional sowing every fortnight or so.

Plant out Cauliflowers sown in September

Cauliflowers raised from a September sowing in a frame may now be planted outdoors if properly hardened off (see February, General Work). Lift the plants with as much soil and root as possible, and plant with a trowel on really good, well-dug soil. Allow 2½ feet between the rows and at least 18 inches between the plants in the rows.

Plant Mint

If you want to make a new plantation of mint now is the time to set about it. Lift some old plants or purchase the necessary roots; divide them up and spread them out thinly over the selected site, which should be in a reasonably open place, and cover with about 1½ inches of finely broken soil.

69

Pot Early Tomatoes and make Further Sowings

Tomatoes from the January sowing (see January, Second Week) should now be ready for their second potting into 4½-inch or 5-inch pots. Use the compost already recommended for general potting on page 62. Pot rather firmly this time and shade for a day or so as before (see February, Third Week).

A sowing of tomatoes made now will provide good sturdy plants for planting outdoors in June. Sow the seeds exactly as before (see January, Second Week) and germinate them in the greenhouse in a temperature of about 60 degs.

THIRD WEEK

Plant Autumn-sown Sweet Peas

Seize the first favourable opportunity to plant out sweet pea seedlings raised in pots in the autumn. Contrary to general practice when planting from pots, no attempt should be made to keep the ball of soil intact around the roots. Instead, very carefully shake the roots clear of soil and then plant equally carefully in deep holes prepared with a trowel. Spread the roots out and work fine soil around them, firming it thoroughly with the knuckles. For exhibition purposes the plants should be at least 9 inches apart in the rows. Common practice is to grow double rows a foot apart with 5-foot alleyways between.

Sow Hardy Annuals

This is a good time to make first sowings of all really hardy annuals, providing the soil is in reasonably good condition. Sow thinly broadcast and cover the seeds with fine soil to about twice their own depth. The seeds should be sown where the plants are to flower. If the seedlings are too thick some of them may be transplanted later on, but the best flowers will be obtained from the untransplanted plants.

Amongst the best annuals for sowing now are sweet alyssum, bartonia, calendula, annual candytuft, annual chrysanthemum, clarkia, collinsia, Convolvulus minor, annual coreopsis, cornflower, eschscholtzia, godetia, annual gypsophila, larkspur, Lavatera rosea, limnanthes, linum (scarlet flax), annual lupins, malope, mignonette, nemophila, nigella, phacelia, cardinal and Shirley poppies, annual rudbeckia, annual saponaria, annual sunflower, Virginian stock, and annual viscaria.

Sow Half-hardy Annuals in a Frame

If you have not a heated greenhouse and were therefore unable to sow half-hardy annuals, etc., as advised in my notes for February, Third Week, you can do so now in a frame. This should be in a sheltered place and it is all the better if it is on a hotbed (see p. 19). The seeds may either be sown directly in the frame or in boxes or pans as in the case of greenhouse-germinated seeds. The latter method does make for easier handling later on. Dahlias usually germinate very well in a frame at this period and make good flowering plants by August.

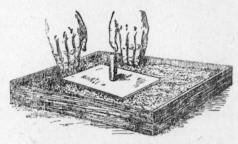

PREPARING A BOX FOR SMALL SEEDS.

If tiny seeds are to be sown it is essential that the surface should be perfectly smooth and level. For this purpose a firming block should be used. Push the compost in around the edge of the box with the fingers.

This, I find, is a good time to make a first sowing of asters. Seed will germinate easily enough earlier in the year, but the plants tend to get too big by planting time, and are much more liable to damp off.

Plant Gladioli and Montbretias

Make a first planting of gladioli, but do not plant all the corms at once. It is much better to make successional plantings over a period of about a month or six weeks, because this will lengthen the flowering period. Cover the corms with about 3 inches of soil. The small "primulinus" varieties may be 3 inches apart in rows 8 inches apart, but the large-flowered gladioli should be at least 6 inches apart in rows 1 foot apart—that is to say, if you want the flowers for cutting. If they are merely to be used for bedding or in groups in the herbaceous border, let them be at least 6 inches apart each way.

Montbretias are also planted now, and all can go out at once.

If you are purchasing dried corms, I advise you to start them into growth first in trays filled with a very light compost mainly consisting of moss peat and sand. Just bury them in this, water moderately, and place in a frame. Then, as soon as growth starts, transfer them to the beds in which they are to flower, planting carefully with a trowel and covering the corms with about 2 inches of soil. A better method of culture is to obtain growing tufts (plants that have never been quite dried off) and plant these as advised for the started corms. Montbretias should be at least 4 inches apart each way—rather more if you are after exhibition flowers.

Start Cannas and Dahlias

Cannas and dahlias can now be started into growth in slightly heated greenhouses, in frames on a mild hotbed, or even in well-constructed frames standing in a really sheltered place. But beware of unheated frames as yet if the sides are thin or have gaps between the wood through which draughts can penetrate. The method of starting dahlias is exactly as in greenhouses (see February, Third Week), except that there is really no need to use boxes. The roots can simply be placed in the frames side by side and nearly covered with dry soil. Old canna roots may be in pots already. There is not any need to repot them for the moment, as this is better done after growth has restarted. If, however, you are purchasing new roots or are dealing with old bedding roots that have been wintered in boxes, pot them singly in 6-inch pots, using a compost of about two parts good loam, one part well-rotted cow manure, or failing this good leaf-mould, and one part moss peat, with enough sand to speckle the whole freely.

Take Dahlia Cuttings

Dahlias introduced to the greenhouse last month will now be making growth, and you can obtain a first batch of cuttings. Sever the firm young shoots when they are about 2 inches in length. Some recommend taking each cutting with a small piece of tuber, but I regard this as wasteful. If the cuttings are severed just above the tuber, leaving a tiny stump still attached to it, this stump will soon send out two or three more shoots which can in turn be taken as cuttings. If the shoot is severed with some of the tuber, no more cuttings will be obtained from there. The cuttings are prepared by trimming the base cleanly just below a joint, removing the lower leaves (if any), and inserting ¾ inch deep in sandy soil. I find the simplest and quickest method in the long run is to put the soil into 2½-inch pots and place one cutting in each. Then there need be no further root disturbance. The cuttings should be rooted in a propagating box with a temperature of from 60 to 70 degs. Any sufficiently deep box with a piece of glass on the top will serve. Water rather freely.

Start Begonia and Gloxinia Tubers

If you have only a small greenhouse or one that is not too well heated and you were therefore not able to follow my advice regarding starting tuberous-rooted begonias and gloxinias into growth in January or February, this is the time to make a start. I have already given full particulars regarding this (see January, Second Week) and there is nothing further to be said, except that you will find it a good deal easier to maintain the required temperature of 55 to 60 degs. in March than in January. Make use of sun heat during the day by closing the ventilators early in the afternoon. An excellent plan with houses that are not too well heated is to have heavy canvas blinds which can be rolled down right over the glass as soon as the sun sets.

Pot Begonia and Gloxinia Tubers

Tubers that were started in January and potted for the first time in February (see February, Third Week) will almost certainly need a shift into their flowering pots, 4 to 6 inches in diameter, according to the size of the plants. Use the same compost and treat as before. Tubers set in fibre in February to start growth will probably be ready for first potting.

Start Hippeastrums

Start another batch of hippeastrums (see January, Fourth Week, and February, Third Week), giving preference to any bulbs that are forming shoots.

Sow Browallia

If you sow seed of browallia now in a slightly heated greenhouse or frame you will have good plants in flower from September to November. Simply scatter the seed thinly in the usual

73

seed compost (see p. 24), cover very lightly with soil, and place a pane of glass and a sheet of brown paper over the pan or box.

POT GREENHOUSE ANNUALS

If you were able to pot some annuals for the greenhouse in February (see February, First Week), the finest should now be ready for a further shift into 7- or 8-inch pots. Use a rather coarser compost than before. That described on p. 62 will do well.

REMOVE VEGETABLE SEEDLINGS TO FRAME

Onions and leeks sown in the greenhouse in January (see January, First and Fourth Weeks), also cauliflowers, peas, lettuces and broad beans sown in February (see February, First Week) will now be better in a frame, where they can be hardened off for planting outdoors in April. Ventilate cautiously at first and be ready with sacks for cold nights, but gradually accustom the plants to full exposure.

SOW CARROTS AND LEEKS OUTDOORS

If the soil is in good working condition, make a small sowing of stump-rooted carrot outdoors, but choose a sheltered place. Sow very thinly, either broadcast or in rows 9 inches apart, and cover with $\frac{1}{4}$ inch of soil. The main sowings will be made in April (see April, Second Week).

As already explained, the best leeks are raised under glass (see

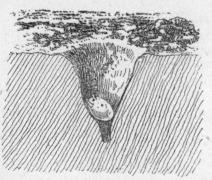

January, Fourth Week), but if you have not got a greenhouse, or even a frame that you can place on a hotbed, you can still have quite good leeks of your own raising by sowing outdoors now. Sow thinly in rows 1 foot apart and cover with $\frac{1}{4}$ inch of fine soil.

BAD POTATO PLANTING.

A dibber has been used, and though this has been worked round and round to enlarge the hole a space has been left beneath the tuber.

PLANT EARLY POTATOES

Even if you are not favoured with a particularly sheltered border you may now make a first planting of early potatoes. I have already given full particulars of the method to be followed in the notes for February, Fourth Week.

Prick off Early Celery

Celery from the February sowing will be in need of pricking off into deeper seed boxes. Use a compost with plenty of leafmould and just a little rotted manure if available, and dibble the seedlings 3 inches apart each way. Water freely and return to the greenhouse in an average temperature of about 55 degs. for the time being, but gradually harden off so that you can remove the boxes to a frame later (see April, Second Week).

Protect Early Fruit Blossom

Outdoor peaches and nectarines should now be coming into flower, and it is an excellent plan to protect these by hanging fishnetting in front of the trees. It might seem that this would afford no protection at all, but actually it makes quite a difference, causing eddies and preventing the slow, unbroken flow of air which always accompanies the worst frosts.

FOURTH WEEK

Prune Roses

This is the time to prune almost all bush and standard roses. The two exceptions are pure tea varieties (there are very few of these now, Lady Hillingdon and Mrs. Herbert Stevens being two of the most familiar) and weeping standards. The teas must be left a week or two longer, while the weeping standards are pruned in the late summer or early autumn. If the roses are required for garden display only, cut back all strong young growths made last year to a length of about 4 or 5 inches. Weaker shoots should be cut back to a couple of inches, while really thin, spindly wood is best removed altogether. If the roses are required for exhibition, they should be pruned rather more severely, strong shoots being cut back 2 or 3 inches, weaker ones removed. Of course, all dead or damaged growth must be removed first of all. Newly planted roses should all be pruned in the same way as those required for exhibition. Climbing roses, as distinct from

75

HOW TO PRUNE A BUSH ROSE.

This very severe annual cutting back is necessary if really high-class flowers are desired. Note that each cut has been made just above a dormant growth bud.

ramblers of the wichuraiana and multiflora types (any catalogue will put you right on this), are also pruned now. Usually it is sufficient to shorten strong growths by about one-third and weaker ones from a half to two-thirds, but occasionally, if a plant has not been making satisfactory progress, rather harder pruning should be carried out.

CLIP IVY ON WALLS

It is an excellent plan to clip ivy growing on walls at this time of the year. The work can be done very quickly with a pair of shears. Simply clip off the leaves, leaving the stems practically bare, and then brush them down with a stiff broom, getting out all dead leaves, dirt, etc. The plants will look very bare at first, but will soon get new leaves and will be much better for a clean up.

PLANT TIGRIDIAS

Tigridias are not everybody's flower, but they are very lovely and even though the individual blooms only last a day, they are followed by a succession of others. The corms are barely hardy and must be given a sheltered and sunny position. Plant now, placing the corms 4 inches deep and about 6 inches apart each way.

PLANT CARNATION LAYERS

Early autumn is usually considered the best time for planting rooted border carnation layers, but in very exposed places I prefer to pot the layers in the autumn and keep them in a cold frame during the winter. Then they are planted outdoors at this time of the year, when conditions are getting steadily more favourable.

Stop Chrysanthemums

Exhibition Japanese chrysanthemums which should be stopped are Autumn Tints, Avon, and Hugh Mitchell. Capt. Kettle, Duchess of Fife, Edith Laundy, and Yorkshire are incurves requiring the same attention (see notes for Second Week of this month).

Sow Spinach Beet

This is a very useful form of beetroot grown for its leaves, which are used like those of spinach. Sow now in drills 1 inch deep and 18 inches apart and thin out the seedlings to 1 foot apart. This plant is sometimes known as perpetual spinach, because it keeps on cropping all the summer and autumn and most of the winter as well.

Sow Lettuces Outdoors

Unless the weather is exceptionally bad or your garden is very cold, it should now be safe to make a first sowing of lettuces outdoors. You can choose a cabbage or a cos variety according to taste. Sow the seeds very thinly in drills $\frac{1}{2}$ inch deep and about 1 foot apart for the large varieties, or 9 inches apart for the Tom Thumb type.

Sow Broad Beans and Peas Outdoors

This is usually a good time to make the first sowing of broad beans outdoors. The place chosen must be open, and really well cultivated. Sow the seeds 6 inches apart in drills rather over 1 inch deep and about 2 feet apart. The dwarf varieties can be grown as close as 15 inches in the rows, but it is a mistake to crowd the bigger kinds.

Make a second sowing of an early culinary pea exactly as advised in my notes for the Second Week in this month.

Sow Celery and Celeriac in a Frame

Celery may be sown in a frame in a very sheltered position and for preference on a mild hotbed. Sow thinly either directly in soil in a frame or in well-drained boxes. Plants from this sowing

77

will provide a succession for planting out after those raised earlier in the greenhouse (see February, Third Week).

Celeriac, which is a moderately good substitute for celery and has the advantage that it will grow on soil that would be much too poor for that crop, is also sown now. The seeds are treated in exactly the same way as those of the celery.

Sow French Beans for Succession

You may now make a third sowing of beans in 8-inch pots for cropping under glass (see January, Fourth Week, and February, Fourth Week). At this season it will be possible to maintain the necessary temperature in a well-made frame placed in a sheltered but sunny position and covered with sacks at night.

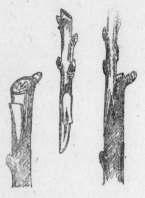

How to Make a Whip Graft.

This method is used when stock and scion are about the same thickness. The cut surfaces must fit exactly together. After fitting them, as shown on the right, bind them together with raffia and cover the whole of the cut area with grafting wax.

Sow Cucumbers on a Hotbed

Good cucumbers can be grown in frames on a hotbed as well as in heated greenhouses. If sown now they will commence to bear in June, just when the earliest hothouse cucumbers are getting past their first vigour. Make a good hotbed as described on page 19. Spread compost prepared as for glasshouse cucumbers (see First Week), with a low mound in the centre of the space covered by each 6 feet by 4 feet light. Place the frames and lights in position, and, as soon as the soil temperature falls to 85 degs., sow two seeds on the centre of each mound. If both germinate, pull out the weaker seedling.

Plant Melons

Melons raised in a warm greenhouse in February (see February, Fourth Week) will be ready for planting. The method followed is exactly the same as for cucumbers (see First Week), and similar watering, syringing, etc., must be carried out.

GRAFT APPLES AND PEARS

Apple and pear stocks that are well established, and also old trees that were cut back for reworking (see January, General Work) may be grafted now. If the stock and the piece of growth, known as the scion, that is to be joined to it are not far off the same size, use a whip graft, but if there is a big difference be-

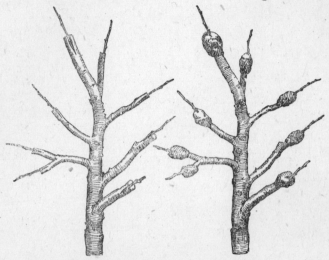

RIND GRAFTING AN OLD TREE.

The scion is prepared as for whip grafting except that no tongue is made. Then a vertical slit is made in the bark of the stock and the graft is slipped beneath it with its cut surface lying snugly against the bared tissue. It is bound in position and the wounded area is covered with wax.

tween the size of stock and scion, as there is sure to be in the case of old trees that are being reworked, employ the method known as rind grafting (see illustrations). Cover the whole of the cut surface and the part immediately above and below it as well with grafting wax, making everything quite airtight.

START VINES IN UNHEATED VINERIES

It is now safe to encourage vines to start into growth even in quite unheated vineries. This is done by closing ventilators altogether at night and opening those at the top only a little by day. Syringe every morning with water that is just slightly warm.

FLOWERS, VEGETABLES, AND FRUITS IN SEASON DURING MARCH

HARDY HERBACEOUS PLANTS.—Adonis *amurensis*, Corydalis *tuberosa*, Doronicum *austriacum*, Helleborus *abschasicus*, H. *atrorubens*, H. *guttatus*, H. *odorus*, H. *orientalis and vars.*, H. *viridis*, Iris *unguicularis*, Pulmonaria *angustifolia*, Primula *elatior (polyanthus)*, P. *rubra*, P. *vulgaris (primrose)*, Saxifraga *ciliata*, S. *cordifolia*, S. *crassifolia*, S. *ligulata*, S. *purpurascens*, S. *Strachyi*.

HARDY BULBS AND TUBERS.—Anemone *coronaria and vars.*, A. *fulgens*, Brodiæa *uniflora*, Chionodoxa *Luciliæ*, Colchicum *montanum*, Crocus *Bolansæ*, C. *biflorus*, C. *candidus*, C. *chrysanthus*, C. *corsicus*, C. *etruscus*, C. *minimus*, C. *stellaris*, C. *susianus*, C. *veluchensis*, C. *vernus*, Cyclamen *coum*, C. *ibericum*, C. *libanoticum*, crocuses *(large-flowering)*, Eranthis *cilicia*, E. *hyemalis*, Erythronium *Dens-canis*, E. *Hartwegii*, Fritillaria *purdica*, Galanthus *byzantinus*, G. *Elwesii*, G. *Fosteri*, G. *latifolius*, Hyacinthus *azureus*, hyacinths *(large-flowered)*, Iris *bakeriana*, I. *persica*, I. *sindjarensis*, I. *rosenbachiana*, Leucojum *vernum*, Narcissus *Bulbocodium*, N. *minor*, narcissus hybrids in var. *(including trumpet daffodils)*, Romulea *rosea*, Scilla *amœna*, S. *bifolia*, S. *sibirica*, Tulipa *biflora*, T. *Kaufmanniana*.

ROCK PLANTS.—Anemone *angulosa*, A. *apennina*, A. *blanda*, A. *nemorosa vars.*, A. *Pulsatilla*, A. *ranunculoides*, A. *vernalis*, Cortusa *Matthiolii*, Daphne *Blagayana*, Doronicum *caucasicum*, Gentiana *acaulis*, G. *alpina*, G. *kochiana*, G. *verna*, Iris *pumila vars.*, I. *verna*, Lithospermum *rosmarinifolium*, Morisia *hypogea*, Omphalodes *cappadocica*, O. *verna*, Primula *cortusoides*, P. *denticulata and vars.*, P. *Forrestii*, P. *glaucescens*, P. *Juliana vars.*, P. *marginata*, P. *viscosa*, Sanguinaria *canadensis*, Saxifraga *apiculata*, S. *arcovalleyi*, S. *aretioides*, S. *Borisii*, S. *Boydii*, S. *burseriana and vars.*, S. *diapensioides*, S. *Faldonside*, S. *Elizabethæ*, S. *Griesbachii*, S. *Haagii*, S. *Irvingii*, S. *Jenkinsii*, S. *juniperifolia*, S. *kewensis*, S. *lilacina*, S. *marginata*, S. *oppositifolia and vars.*, S. *Paulinæ*, S. *Petraschii*, S. *porophylla*, S. *racemiflora*, S. *sancta*, S. *scardica*, S. *Sibthorpii*, S. *Sundermannii*, S. *Vandellii*, Schizocodon *soldanelloides*, Sisyrinchium *grandiflorum*, Soldanella *alpina*, S. *minima*, S. *montana*, Synthyris *reniformis*, Viola *calcarata*, V. *canadensis*, V. *florariensis*.

HARDY AQUATICS AND BOG PLANTS.—Caltha *palustris*, Primula *giraldiana*, P. *rosea*, P. *sino-purpurea*.

HARDY EVERGREEN SHRUBS.—Arctostaphylos *Manzanita*, Azara *integrifolia*, A. *microphylla*, Berberis *aquifolia*, B. *buxifolia*, B. *japonica and vars.*, B. *nepalensis*, B. *replicata*, Camellia *japonica vars.*, Daphne *collina*, D. *Dauphinii*, D. *Laureola*, D. *tangutica*, Epigæa *repens*, Erica *arborea and vars.*, E. *carnea*, E. *darleyensis*, E. *lusitanica*, E. *mediterranea*, Lonicera *fragrantissima*, Pieris *floribunda*, P. *japonica*, P. *taiwanensis*, Raphiolepis *Delacourii*, Rhododendron *arboreum (shelter)*, R. *calophytum*, R. *neriiflorum*, R. *præcox*, R. *strigulosum*, R. *sutchuenense*, R. *Thomsonii*, Ulex *europæus vars.*, Viburnum *Tinus*.

HARDY DECIDUOUS SHRUBS.—Cassandra *calyculata*, Colletia *infausta*, Cornus *Mas*, Corylopsis *Griffithii*, C. *pauciflora*, C. *platypetala*, C. *spicata*,

1. Drawing a drill for seed sowing.   2. Sowing the seeds thinly and evenly in the drill.   3. Covering the seeds and firming the soil by scuffling with the feet.   4. Planting a sweet pea.   Note the way in which the roots have been shaken free of soil.   5. Firming in the sweet pea after planting.

1. Potato planting. It only remains to cover the tubers with soil drawn from between the rows. 2. Planting seakale thongs with a dibber. 3. Pruning a bush hybrid tea rose. 4. Removing a briar growing from a standard hybrid tea rose. 5. Pruning the standard rose to obtain a shapely head.

Cydonia *japonica*, Daphne *Mezereum*, Forsythia *intermedia vars.*, F. *ovata*, F. *suspensa*, Lonicera *Standishii*, L. *syringatha*, Magnolia *stellata*, Nuttalia *cerasiformis*, Prinsepia *sinensis*, Prunus *nana*, P. *spinosa* (*sloe, blackthorn*), P. *tomentosa*, Salix *gracilistyla*, S. *Caprea* (*palm, goat willow*), Spiræa *Thunbergi*, Stachyurus *præcox*, Viburnum *grandiflorum*.

HARDY EVERGREEN TREES.—Arbutus *Andrachne*.

HARDY DECIDUOUS TREES.—Acer *Opalus*, A. *rubrum*, Alnus *cordata*, A. *firma*, A. *japonica*, A. *oregona*, Magnolia *Campbellii* (*shelter*), Parrotia *persica*, Prunus *Amygdalus* (*almond*), P. *Blireana*, P. *Conradinæ*, P. *dasy-*

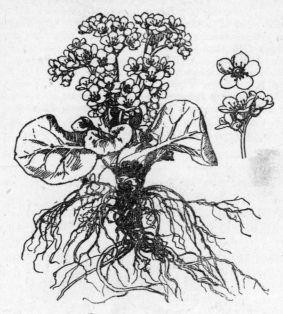

SAXIFRAGA STRACHEYI.

carpa, P. *Davidiana*, P. *incisa*, P. *Mume*, P. *pendula*, P. *Persica and vars.* (*peach*), P. *Pissardii* (*purple plum*), P. *subhirtella and vars.*, P. *triloba*, P. *yedœnsis*, Salix *Smithiana*.

HARDY CLIMBING PLANTS.—Clematis *calycina*, Ercilla *volubilis*.

GREENHOUSE PLANTS.—Abutilons, acacias, arum lilies, astilbes, azaleas (*Indian and mollis*), Boronia *megastigma*, carnation (*perpetual-flowering*), cinerarias (*hybrids*), Coleus *thyrsoideus*, correas, Epacris *hyacinthiflora*, forget-me-nots, freesias, hippeastrums, hyacinths (*large-flowered*), lachenalias, Leucocoryne *ixioides*, lilies of the valley, Lilium *Harrisii*, narcissi (*including trumpet daffodils*), Primula *obconica*, P. *sinensis and stellata*, P. *malacoides*, primroses, polyanthuses, rhododendrons (*Javanese*), roses, tulips (*earlies and May-flowering*), wallflowers, *also shrubs in pots such as* cherries, deutzias, genistas, lilacs, peaches, etc.

F

Plant Alpines

Alpine plants are almost invariably grown by nurserymen in small pots and can be transplanted to the rock garden from these at any time of the year, providing sufficient care is taken. But April is the ideal month, and the one in which there is least risk. Even plants grown in the open ground can be shifted now, unless they happen to be in flower— *e.g.,* aubrietias, arabis, early saxifrages, etc.—in which case they should be transplanted as soon as they have finished flowering. When planting from pots, simply tap the plants out, remove the crocks from the bottom of the pot ball, and loosen the mass a little with the fingers, but not so much as to damage any of the roots. Plant with a trowel and make firm. Only when planting in the moraine is it advisable to shake all the soil away from the roots and then spread these out carefully in the new compost.

PREPARING FOR REPOTTING OR PLANTING.

When plants have been removed from pots the old crocks in the bottom of the pot ball must be removed and the roots loosened a little. This is most important when planting out pot-grown alpines.

Plant Evergreen Shrubs

There is no doubt that the best time for planting evergreen shrubs is in the early autumn (see September, Third Week), but it is not always possible to complete the work then, and April is a good second best time. In many seasons April-planted evergreens do quite as well as those planted in late September or early October, but difficulties arise if, instead of the proverbial sunshine and showers, we have continued spells of cold east wind. The only remedy then is to erect some kind of protection around the shrubs, either by making screens of sacking or placing wattle hurdles or evergreen boughs in position, paying particular attention to the east and north sides. Later on, as the weather becomes warm, a nightly syringing with tepid water will do good.

PROPAGATE SHRUBS, ETC., BY LAYERING

Layering is a very simple method of propagating quite a number of shrubs, fruit trees, etc. It is worth trying practically any variety, with the exception of the big fruits such as apples, pears, cherries, plums, etc., and also very hard-wooded shrubs such as hawthorns, beech, etc. Many evergreens grow freely from layers; rhododendrons, for example, and also laurels and aucubas. Rambler roses form roots without difficulty, and so do many of the more vigorous climbing varieties.

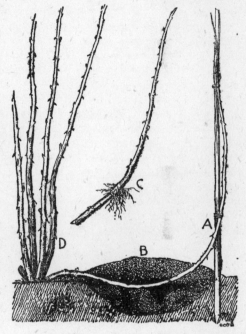

The method is similar in all cases. Choose a good, supple branch or stem, preferably one formed last year, make an upward incision through one of its joints, not too near the tip but at a point that can easily be bent down to soil level, press the cut portion of stem into the soil and hold it in position with a wooden peg or a heavy stone.

HOW TO LAYER A ROSE.

A stray shoot (A) from the parent plant (D) is bent down, covered with good soil (B), and tied to a stake. After a few months roots will be formed, and the layer (C) can be severed and planted on its own.

If the soil is very heavy or poor, make up a good mixture of loam, peat moss, and sand in about equal parts, and peg the layer into this. Keep well watered during the summer and by the autumn the branch will have formed roots around the cut surface and can be detached from the parent plant and established on its own.

Greenhouse General Management

There will now be much less difficulty in maintaining sufficient temperature in the greenhouse. It may even be necessary to have some temporary shading for a good many plants during the hottest part of the day, especially in small houses which heat up very quickly, but permanent shading will not be needed as yet. It is not wise to have the temperature running much above 70 degs. in the general utility greenhouse in April, which means ample top ventilation on all sunny and fairly still days. Do not use the side ventilators as yet, nor leave the door open, for fear of admitting damaging draughts.

Bedding plants and half-hardy annuals generally must be gradually hardened off. Later in the month (see Third Week) you should remove them to frames, if possible, but you must prepare them gradually for this in the early part of the month by giving increased ventilation whenever the weather is favourable, and keeping them as close to the glass as possible. In a mixed greenhouse it is sometimes difficult to reconcile the needs of all the plants at this stage, but much can be done by erecting shelves, a little below the top ventilators, where the plants that need cool conditions can be placed. Those varieties that require warmth can be kept on the staging and as near to the heating apparatus as possible. Usually one end of the greenhouse is considerably warmer than the other.

From now onwards you will have to keep a sharp look-out for pests such as greenfly, thrips, and red spider. Should any of these appear, fumigate at once with an appropriate fumigant—nicotine for greenfly, and naphthalene for red spider and thrips. Naphthalene fumigation, however, is a rather tricky business, and you should only attempt it with the aid of a special naphthalene fumigating lamp which you can purchase from any dealer in horticultural sundries. The correct dose is 4 ounces of Grade 16 naphthalene per 1,000 cubic feet of glasshouse area.

The main batch of calceolarias and autumn-sown schizanthuses will be approaching their flowering period and will benefit by fairly constant feeding, providing you use the manure water or fertiliser really weak. The former should only just colour the water, while in the case of proprietary fertilisers you should consult manufacturers' instructions and certainly not exceed them; I find that it is usually better to halve the strengths they recommend. Similar remarks apply to hippeastrums which are forming their flower stems.

HARDEN OFF PLANTS IN FRAMES

Onion, leek, cauliflower, pea, broad bean, and lettuce seedlings in frames (see March, Third Week) will require full ventilation whenever the thermometer is above freezing point and the wind is not very cold, for they must be hardened fully for planting out later in the month (see Third Week). Similar remarks apply to violets, violas, pansies, pentstemons, autumn-sown antirrhinums, and other nearly hardy plants, but more tender kinds must still be ventilated with some caution.

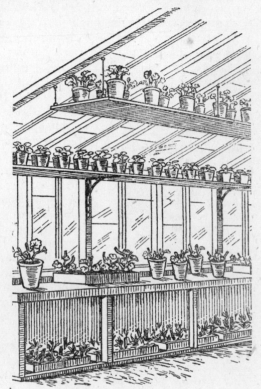

MAKING THE MOST OF SPACE.

Dahlias are being started into growth beneath the staging, stock geraniums are growing above them, while the shelves are occupied by rooted geranium cuttings that are hardening off.

PRICK OFF SEEDLINGS

Throughout the month you will be kept busy pricking off many seedlings from sowings made earlier (see March, General Work, for details).

GENERAL POTTING

In addition to pricking off there will be a considerable amount of potting to do. Seedlings pricked off earlier may be getting overcrowded. Pot them singly into 2½- or 3-inch pots directly their leaves touch. The later chrysanthemum and carnation cuttings will be needing a shift (see January, General Work, and March, General Work), while dahlia cuttings can be potted into 3-inch receptacles directly they are rooted, unless you inserted them singly in pots, in which case no further move will be needed as yet. This also applies to miscellaneous greenhouse plant cuttings such as abutillons, petunias, daturas, etc. (see March, General Work). Begonias and gloxinias started as tubers in January and February and already potted once will be in various stages of growth, and the same applies to many other young greenhouse plants and tomatoes. The safe plan is to tap a typical plant out of its pot occasionally and examine the roots. If the soil is just nicely moist right through, you can do this quite easily without disturbing the plant at all. Simply turn the pot upside down, place one hand over the soil, and give the rim of the pot a sharp rap on the edge of the potting bench. As soon as you see white rootlets forming freely all round the side of the pot ball, transfer the plants to larger receptacles. The usual practice is to shift from 3-inch pots into 4- or 5-inch pots, and from these into 6- or 7-inch pots, or, in the case of tomatoes, directly into the 10-inch pots or large boxes in which they will fruit. But too big a shift at one time is not generally desirable. The compost I have already mentioned several times—namely, seven parts good fibrous loam, three parts best moss peat, and two parts coarse sand, with 1½ ounces hoof and horn meal, 1½ ounces superphosphate of lime, ¾ ounce sulphate of potash, and ¾ ounce ground chalk added to each bushel of the mixture—can still be used for the majority of plants. Most plants should be returned to the greenhouse im-

UNPOTTING A PLANT.

This is done by reversing it, as shown, and giving the rim of the pot a sharp tap on the edge of the potting bench.

mediately after potting, but chrysanthemums are better in an unheated frame, where they may be hardened off gradually.

Repot Indian Azaleas and Camellias

Both Indian azaleas and camellias may be repotted if necessary as soon as they have finished flowering. Use a compost of loam and moss peat in about equal parts with half a part of sand and a good sprinkling of bone meal. At the most only use a pot one size larger than that occupied formerly—it is all the better if they can go back into the same size pots after teasing out some of the old soil with the point of a stick. After potting the plants must be returned to the greenhouse for a few weeks and should be syringed every morning with tepid water.

Prune Azaleas, Genistas, and Deutzias

As soon as they have finished flowering remove the faded flower heads from Indian azaleas and cut back the flowering branches of deutzias and genistas quite close to the base.

Take Cuttings of Winter-flowering Begonias

It should be possible to take further cuttings of winter-flowering begonias during the month (see March, General Work). Semi-tuberous rooted begonias of the Optima type will now be starting into growth again, and you may encourage them to do so by giving them rather more water. As soon as the basal growths are a couple of inches in length you can remove some of them

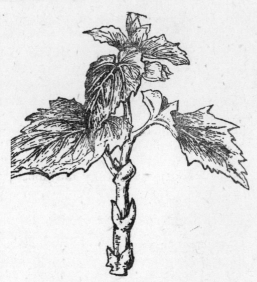

A Winter-Flowering Begonia Cutting.

Note the method of trimming the cutting immediately below a joint and removing the lower leaves.

89

as cuttings, treating them exactly as the other winter-flowering types.

Rest Freesias, Lachenalias, etc.

Freesias and lachenalias that have been flowering during the winter must now be allowed to go to rest gradually. To effect this, place them on a shelf quite near the glass and gradually reduce the water supply. Rather similar remarks apply to arum lilies that have been used for winter flowering. These cannot be stood near the glass, but they must be kept in a cooler atmosphere. Old cyclamen that have finished flowering may be treated just like freesias, but the young seedlings must be kept growing.

Take Cuttings of Bedding Plants, etc.

It is still possible to take cuttings of bedding and greenhouse plants in exactly the same manner as I described in the notes for General Work during March. It is true that the bedding plants will be comparatively late in flower, but they may be none the less useful for that. Some late-struck fuchsias, geraniums, and salvias make admirable pot plants for the greenhouse in autumn. Continue to take cuttings of dahlias as they become available (see March, Third Week).

Stop Early-Flowering Chrysanthemums

From time to time during the month you should pinch out the growing tips of the rooted cuttings of early-flowering chrysanthemums required for spray flowering. The ideal moment to do this is when the cuttings are well rooted, growing freely, and are about 6 inches in height. In the case of February and March rooted cuttings, most will reach this stage before the end of April. Note particularly that this stopping applies only to plants that are to be grown for garden decoration or to produce a lot of flowers. The object is to produce a number of branches on each plant, and with this end in view the plants will be stopped again in June. In the case of plants that are grown for large individual flowers, either for exhibition or for cutting, a different method is followed (see May, Third Week), and they must not be stopped now.

Prepare Celery Trenches

Some time during the month you should prepare the trenches for celery. They will not actually be wanted until June, but it is an advantage to prepare them well in advance so that manure and soil may become blended together. The trenches should be 15 inches wide for single rows and 18 inches wide for double rows, and they must be at least 3 feet apart. You can use the ground between the trenches for various salad crops. Remove the soil to a depth of 18 inches and then break up the bottom as deeply as possible with a long fork, mixing well-rotted manure or decayed vegetable refuse with it. Place a layer of manure and good top-spit soil in about equal parts 9 inches deep on top of the forked subsoil and a further layer of 6 inches of good top-spit soil on top of this. This, you will see, leaves you with a depression about 3 inches deep in which the celery will be planted later on. This shallow trench gives some protection to the young plants and makes it very easy to flood them with water.

MAKE SUCCESSIONAL SOWINGS

You will need to make sundry successional sowings during the month if you wish to maintain an unbroken supply of vegetables later on. In the main these are the same as for last month (see March, General Work). Radishes and mustard and cress may now be sown outdoors, but choose a warm, sheltered place for preference. You should make two further sowings of lettuce at fortnightly intervals (see March, Fourth Week). Similar instructions apply to spinach (see March, First Week). A further sowing of broad beans outdoors (see March, Fourth Week) made towards the end of the month will ensure a crop in the early autumn. Further sowings of carrots will be necessary, but these I have dealt with separately (see Second Week). Most important of all are at least two sowings of peas (see March, Second Week). These are treated as before, but you should now choose a main-crop variety, such as Quite Content or Duke of Albany, in place of the early kinds recommended before.

TRAIN AND TOP-DRESS EARLY CUCUMBERS

Side shoots formed on the main stems of cucumbers planted in March (see March, First Week) must be stopped from extending too far or there will soon be such a mass of foliage in the house that the plants will get unhealthy. Pinch out the soft tip of each side shoot as soon as it carries two tiny fruits, or when it is

2 feet in length if it reaches that before it has two fruits. If secondary side shoots appear, pinch them when they have made a couple of leaves. The tip of the main stem must be pinched out as soon as it reaches the apex of the house.

Keep a sharp watch and as soon as white rootlets appear on the surface of the bed give a top-dressing, a couple of inches thick, of a mixture of equal parts good fibrous loam and well-rotted manure. Repeat this later if necessary. The plants will want a

HOW A GREENHOUSE CUCUMBER IS TRAINED.

The fruit-bearing laterals have been stopped some time previously by pinching out their tips, as indicated by the black lines. Further laterals are allowed to form all up the main stem, which is stopped when it reaches the ridge.

lot of water now that they are growing freely. You should also syringe them twice daily with tepid water and damp down the paths as well to maintain plenty of moisture in the atmosphere. Open the top ventilators a little when the thermometer reaches 75 degs. A light permanent shading on the glass will be advisable from now onwards. You can use ordinary limewash with a little white of egg mixed in to make it stick. Syringe the glass quite lightly with this. Heavy shading is not desirable as yet.

Cucumbers growing on hotbeds (see March, Fourth Week) are trained in a slightly different manner from those growing in greenhouses. The tip of each plant is pinched out when it has made four leaves. Then the laterals which form are trained evenly over the bed, being held in position with wooden or wire pegs, and are stopped again as soon as they reach the edge of the frame or interfere with neighbouring plants. Sub-laterals, bearing flowers and subsequently fruits, are pinched from time to time one or two leaves beyond the flowers to prevent gross overcrowding with foliage. Later on some old growths that have finished bearing may be cut out to make room for new growths (see June, General Work).

Water the frame plants freely and ventilate very sparingly on mild days only. Spray overhead when closing for the day in sunny, warm weather.

Train and Pollinate Melons

The training of melons (see March, Fourth Week) is not unlike that of cucumbers. It is, however, necessary to restrict each plant to about four fruits. These should be placed as evenly as possible over the plant. There are two kinds of flowers, male and female, and only the latter will produce fruits. You can recognise the females because each will have a tiny fruit on its stalk just beneath the petals. These flowers must be pollinated by hand, and all on any one plant at the same time. You can arrange to get four

FERTILISING MELON FLOWERS.

Male flowers are shown at A and B, while one has been partially stripped for pollinating at C. Female flowers, distinguished by the embryo fruits to which they are attached, are shown at D. The work of pollination is beng carried out at E.

93

suitable blooms open at once by judicious pinching. Backward blooms can be hastened by stopping the shoots on which they are growing one leaf beyond the flower, while forward blooms can be retarded by allowing the shoot to grow unstopped. Scatter pollen from the male blooms on to the females when the sun is shining.

MANAGEMENT OF THE VINERY

The vinery, whether heated or unheated, will require fairly constant attention throughout the month. In unheated houses growth can be encouraged now by giving less ventilation and rolling down heavy canvas blinds (see notes on starting begonias and gloxinias, March, Third Week) an hour before sunset, so as to trap sun heat for the night. In a heated vinery growth will be in full swing, and will be in various stages according to the time at which the house was closed. Some vines will be in flower, and will need a slightly higher temperature and a drier atmosphere; more ventilation should be given and syringing discontinued for the time being (see February, General Work). These will also require training and stopping, as I explained in the same place. Other vines a little more advanced will be in need of fruit thinning, as described in the notes for March, General Work. The earliest vines, started in January, will be forming their pips (this is technically known as stoning), and you must make every effort to avoid severe fluctuations of temperature. A minimum night temperature of 60 degs., rising to 80 by day with direct sun heat is ideal.

THIN PEACHES, NECTARINES, ETC.

In the early orchard house peaches and nectarines will have completed stoning by this period, and it will be all the better if you can increase the temperature by 5 or 10 degs. by day and night. Thinning can be completed as soon as the stones are formed. You can easily ascertain how far things have gone by removing a typical fruit and cutting into it. If the stone is hard and almost full size, with a well-developed kernel, the stoning period is over. Leave an average of one fruit per square foot of tree area. Peaches in unheated houses should be nicely set and you can commence thinning as advised in the General Notes for March.

FIRST WEEK

Sow Grass Seed

This is usually the most favourable time for sowing grass seed, but wait a little if the ground is sticky. Rake the surface of the ground quite level and scatter the seed as evenly as possible at the rate of 2 ounces per square yard. Cover with a light sprinkling of fairly

A Good Method of Sowing a New Lawn.

The plot is divided into yard-wide strips with the aid of two lines and one strip is sown at a time. Measure the length of the strip in yards, multiply by two, and you will have the correct weight in ounces of grass seed for the marked area.

dry soil and then stretch black thread between small sticks placed about the seed bed. This, I find, is the most effective method of keeping off birds. They fly into the fine black thread without, apparently, seeing it, and the fright they get keeps them away for quite a long time.

Complete Rose Pruning

You should now prune the more delicate tea roses that I advised you to leave alone last month (see March, Fourth Week). Treatment is the same as for the hybrid teas except that cutting back

95

should be a little more severe, as most of these varieties tend to make weakly growth if pruned insufficiently.

APPLY TONK'S FERTILISER TO ROSES

Give all your roses a dressing of Tonk's fertiliser. It will provide them with most of the food they require throughout the summer. You can purchase this fertiliser ready for use, or, if you prefer, you can make it yourself. The ingredients are twelve parts superphosphate of lime, ten parts nitrate of potash, two parts sulphate of magnesia, one part sulphate of iron, eight parts gypsum. Mix thoroughly, crush up fine, and use at 4 ounces per square yard.

PRUNE FLOWERING SHRUBS

Shrubs to prune now include the hardy fuchsias such as F. macrostemma, F. gracilis, and F. Riccartoni; Buddleia variabilis, and its varieties, Leycesteria formosa, Perowskia atriplicifolia, Romneyas Coulteri and trichocalyx, also all varieties of cornus and salix (willow) grown for bark effects. In all cases pruning should be hard, last year's growth being cut back quite close to the older wood, but in the case of the buddleias you can allow a few branches to remain at three-quarter length to build up a main framework of growth (see February, First Week).

STOP JAPANESE CHRYSANTHEMUMS

There are two well-known Japanese chrysanthemums which should be stopped early in April, in the south of England, to give flowers by Mid-November—namely, Rise of Day and Thames. If you wish to grow the Japanese chrysanthemum Edward Page, also known as Chiltern White, as an outdoor variety, you must stop it now. The same remark applies to the sport of this variety, Yellow Edward Page.

POT CYCLAMEN SEEDLINGS

If you were able to raise any cyclamen from seeds last summer (see August, Second Week), the seedlings will now be ready for transferring singly to 3-inch pots. Use a compost rather rich in humus; two parts loam and one part of either leaf-mould or moss peat, with a liberal sprinkling of sand and powdered mortar rubble and a dusting of bonemeal and old soot will do well. The corms should be kept on the surface of the soil, not buried. Pot moderately

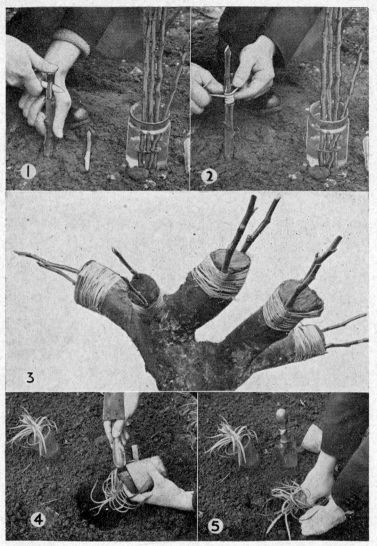

1. Preparing a young apple stock for a whip graft. The prepared scion is lying between the operator and the jar containing more shoots from which grafts will be cut. 2. Binding the scion on to the stock. 3. An old fruit tree headed back and rind grafted. 4. Knocking a border carnation out of its pot prior to planting out. 5. Firming the soil around a newly-planted carnation.

1. A seedling cyclamen rooting through the drainage hole in its pot. This is an indication that the plant needs a shift to a larger size pot. 2. Tapping a gloxinia out of its pot prior to repotting. 3. Building a plant into the rock garden. 4. Planting an asparagus bed. 5. A temporary shelter of stakes and straw mats for a newly-planted shrub.

firm, water freely, and then stand the plants on a shelf or staging in a light, airy part of the greenhouse. The temperature should not fall below 50 degs. An average of just over 60 degs. is ideal at this stage.

Sow Zinnias in a Frame

If you make a sowing of zinnias in a warm, sheltered frame and keep the seedlings growing strongly without check, the plants

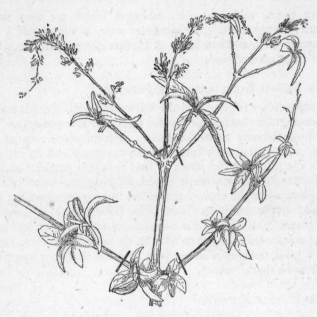

Pruning a Buddleia variabilis.

This bush has been allowed to form a fairly extensive framework of old wood, and young growths are cut back as indicated by the black lines. Pruning can be even more severe, if desired, growth being cut back annually to within a foot or so of the ground.

will flower by July. The secret of success with zinnias is to maintain steady growth. Any kind of check is fatal, and sometimes it is almost impossible to avoid a check with seedlings from an earlier sowing. Sow thinly in boxes or directly in the frame and cover with ¼ inch of fine soil.

G

lime sulphur wash at the usual winter strength recommended by the manufacturers.

Black currants sometimes get very badly attacked by a minute pest which breeds within the buds and causes them to swell up to a great size. This condition is appropriately known as " big bud " and, if any of your black currants are suffering from it, you should spray them at once with lime sulphur wash at twice the normal winter strength recommended by the manufacturers. The effect of this will be to scorch the tiny leaves that are just appearing, but the bushes will recover later on and the mites will be killed.

Finish Grafting Fruit Trees

Early April is a good time for grafting fruit trees in the open—but the earlier the better. I have already given instructions in March, Fourth Week.

Big Bud.

These swollen black currant buds are full of minute insects.

SECOND WEEK

Plant Violets

It is time to make a new violet plantation out of doors to provide clumps for forcing next winter. If cuttings were rooted the previous autumn, as described in the notes for September, General Work (and there is no better way of growing good, clean violets), the old clumps that have been flowering during the past winter can be discarded altogether. However, if you have no cuttings you will have to be satisfied with young rooted pieces pulled from the out-side of the old clumps to make the new plantation. The central portion of each clump should be thrown away, however, for it is very unlikely to give good results another season. Whether you use rooted pieces pulled off the clumps or rooted cuttings the method of making a plantation is the same. Choose a partially shaded border and rather heavy, rich soil if there is any choice

"...leaving her for good! She **COOKED** my Seed Potatoes!!"

Moscow's Move For 'Improved' Agreement

THE Soviet Government has notified Turkey that it wishes to terminate the existing Soviet-Turkish Treaty of friendship and neutrality on the grounds that in view of changed conditions it needs "considerable improvement."

A statement issued by the Information Bureau of the Soviet Foreign Affairs Department, quoted by Moscow radio to-day, said:

"On March 19 the People's Commissar for Foreign Affairs of the U.S.S.R., M. Molotov, in connection with the impending termination of the validity of the Soviet-Turkish agreement of friendship and neutrality on December 17, 1945, made to the Turkish Ambassador, M. Sarper, on behalf of the Soviet Government, a statement to be transmitted to the President of the Turkish Republic.

Mr. Thomas Crane Davi
Ystrad Mynach, and Miss
garet Olwyn Rees, of Ba
after their wedding at St.
Church, Maindee, Newpe

WELSH RUGB'

Great Changes

in the matter. Plant the big single varieties 1 foot apart in rows 18 inches apart and the doubles 6 inches apart in rows 1 foot apart.

Sow Hardy Annuals

Seed of the various hardy annuals will usually germinate more readily and certainly in mid-April than in March, particularly if the soil tends to be heavy and cold. I gave particulars for an early sowing in the notes for March, Third Week, and these apply with equal force now, except that to the list of varieties there given a number of other kinds can now be added, notably nasturtiums of all types, calandrinia, sweet sultan, layia, leptosiphon, canary creeper, Tagetes signata pumila, Mesembryanthemum criniflorum, ursinia, venidium, dimorphotheca, salpiglossis, and jacobæa. In sheltered gardens it is even possible to sow a number of half-hardy annuals outdoors with success, but if your garden is at all exposed I advise you to leave this until the first week in May. In any case it is bound to be a bit of a gamble at the moment.

A GOOD VIOLET DIVISION.
Young rooted pieces such as this, pulled from the outside of old clumps, are almost as good as cuttings.

Stop Japanese Chrysanthemums

A number of popular Japanese chrysanthemums should be stopped in the Midlands and South if fully developed blooms are required by mid-November. The varieties in question now are Mrs. G. Stacey, Mrs. H. Habgood, and William Wigley in the Japanese exhibition class and Charles Curtis, H. W. Thorp, J. W. Streeter, Lord Somers, Mahogany, Mrs. F. Judson, Mrs. G. Denyer, Mrs. J. P. Byce, Mrs. T. E. Wiseman, Mrs. S. Dove, Madame E. Roger, and Pink Thorp in the incurved section. It is also a good time to stop all decoratives and single chrysanthemums that are well rooted and growing freely.

Late Queen, ready from April to June. Sow some of each kind now and you will be assured of a succession later on. As regards cabbage, choose a quick-maturing variety such as Winnigstadt or Greyhound.

Sow Celery in Frame

To supplement earlier sowings of celery made in a warm greenhouse, or as an alternative to these if they could not be made, celery may now be grown in an unheated frame. The method is just the same as before (see February, Third Week), the seed being sown thinly in well-drained seed trays filled with a light, sandy compost.

Remove Early Celery to Frame

Early celery pricked off last month (see March, Third Week) will now be better in a frame, where it can be still further hardened off for planting out.

Prick off Cabbages, Cauliflowers, etc.

Cabbages, cauliflowers, broccolis, and Brussels sprouts raised in frame or greenhouse in March (see March, First Week) will be in need of pricking off, 3 inches apart each way, in a frame or, providing the weather is mild and they have been properly hardened off, in a sheltered border outdoors.

Plant out Vegetable Seedlings

Culinary peas, onions, leeks, cauliflowers, broad beans, and lettuces raised in the greenhouse and transferred to a frame last month for hardening off (see March, Third Week) may now be planted out in the beds in which they are to mature, providing the weather is fairly mild. If it is frosty or winds are cold, wait a further week. All the ground should have been well dug and manured. The position chosen for the cauliflowers should be sheltered from north and east if possible. Exhibition leeks are usually grown in trenches prepared exactly as for celery (see April, General Work), but quite good leeks can also be grown in ordinary beds if the plants are dropped into holes about 9 inches deep made with a dibber. With this exception, all other planting of seedlings mentioned above is best done with a trowel. Plant the celery 1 foot apart (if there are two rows in an 18-inch-trench, set the rows 1 foot apart). Leeks should be 9 inches apart in rows 18 inches apart for ordinary purposes and 1 foot apart in the trenches for exhibition. Onions are set 9 inches apart in rows 1 foot apart; lettuces from 6 to 9 inches apart, according to the size of the variety, the rows being 1 foot apart to allow easy use of the hoe; cauliflowers 2 feet apart in rows 2½ feet apart; broad beans 6 inches apart in rows from 15 to 30 inches apart, according to the size of the variety; and peas 4 inches apart in double rows 10 inches apart, with from 3 to 6 feet between each pair of rows, according to the height of the variety.

Place Early Tomatoes in Final Pots

Tomatoes from a January sowing should now be ready for their final pots. You can, if you prefer, grow them in boxes or plant them out directly into a border of

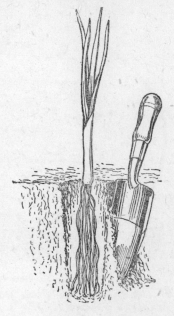

ONION PLANTING.

A hole has been prepared sufficiently large to take all the roots without any unnatural cramping.

compost prepared on the staging, or on the floor if the house is a light one with low walls or glass right to ground level. Nevertheless, I think 9- or 10-inch pots are best for the first crop, as plants seem to come to maturity more rapidly in them than when grown in any other way. The compost should consist of about four parts good loam, one part of old, well-rotted manure and sweet leaf-mould, well mixed, and a 5-inch potful of bone-meal added to each bushel of this mixture. Be sure to make it really firm around the roots, for tomatoes get soft-stemmed and fruit badly in loose soil.

Spray Apples and Pears

If apples were attacked last year by scab disease, spray now with lime sulphur wash at full winter strength as recommended by the manufacturers. Pears similarly attacked should be treated

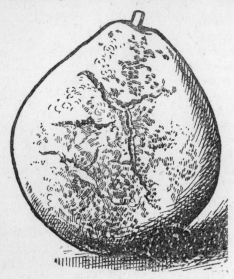

DAMAGE CAUSED BY PEAR SCAB.

Dry cracks in the fruit are an almost certain sign that this disease has been at work. The fungus also attacks apples.

with Bordeaux mixture rather than lime sulphur, as the latter is inclined to cause scorching. The Bordeaux should be used at full strength as recommended by the manufacturers.

THIRD WEEK

THIN HARDY ANNUALS

Hardy annuals sown in March outdoors where they are to bloom (see March, Third Week) will be in need of a first thinning out. Simply pull out the feeblest seedlings until the remainder are left a clear 2 or 3 inches apart each way and have room to develop. A further thinning will be necessary in May. You can transplant some of the seedlings elsewhere if you wish, but as a rule those with long, unbranched roots (the gardener calls them tap roots) do not recover well from the shift. These include annual lupins, eschscholtzias, poppies, clarkias, godetias, gypsophilas, Virginian stocks, and mignonette. Be sure to firm the soil around the seedlings you leave, because in pulling out the others you are likely to loosen their roots.

PLANT OUT AND STAKE SWEET PEAS

Sweet peas that you raised in the greenhouse during January will be ready for planting out, providing you have hardened them off properly. The method to follow is exactly the same as that for planting out September-sown sweet peas (see March, Third Week).

Sweet peas planted in March should be well established, and it will be time to provide each plant with a bamboo cane at least

7 feet long. This must be pushed really firmly into the soil, and it is a good plan to link all the canes together at the top with string or wire, securing this at each end to a stronger post. Reduce the number of shoots to one per plant, choosing the sturdiest, and lead this towards its cane with a raffia tie.

If the March-sown peas (see March, First Week) have made 2 or 3 inches of growth, as they should by this time, pinch out the tip of each plant. These late-sown peas are usually grown naturally on bushy pea sticks and are not trained to a single stem on bamboos, so there will not be any need to reduce the number of shoots that form as a result of the stopping.

Plant Violas and Pansies

Plant out violas and pansies, both seedlings and rooted cuttings, if they have been properly hardened off. A rather cool, semi-shaded position is best, though both plants will grow in full sun. The drawback is that they tend to finish flowering sooner. Well worked, rather liberally manured ground will ensure fine blooms. Plant with a trowel and water in freely.

Start Dahlias in Frames

If you were unable to start dahlias early, as recommended in the February and March notes (see February, Third

Sweet Pea Seedling.

Contrary to practice with most other seedlings, the soil should be shaken from the roots of sweet peas when these are planted out.

Week, and March, Third Week), you can do so now in an unheated frame. Simply arrange the roots close together in a frame and cover the tubers with light soil. Water moderately, but give increasing supplies as growth commences. Cover the frame with plenty of sacks every night, and remove these in the morning, unless it is very frosty.

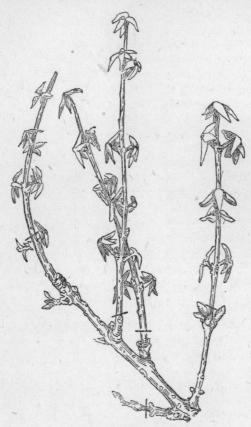

PRUNING A FORSYTHIA.

The shoots that have just borne flowers are cut back to shoots or growth buds, as indicated by the black lines.

PRUNE FORSYTHIAS

This is the time to prune forsythias if you want to keep them as moderately small specimens, or to train them against a wall. The method is to cut back as many as possible of the flowering branches to within a few inches of the older wood, but to retain all strong growth that has not flowered. In the case of wall specimens, any small laterals that have not flowered and cannot conveniently be tied in can be cut back severely.

PRUNE EVERGREENS GROWN FOR FOLIAGE

Hardy evergreen shrubs that are grown principally for their foliage, either in hedges or as topiary specimens, etc., can also be pruned with safety. If there is any really hard cutting back to be done, this is certainly the time to do it. Light trimming can be practised during the summer, but severe pruning is out of place then. Old, worn-out laurel hedges can often be renovated by cutting them back to within a foot of the ground at this time of the year. Of course, the stumps look terrible for a while, but given a little luck and some warm, showery weather, they will soon be a forest of healthy new shoots, with fine, vigorous leaves.

Stop Japanese Chrysanthemums

Japanese chrysanthemums to stop now for flowers in mid-November are Canada, Catherine Cameron, Golden Shell, Joseph Bradford, Kingsford Smith, Lancashire, Leicester, Mrs. G. Drabble, Princess Mary, Queen Mary, Robert Radcliffe, Robert O. Jones, Strawberry, Thomas Glidden, Winifred Greenfield, W. Cresswell, William Rigby, W. H. Walker, and Worcestershire. Incurves are Emblème Poitevene and Calypso.

Transfer Bedding Plants to Frames

You may now transfer most of the bedding plants and half-hardy annuals which till now have been in the greenhouse to frames for the next stage in hardening off. For the first few days after this move you should keep the frames closed, and cover them well with sacks at night. Then admit a little air by day if it is fine, steadily increasing the amount until by the end of the month the lights are removed altogether for several hours on all mild days. Your object should be thoroughly to accustom the plants to full exposure, day and night, by the end of May.

Sow Vegetable Marrows, Ridge Cucumbers, and Melons

Later on you are sure to want vegetable marrows, and you may be glad of a few ridge cucumbers as well. Sow some seeds now, singly, in 2½- or 3-inch pots, and germinate them in the greenhouse or in a frame on a hotbed in a temperature of 60 degs. or thereabouts. They will germinate more quickly if you cover the pots with a piece of brown paper, but this must be removed as soon

Hardening Off in Frames.

As spring advances bedding plants in frames must be given more and more ventilation. On mild days the lights can be slid right off for most of the day.

109

as the seed leaves appear. Melons that are to be grown in a frame should also be sown now and germinated in exactly the same way.

Sow Parsley Outdoors

Make a small sowing of parsley outdoors to provide a successional crop after that sown in February (see February, Fourth Week). Details of sowing are exactly as before, except that there is no need now to choose a specially sheltered or warm position.

FOURTH WEEK

Plant Antirrhinums and Pentstemons

Antirrhinums raised in the autumn from seeds or cuttings and also pentstemons from autumn cuttings may be planted in their flowering quarters if they have been thoroughly accustomed to full exposure.

Take Chrysanthemum Cuttings for Dwarf Plants

This is the time to commence taking cuttings of chrysanthemums that are to make dwarf specimens in pots. You can root them in boxes or beds of soil exactly as the earlier chrysanthemum cuttings, though I think a better method is to insert them singly in $2\frac{1}{2}$-inch pots, or three around the edge of a 3-inch pot. Allow them to root either in a cool greenhouse or a frame. By no means all varieties are suitable to this method of culture. Three of the best are Blanche Poitevene, Poupre Poitevene, and Pink Poitevene, while others that you might try are Jean Pattison, and its sports, Golden and Red Pattison, Alba, Rose Chochod, Bronze and Pink Marcus, Fifi, Lydia, Kathleen Thompson, Vermilion and Caprice du Printemps.

Sow Greenhouse Primulas

Make a first sowing of the various primulas that flower in the greenhouse during winter—*i.e.*, Primula sinensis and its variety stellata, P. obconica, and P. Kewensis. Do not sow all your seeds of the first three now, however, but keep some for a second batch in June (see June, Third Week). Sow the seeds thinly in the usual seed compost (see p. 24). I think they are better sown in well-drained pots or pans rather than boxes. Cover the seeds very lightly with fine soil and germinate in the greenhouse in a temperature of about 60 degs. Cover each seed vessel with a pane of glass until germination takes place. If water is needed, give this by holding the pots nearly to their rims in a tub and not by watering overhead.

Sow Annuals for the Greenhouse

You can now make a second sowing of hardy and half-hardy annuals, for flowering in pots in the greenhouse (see February, Third Week, and March, First Week). Plants from this late sowing will provide a succession of flowers after the first batch is over.

Sow Runner Beans

Make a small sowing of runner beans in exactly the same way as the early sowing of French beans (see Second Week). If you germinate them in the greenhouse you will have some nice forward plants for putting out the first week in June, and these will give you a crop of beans several weeks earlier than would be possible from the earliest outdoor sowing.

Sow Globe Beetroot

You can now make a sowing of globe beetroot in a fairly sheltered border out of doors. This earliest sowing need not be a very large one, as it will be followed by another in May, and also by a much bigger sowing of long beet in the same month. Sow the seeds 2 inches deep in rows 15 inches apart. I find the most economical method is to place three seeds every six or eight inches along the rows and then reduce the seedlings to one at each point later on.

Sow Endive

Make a small sowing of endive; it makes a welcome change from lettuce in summer salads. Sow the seeds thinly in drills ½ inch deep and 1 foot apart.

Spray Gooseberries

If you considered it necessary to spray your gooseberries with lime sulphur before flowering (see April, First Week), you should certainly repeat the treatment as soon as the petals have fallen and

AMERICAN GOOSEBERRY MILDEW.
This disease causes a mould-like outgrowth on leaves and fruits. Bushes that have been attacked in former years must be sprayed with lime sulphur as a preventive.

you can just see the tiny, fertilised fruits. But for this second spraying you must use the lime sulphur at summer strength. Consult manufacturers' instructions regarding this.

REMOVE GREASEBANDS FROM TREES

You should now remove and burn greasebands that have been round the main trunks or branches of apples, pears, etc., since September.

THIN OUTDOOR PEACHES AND NECTARINES

The young fruits on outdoor peaches and nectarines should now be about the size of marbles and you must commence to thin them out. The work is done in exactly the same way as with indoor peaches (see March, General Work), and so I need not go into it again in detail here. Do not forget that there may be a natural fall during the stoning period with outdoor peaches and nectarines just as with glasshouse-grown varieties, and that it is not wise to complete thinning until this is over. Disbudding (*i.e.*, removal of unwanted young shoots) is

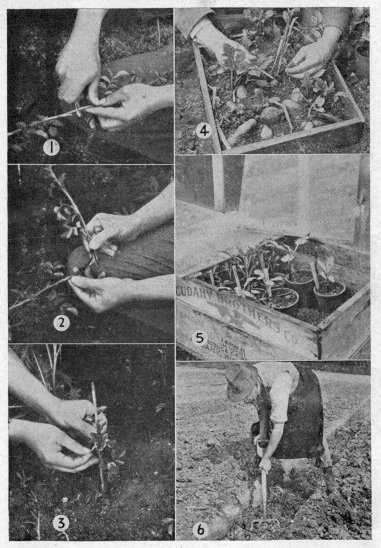

1. Layering a rambler rose. An incision is being made through a joint.
2. The incision opened and ready for pegging down into the soil. 3. The
layer completed and made secure to a small cane. 4. Taking a dahlia
cutting. 5. Dahlia cuttings rooting in an improvised close frame placed on
the greenhouse hot-water pipes. 6. Forking manure into the bottom of a
celery trench.

1. Placing clean straw around strawberry plants to protect the fruits from mud splashes. 2. A strawberry bed covered with nets to keep birds from damaging the fruits. 3. The first stage in training cucumbers. 4. Pollinating the first trusses of tomato flowers. 5. Removing a side shoot from a tomato plant.

carried out with the outdoor trees as with those in the orchard house.

In the case of apricots, trees may be allowed to carry more fruits (three or four per square foot), and disbudding is nothing like so drastic, well-placed laterals being merely stopped and not rubbed right out.

FLOWERS, VEGETABLES, AND FRUITS IN SEASON DURING APRIL

HARDY HERBACEOUS PLANTS.—Achillea *rupestris*, Adonis *vernalis*, Anchusa *myosotidiflora*, A. *officinalis*, Bellis *perennis monstrosa (double daisy)*, Cheiranthus *Allioni (Siberian wallflower)*, C. *Cheiri (wallflower)*, Doronicum *plantagineum*, Dracunculus *vulgaris*, Helleborus *orientalis and vars. (Lenten rose)*, Heuchera *tiarelloides*, Myosotis *hybrids (forget-me-nots)*, Polygonatum *multiflorum (Solomon's Seal)*, P. *macrophyllum*, Primula *elatior polyanthus (polyanthus)*, P. *vulgaris vars. (primrose)*, Pulmonaria *angustifolia*, Ranunculus *bullatus plenus*, Saxifraga *ciliata*, S. *cordifolia and vars.*, S. *crassifolia*, S. *purpurascens*, S. *Stracheyi*.

HARDY BULBS AND TUBERS.—Anemone *coronaria and vars.*, A. *fulgens and vars.*, Chionodoxa *Luciliæ*, Convallaria *majalis (lily of the valley)*, crocuses *(large-flowering)*, Cyclamen *repandum*, Erythronium *californicum*, E. *Dens-canis*, E. *grandiflorum*, E. *Hartwegii*, E. *Hendersonii*, E. *revolutum*, E. *tuolumnensis*, Fritillaria *citrina*, F. *Imperialis*, F. *Meleagris*, F. *oranensis*, F. *pluriflora*, F. *Purdyi*, F. *pyrenaica*, F. *recurva*, F. *verticillata*, hyacinths *(large-flowered)*, Iris *bucharica*, I. *melanostricta*, I. *orchioides*, I. *tingitana*, I. *warleyensis*, Leucojum *vernum*, Milla *uniflora*, Muscari *botryoides*, M. *Heavenly Blue*, M. *latifolium*, M. *moschatum*, M. *paradoxum*, Narcissus *Bulbocodium*, M. *minor*, narcissus hybrids in var. *(including trumpet daffodils)*, Pushkinia *scilloides*, Romulea *rosea*, Scilla *amœna*, S. *bifolia*, S. *nonscripta (bluebell)*, S. *sibirica*, S. *pratensis*, Tecophilæa *cyanocrocus (shelter)*, Trillium *erectum*, T. *grandiflorum*, T. *ovatum*, T. *recurvatum*, T. *sessile*, T. *stylosum*, Tulipa *australis*, T. *chrysantha*, T. *Clusiana*, T. *dasystemon*, T. *Didieri*, T. *Eichleri*, T. *Fosteriana*, T. *Greigii*, T. *Hageri*, T. *ingens*, T. *Kushkensis*, T. *linifolia*, T. *orphanidea*, T. *præstans*, T. *primulina*, T. *pulchella*, T. *saxatilis*, T. *sylvestris*, T. *Wilsoniana*, tulips in var. *(early singles and doubles, Mendels and Triumphs)*.

ROCK PLANTS.—Æthionema *coridifolium*, Æ. *iberideum*, Æ. *grandiflorum*, Æ. *pulchellum*, Æ. *Warley Rose*, Alyssum *saxatile and vars.*, A. *serpyllifolium*, A. *spinosum*, Androsace *carnea*, A. *lactea*, A. *pyrenaica*, A. *sarmentosa and vars.*, Anemone *angulosa*, A. *apennina*, A. *Pulsatilla*, A. *ranunculoides*, A. *sylvestris and vars.*, A. *vernalis*, Arabis *albida and vars.*, A. *alpina*, A. *aubrietioides*, Arctostaphylos *Uva-ursi*, Armeria *cæspitosa*, Arnica *montana*, Aubrietia *deltoidea and vars.*, Bellis *perennis vars.*, Bellium *bellidioides*, Calceolaria *biflora*, Cheiranthus *alpinus*, Cornus *canadensis*,

Corydalis *tuberosa,* C. *Wilsonii,* Cortusa *Matthiolii,* Cotyledon *simplicifolius,* Daphne *arbuscula,* D. *Blagayana,* D. *Cneorum,* D. *tangutica,* Dicentra *eximia,* Doronicum *caucasicum,* Draba *Aizoon,* D. *Dedeana,* D. *imbricata,* D. *olympica,* Epigæa *repens,* Epimedium *alpinum,* E. *concinnum,* E. *macranthum,* E. *pinnatum,* E. *rubrum,* Gentiana *acaulis,* G. *verna,* Geum *Borisii,* G. *montanum,* Houstonia *serpyllifolia,* Iberis *saxatilis,* I. *sempervirens,* Iris *cristata,* I. *ensata,* I. *pumila and vars.,* Isopyrum *thalictroides,* Lathyrus *vernus,* Lithospermum *rosmarinifolium (shelter),* Macrotomia *echioides,* Mazus *Pumilio,* M. *reptans,* Morisea *hypogæa,* Myosotis *rupicola,* Omphalodes *cappadocica,* O. *verna,* Orobus *vernus,* Papaver *alpinum,* Primula

Anemone Pulsatilla.

Allioni, P. *Auricula and vars.,* P. *cortusoides,* P. *darialica,* P. *denticulata and vars.,* P. *frondosa,* P. *glaucescens,* P. *Juliæ,* P. *Juliana hybrids,* P. *marginata,* P. *minima,* P. *nutans,* P. *pubescens,* P. *Reinii,* P. *Sieboldii,* Ranunculus *alpestris,* R. *amplexicaule,* R. *glacialis,* R. *gramineus,* R. *pyrenæus,* Sanguinaria *canadensis,* Saxifraga *arco-valleyi,* S. *aretioides,* S. *Boydii,* S. *cæsia,* S. *decipiens in var. (mossy saxifrages),* S. *diapensioides,* S. *hypnoides (mossy saxifrages),* S. *kewensis,* S. *lilacina,* S. *marginata,* S. *Obristii,* S. *oppositifolia and vars.,* S. *Petraschii,* S. *sancta,* S. *tombeanensis,* S. *valdensis,* Shortia *galacifolia,* S. *uniflora,* Soldanella *alpina,* S. *montana,* Synthyris *reniformis,* Tiarella *cordifolia,* Townsendia *Wilcoxiana,* Viola *biflora,* V. *gracilis and vars.*

HARDY AQUATICS AND BOG PLANTS.—Caltha *palustris and vars.*, C. *poly-petala*, Cardamine *pratensis plena*, Chrysosplenium *oppositifolium*, Dodecatheon *Meadia and vars.*, Primula *Cockburniana*, Saxifraga *peltata.*

HARDY EVERGREEN SHRUBS.—Arctostaphylos *Manzanita*, Berberis *aquifolium*, B. *buxifolia*, B. *Darwinii*, B. *hakeoides*, B. *japonica and vars.*, B. *replicata*, Ceanothus *rigidus (wall)*, Choisya *ternata*, Coronilla *glauca (shelter)*, Daphne *Dauphinii*, Erica *arborea*, E. *australis Mr. Robert*, E. *carnea and vars.*, E. *darleyensis*, E. *mediterranea*, Euphorbia *Wulfeni*, Kalmia *glauca*, Osmanthus *Delavayi*, Osmarea *Burkwoodii*, Phillyrea *Vilmoriniana*, Photinia *serrulata*, Pieris *floribunda*, P. *japonica*, Rhododendron *arboreum (shelter)*, R. *agrophyllum*, R. *Augustinii*, R. *calophytum*, R. *campanulatum*, R. *campylocarpum and hybrids*, R. *cephalanthum*, R. *Falconeri*, R. *fastigiatum*, R. *hippophæoides*, R. *impeditum*, R. *neriiflorum*, R. *racemosum*, R. *rubiginosum*, R. *scintillans*, R. *spinulosum*, R. *Valentinianum*, R. *Williamsonianum*, Skimmia *Fortunei*, S. *japonica*, Viburnum *Burkwoodii*, V. *Tinus*, Vinca *minor.*

HARDY DECIDUOUS SHRUBS.—Azalea *amœna*, A. *Rhodora*, A. *Vaseyi*, Cassandra *calyculata*, Colletia *infausta*, Corylopsis *Veitchiana*, C. *Willmottiæ*, Cydonia *japonica*, C. *Maulei*, Cytisus *præcox*, Elæagnus *multiflorus*, Enkianthus *campanulatus*, Exochorda *Korolkowii*, Forsythia *intermedia and vars.*, F. *suspensa*, F. *viridissima*, Fothergilla *Gardeni*, Genista *radiata*, Magnolia *obovata*, M. *salicifolia*, M. *stellata*, Prunus *dehiscens*, Rhodora *canadensis*, Ribes *aureum*, R. *sanguineum and vars.*, R. *speciosum*, Rosa *Hugonis*, Spiræa *arguta*, S. *prunifolia*, S. *Thunbergii*, Ulex *europæus plenus*, Viburnum *Carlesi*, Xanthorrhiza *apiifolia.*

HARDY EVERGREEN TREES.—Arbutus *Andrachne*, A. *hybrida.*

HARDY DECIDUOUS TREES.—Acer *circinnatum*, A. *macrophyllum*, A. *Opalus*, A. *platanoides (Norway maple)*, A. *rubrum*, Alnus *firma*, Amelanchier *canadensis*, A. *grandiflora*, A. *vulgaris*, Magnolia *Campbelli (shelter)*, M. *conspicua*, M. *Lennei*, M. *Sargentiana*, M. *Soulangeana*, Prunus *Amygdalus (bitter almond)*, Prunus *Avium*, P. *Cerasus (wild cherry)*, P. *incisa*, P. *lannesiana (Japanese cherry)*, P. *Mahaleb and vars.*, P. *Padus (bird cherry)*, P. *Persica and vars. (peach)*, P. *Sargentii*, P. *serrula*, P. *serrulata and vars. (Japanese cherry)*, P. *subhirtella*, Pyrus *aldenhamensis*, P. *baccata (Siberian crab)*, P. *communis (pear)*, P. *Eleyi*, P. *floribunda*, P. *theifera*, P. *spectabilis*, Robinia *pseudo-acacia.*

HARDY CLIMBING PLANTS.—Akebia *lobata*, Clematis *alpina*, C. *Armandii*, Ercilla *volubilis*, Schizandra *chinensis*, Stauntonia *hexaphylla.*

GREENHOUSE PLANTS.—Abutilons, acacias, arum lilies, astilbes, azaleas *(Indian, mollis, etc.)*, Boronia *megastigma*, bougainvilleas, Callistemon *speciosus*, calceolarias *(herbaceous)*, Cantua *dependens*, carnations *(perpetual-flowering)*, chorizemas, cinerarias *(hybrids)*, clivias, Coronilla *glauca*, Deutzia *gracilis*, Dicentra *spectabilis*, Dillwynia *floribunda*, eriostemons, freesias, Genista *fragrans*, hippeastrums, Hydrangea *hortensis in var.*, hyacinths *(large-flowered)*, kennedyas, Leucocoryne *ixioides*, Lilium *Harrisii*, pelargoniums *(show and regal)*, rhododendrons *(Javanese)*, roses, schizanthus *and other* annuals *(see list, September, First Week)*, stephanotis, tulips *(Cottage, Darwin)*, wallflowers.

VEGETABLES IN STORE.—Same as March.

VEGETABLES OUTDOORS.—Broccoli *(late)*, sprouting broccoli, cabbage *(sown*

July, August), kale, leeks, lettuce, spring onions, rhubarb, seakale, spinach beet, turnip tops.

VEGETABLES UNDER GLASS.—French beans, carrots, cucumbers, lettuces, mustard and cress, radishes.

FRUITS IN STORE.—Apples : *Allan's Everlasting (D), Annie Elizabeth (C), Barnack Beauty (CD), Belle de Boskoop (CD), Bramley's Seedling (C), Brownlees' Russet (D), Cornish Gillyflower (D), Crawley Beauty (C), D'Arcy Spice (D), Duke of Devonshire (D), Easter Orange (D), Edward VII. (C), Encore (C), King George V. (D), King of Tompkin's County (D), Laxton's Pearmain (D), Lord Burghley (D), Lord Hindlip (D), May Queen (D), Monarch (C), Newton Wonder (C), Ontario (CD), Sanspareil (CD), Stark (D), Sturmer Pippin (D), Wagener (C).* Grapes: *Mrs. Pince, Prince of Wales.* Pears: *Bergamotte d'Esperen (D), Catillac (C), Josephine de Malines (D), Uvedale's St. Germain (C).*

FRUITS UNDER GLASS.—Strawberries.

SANGUINARIA CANADENSIS.

MAY

GENERAL WORK

Thin and Stake Herbaceous Perennials

IT is usually a mistake to allow herbaceous perennials to retain all the growth they produce. Much better results can be obtained by thinning out the shoots a little at this time of the year. Delphiniums and Michaelmas daisies in particular repay rather drastic thinning. Retain some of the sturdiest shoots and nip off the rest. Before the stems get too long and begin to flop about, place bamboo canes in position and loop the stems to these. In most cases it is best to have several canes per plant, thrust in close to the clump but leaning outwards towards the top so that, as growth extends and is tied to the canes, it will be spread out and get its full ration of light and air.

Thin Out Rose Growth

It is an excellent plan to examine rose bushes and standards occasionally during the month and to pinch out any badly placed or overcrowded shoots. Those growing inwards and so tending to crowd the centre of the plant are the ones most likely to cause trouble later on.

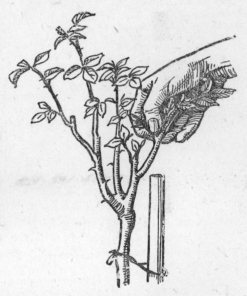

THINNING A ROSE.

A young shoot growing inwards is being pinched out to prevent overcrowding.

KEEP A WATCH FOR GREENFLY

Greenfly is likely to make its first appearance during the month. Keep a sharp look out for this pest especially on the young growths of roses and plum trees. At the outset it is easy enough to kill all the insects by spraying once or twice at short intervals with any good nicotine insecticide, but if you neglect to do this the leaves will very soon cockle and curl to such an extent that the aphides (greenflies) will be almost completely protected within their folds.

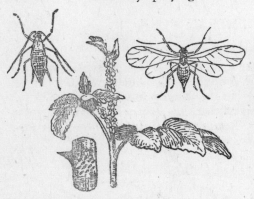

GREENFLIES OR APHIDES.

Both winged and wingless forms are found. Young growth is attacked first and the insects crowd thickly on the soft tips of shoots (centre). The small section of an old rose shoot is covered with eggs.

KILL SLUGS

Slugs are also likely to be much in evidence now and may do a lot of damage to tender seedlings, lettuces, delphiniums, etc., unless you take measures against them. There are numerous proprietary powders which may be sprinkled around plants to protect them. An effective home-made slug killer can be prepared by mixing 4 ounces of Paris green with 7 lb. of bran. This should be broadcast thinly over the soil, preferably when the weather is damp and mild. Paris green is an arsenical poison, so should be used with due care, but in the small quantities advised is not likely to do any harm.

USE LAWN SAND ON WEEDY LAWNS

May is a good month for using lawn sand or finely powdered sulphate of ammonia to kill small, broad-leaved weeds on the lawn. What actually happens is that the chemical lodges on broad leaves and scorches them but slips harmlessly off the upright narrow blades of grass. It is most effective in dry weather. If you use sulphate of ammonia, be certain to distribute it as evenly as possible and not to use more than ½ ounce per square yard. You can give a second application a few weeks after the first providing there has been some rain meanwhile to wash the former dose away. Commercial lawn sand should always be used strictly according to manufacturers' instructions.

Feed Plants that are in Full Growth

It is a very good plan to feed plants that are growing fast. At this time of the year most herbaceous plants are making a big effort and many of them are forming their flower stems. Spring-sown vegetables are also growing freely and need plenty of nourishment. Early in the month give all such plants a small top dressing of a compound, quick-acting fertilizer and hoe this in. There are plenty of good fertilizers on the market for this purpose or, if you prefer, you can make your own mixture with seven parts superphosphate of lime, five parts sulphate of ammonia, two parts sulphate of potash, and one part steamed bone-flour well mixed and applied at the rate of 3 ounces per square yard. Repeat the application after about three weeks. The mixture mentioned above is suitable for a great variety of plants, but in the case of vegetables grown principally for their leaves, and also peas, you can increase the proportion of sulphate of ammonia to three parts with advantage. An occasional thorough soaking with weak liquid manure, made by soaking a small sack of well-rotted farm-yard, stable, or sheep manure, or old soot in a tub of water, will also do these vegetables a lot of good.

Plant Aquatics

May is the best month of the year for planting water lilies and other aquatic plants. These may either be planted direct in soil, spread on the bottom of the pool to a depth of at least 6 inches, or they may be planted in baskets or pots which are then sunk into position. If you adopt the former method, empty the pool first, place the soil in position and plant the roots with a trowel exactly as if you were dealing with herbaceous perennials. Then run a little water into the pool, but only a few inches at first. Add more as the plants grow, the idea being to keep the leaves of water lilies just floating on the surface. If the plants are placed in boxes or pots these may be stood on bricks temporarily to keep the crowns near the surface. When growth is well started the bricks are removed and the receptacles sunk to their normal positions.

HARDEN OFF BEDDING PLANTS IN FRAMES

During the early part of May bedding plants in frames must receive as much ventilation as possible, though it is still unwise to expose any of them to frost. Take the lights right off by day if the weather is fine, but replace them in the afternoon should there be a threat of frost. A clearing sky in the afternoon is to be

HOW TO PLANT A LILY POOL.

The inset sketch shows the method of spreading soil to form a bed and covering with clean gravel to prevent water discolouration.

regarded with suspicion at this time of the year, as, more often than not, it is an indication that there will be a sharp frost at night. Geraniums, fuchsias, and marguerites, also almost all half-hardy annuals sown in February (see February, Third Week), should be fully hardened off and ready for the open ground by the last week in May; but it is advisable to give dahlias, heliotropes, scarlet salvias, and cannas a further week as they are more susceptible to cold.

GENERAL GREENHOUSE MANAGEMENT

As sun heat gains still more in power you will have to be increasingly careful in shading plants. Foliage plants in general, and particularly many ferns, suffer a lot if exposed too long to intense light and heat. Tuberous-rooted begonias also take it badly, and gloxinias appreciate a measure of shade.

Another consequence of the increased sun heat is that plants will require considerably larger supplies of water. This is particularly so in the case of cucumbers and tomatoes. The earlier raised plants should be growing very freely and will transpire a lot of water on a warm day. You must certainly examine all the plants in your greenhouse daily. It does not follow that all the plants will require water every day, though it is quite possible some will, but you should examine the soil carefully to make quite certain how things are. In the case of plants in pots, rap these with a hard piece of wood or the leg bone of a chicken. If the pot gives a ringing note the soil within it is dry, but if it has a dull heavy sound the soil is probably moist enough. I say " probably " because the test is valueless if the pot happens to be cracked. Broken pots always give a dull note, so see that you are not misled.

More ventilation can be given by day and in most cases it is safe to give a little ventilation at night, but I still prefer to rely exclusively on the top ventilators, except in the case of plants that have been grown under cool conditions from the outset—trees in the unheated orchard house, for example. Side ventilators are well enough in the summer, but in the spring they are liable to cause damaging draughts. One thing that you must particularly guard against from now onwards is a sudden rise of temperature early in the morning. As soon as direct sunlight first strikes the greenhouse, this quick rise in temperature is likely to take place, and the wise gardener will be at hand to increase ventilation and so steady the thermometer. A vast amount of damage in amateurs' greenhouses must be done every year during the spring and summer on bright mornings between about 5 and 8 a.m.

Pot on Spring Rooted Pelargoniums, etc.

If you struck cuttings of fuchsias and pelargoniums in March (see March, General Work) and you wish to grow on some of the plants in pots for autumn and winter flowering, they will need potting now into 5-inch pots. Use the compost described on page 62. Pinch the points out of fuchsias to encourage bushy growth. Return the plants to the greenhouse for a week or so after potting. At the end of the month they may go to a sunny frame for the summer. Similar remarks apply to rooted cuttings of coleuses and other greenhouse plants. Some of the later cuttings of all these plants will be in need of first potting into 3-inch pots.

Cuttings of winter-flowering begonias rooted last month (see April, General Work) must be potted as soon as they are well rooted. Pot them singly in 3-inch pots, using the compost described on page 62. Place them on the staging in the greenhouse with an average day temperature of 65 degs., not falling below 55 degs. at night, and shade from direct sunshine.

Allow Nerines, Arums, etc., to go to Rest

Gradually reduce the amount of water given to nerines, and place the plants in the sunniest part of the greenhouse. The object of this is to ripen the bulbs and allow them to go to rest. The foliage will gradually turn yellow and die down. Freesias and lachenalias (see April, General Work) will benefit from a similar thorough baking on a shelf near the glass or in some such sunny place. Once their foliage dies down no water need be given until July or August. Arum lilies must also be allowed to go to rest (see April, General Work). This now applies to the later batches that have flowered in a cool house as well as to the earlier forced roots. Do not attempt to bake them in the sun after the fashion of nerine bulbs, but simply reduce the water supply gradually and then, when the foliage dies down, lay the pots on their sides and give no more water until August.

Pot and Stop Perpetual-flowering Carnations

Carnations grown from cuttings taken during the winter and early spring are all likely to be ready for their final shift into pots 6 or 7 inches in diameter some time during the month. Do the work as soon as the 3-inch pots are comfortably filled with roots but before they show the slightest tendency to become pot-bound. Use a compost of twelve parts good yellow loam, two parts well-rotted manure, one part wood ashes, one part old mortar rubble, and from one to two parts coarse sand, according to the nature of the loam. Pot firmly and then arrange the plants in a frame, keeping the lights on if it freezes or the wind is very cold, but removing them altogether when it is mild.

From time to time break out the ends of the first side shoots resulting from the earlier stopping (see March, General Work). The ideal time to do this is when the shoot has made about eight joints, and two complete joints should be broken out. Do not deal with more than one shoot per plant at a time but spread the work over a period so that the plant does not suffer any severe check to growth.

THIN OUT CHRYSANTHEMUM GROWTHS

During the month chrysanthemums that were stopped during March and April will be making new growths—" breaks " the chrysanthemum expert terms them. You will have to decide just how many of these you require per plant and then rub the rest out as soon as possible. The actual number retained will depend upon the type of chrysanthemum and the purpose for which you are growing it. In the case of exhibition Japanese chrysanthemums that are being grown for the very biggest flowers possible, only one shoot must be retained per plant. If prize winning is not the main object you may be satisfied to leave three stems per plant, and this is usually the ideal number to leave on incurved varieties that are being grown for exhibition. The reason for leaving more in their case is that great size is not desirable, quality and form are the imperative points and these are best obtained by having several blooms per plant. Decoratives that are being grown for cutting may also have three stems from the present stopping. They will be allowed to carry still more when they break again (see June, General Work).

EXHIBITION CHRYSANTHEMUMS.

After stopping only three shoots have been retained, all others having been rubbed out at an early stage.

MAKE SUCCESSIONAL SOWINGS

Once again there will be a number of sowings to be made during the month to provide a succession of vegetables after those

DECORATIVE CHRYSANTHEMUMS.

As the flowers had not to be of great size, three shoots were retained after the first stopping, and from two to three further shoots on each of the first "breaks" after the second stopping.

raised from earlier sowings. Lettuces, spinach, turnips, radishes, and mustard and cress should be sown exactly as explained in the notes for April, General Work, with the one exception that it is now more than ever advisable to sow the three first-named in a partially shaded position. They will not stand a great amount of summer heat, as this makes them run to seed. You should make a couple of sowings of maincrop peas to give you a chance of continuing the crop well on into the autumn. Make a further sowing of endive (see April, Fourth Week) towards the end of the month, and another sowing of kohl rabi about the middle of the month (see April, First Week).

STAKE CULINARY PEAS

Successional batches of culinary peas will be growing freely during the month and these must be staked as soon as they are a couple of inches in height. Even the dwarf peas should have small brushy twigs to keep them erect. At the same time draw a little soil into a ridge on each side of the row. This will serve to protect the young plants and will also make a trough into which you can pour water and liquid manure later on.

EARTH UP EARLY POTATOES

As the earlier crops of potatoes push their shoots through the ground draw more soil around them for protection. A few degrees of frost will injure these shoots and there can be no certainty about the weather until May is well advanced. The very earliest outdoor crops, on sheltered borders (see February,

Fourth Week) will be well advanced in growth and it will not be possible to protect them with soil alone. Keep some dry straw, bracken, or evergreen boughs at hand and strew these thickly over the bed when frost threatens.

Potatoes in frames must be ventilated as freely as possible on all mild days, but be sure to place the lights in position again early in the afternoon if frost threatens. Incidentally, it is wasteful

EARTHING UP POTATOES.
The sectional drawing shows the way in which tubers are formed in the mounded soil.

to lift whole roots of frame potatoes when the tubers form. Scrape away the soil from them as they grow, remove the biggest tubers and then return the soil once more. The smaller tubers will continue to swell and you can collect them later on. You should get some tubers early this month.

THIN ONIONS, ROOT CROPS, ETC.

Various crops sown in drills out of doors will be in need of thinning during the month. The sooner this can be commenced the better, once the seedlings can be clearly seen, but I do not advise you to complete the thinning all at one operation as there may be some casualties yet. Your ultimate object is to leave onions from 6 to 9 inches apart, turnips 5 or 6 inches apart, kohl rabi 9 inches apart, shorthorn carrots 3 inches and long or intermediate carrots 6 inches apart, lettuces 6 inches to a foot apart according to the size of the variety, and leeks 4 inches apart (they will be transplanted in July). If you sowed globe artichokes and asparagus last month (see April, First Week) the seedlings will also need thinning, the former to 6 inches and the latter to 1 foot apart. In all cases it is advisable to increase these distances if you wish to have big produce for exhibition. Seedlings of lettuce may be transplanted elsewhere if you water them in well. The seedlings of root crops are not of any value for transplanting. Pull out the weakest and least promising seedlings first, and be careful not to disturb those you leave more than you can help. Make

A LESSON IN THINNING ONIONS.

Proper bulb development is impossible unless the plants have plenty of room, as shown on the left.

the loosened soil firm again with the knuckles. This is particularly important in the case of onions, as the dreaded onion fly frequently lays its eggs in the loose soil caused by careless thinning.

FEED, DISBUD, AND POLLINATE TOMATOES

Tomatoes will be in various stages of growth. The earliest will have set some fruits by this time, later batches may be just coming into flower, while yet others from March sowings will be ready for potting on into 5-inch pots early in the month. In all cases you must remove side shoots regularly.

It is advisable to continue to fertilise flowers by hand either by tapping the plants or by scattering dry pollen from flower to flower with a camel's hair brush. This is most effective if done about midday when the sun is shining.

The earliest plants will benefit from a top dressing of old, well-rotted manure thoroughly broken up and spread evenly all over the existing compost to a depth of about 1 inch. You can give additional food in liquid form once a week. There is nothing better than a good proprietary fertiliser for this purpose—only be sure to use it weak. I prefer to dilute with twice as much water as the manufacturers recommend and then give the feed rather more frequently. If you prefer to make your own mixture use three parts superphosphate of lime, two parts sulphate of ammonia, and two parts sulphate of potash well mixed and dissolved in water at the rate of 1 teaspoonful per gallon.

Keep the main stems tied up regularly and pinch out the points of the most forward plants as soon as they reach the ridge.

TRAIN AND FEED MELONS

You will now be able to see the result of your pollination last month (see April, General Work). If sufficient fruits have set per plant, well and good; but if only one or two have set, remove them and start all over again, fertilising the requisite number of female flowers all on the same day. As soon as white rootlets

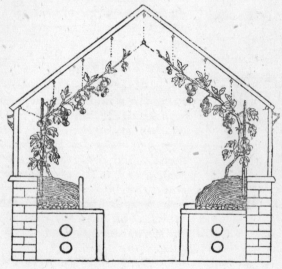

METHOD OF TRAINING TOMATOES IN A SPAN HOUSE.
*Each plant is stopped—that is to say, the growing tip is pinched out—
as soon as it reaches the ridge of the house.*

appear on the surface of the bed, top dress with an inch of well-rotted manure thoroughly broken up. Water very freely. Continue to pinch out points of side shoots so that the house does not get overcrowded with foliage. Maintain a rather moist atmosphere and a day temperature averaging 70 degs.

TRAIN AND FEED CUCUMBERS

Cucumbers in heated greenhouses and in frames on hotbeds will be in various stages of growth. All will require regular

127

training and stopping as already described (see April, General Work), and all must be watered freely and ventilated very sparingly. A damp, warm atmosphere is what the cucumber likes, and only on really mild days should a little air be admitted. From this time onwards a permanent shading of lime wash will be needed on the glass to prevent sun scorch.

The earliest plants in full bearing will need regular feeding with very dilute liquid manure (horse, cow, and sheep dung steeped in water are all good, and so is old soot); while if you note white rootlets on the surface of any of the beds, top dress at once with an inch-thick layer of old manure, well broken up.

LIQUID MANURE.

This is prepared by soaking a small sack of manure (B) in a tub of water. The simplest method is to attach the sack to a stick (A) long enough to span the tub easily (C D).

MULCH FRUIT TREES

Spread a fairly thick layer of well-rotted farmyard or stable manure, or failing this spent hops (not hop manure, which contains chemicals), around fruit trees and bushes of all types, also raspberries. This is known technically as a mulch, and it is very valuable for two reasons : it provides the trees with much-needed nourishment while they are in growth, and helps to retain moisture in the soil by preventing surface evaporation.

DISBUD AND THIN PEACHES, NECTARINES, ETC., OUTDOORS

During the month peaches, nectarines, and apricots on walls will be growing freely, and you must continue to disbud them in the same way as those grown under glass (see February, General Work). The fruits must also be thinned a little, but do not complete this process until the stones are formed (see April, General Work).

MANAGEMENT OF ORCHARD HOUSE

Peaches and nectarines that were started into growth in January will be ripening their fruits during May and you must no longer syringe them. Ventilate as freely as possible without letting the

128

1. A chrysanthemum which has been stopped once and, as a result, has produced three sturdy shoots. 2. Staking a delphinium in such a way that growth is spread out. 3. Placing sticks to culinary peas. 4. Tying in sweet peas that are to be trained on the single stem system. Note the small bushy twigs which afforded the plants support until they were big enough to be tied to the canes.

1. Damping down the pathway of a greenhouse to maintain moisture in the atmosphere. 2. Planting a brussels sprout with a dibber. A drill has been drawn to mark the row and hold water. 3. Planting an antirrhinum. 4. Planting celery in a shallow trench. 5. Watering in celery after planting. 6. Hippeastrums gradually ripening off on the greenhouse shelf after flowering.

temperature fall below 60 degs. by day or 50 degs. by night. Later trees will be in various stages of growth and will require thinning, disbudding, etc., as described in my notes for General Work during March and April. Apricots should be thinned moderately if overcrowded, and laterals must be pinched from time to time to prevent unnecessary formation of wood.

TREATMENT OF VINES

Outdoor vines will be growing freely now and you must regulate their growth in much the same manner as that of indoor varieties. Reduce the number of laterals to one per spur, retaining those that are showing flower trusses. Stop them beyond the truss but before they have grown so far as to interfere with neighbouring vines or the laterals from other rods.

Indoor vines will be in various stages of growth according to the time at which you started them, and I refer you to my notes in the General Work for February, March, and April for information on such matters as pollination,

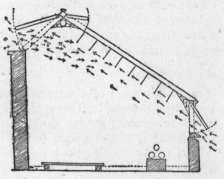

SIDE VENTILATION IN THE VINERY.

The arrows show the currents of air caused by using both side and top ventilators and emphasize the danger of causing cold draughts with this dual ventilation.

stopping, thinning, etc. The earliest vines started in January will now be commencing to ripen, and you must give increased ventilation, using side ventilators as well as those at the ridge. This, of course, applies in measure to all vineries now that the weather is getting warmer, but in particular to the earliest house, because a heated, stagnant atmosphere is a certain cause of cracking. There is no need to keep the evaporating trays filled with water any longer in the forward house as a rather dry atmosphere is an advantage. Keep the top ventilators a little open throughout the night, even though this necessitates the use of a little more artificial heat when the weather is cold.

I

FIRST WEEK

PLANT DAHLIA TUBERS OUTDOORS

If you have not been able to start dahlia tubers into growth in either a greenhouse or frame you can plant them outdoors now. Cover the tubers with 3 inches of soil and then they will be quite secure against frost. It will be some weeks before shoots appear above ground.

SOW HARDY AND HALF-HARDY ANNUALS

If you want flowers of hardy and half-hardy annuals outdoors in early autumn, now is the time to sow them. The seeds should be scattered broadcast where the plants are to flower and should be covered lightly with soil exactly as described for earlier sowings (see March, Third Week, and April, Second Week).

SOW CINERARIAS

Sow a few seeds of cinerarias if you want to have plants in flower by December. The seeds will want a little warmth to encourage germination so early, but the ordinary greenhouse temperature of 55 to 60 degs. will be ample. Sow very thinly in well-drained sand, using the usual seed compost (see p. 24). Cover lightly with fine soil and sand, and shade until germination commences.

STOP EXHIBITION CHRYSANTHEMUMS

Japanese chrysanthemums which should be stopped during this week if you require blooms for a mid-November show are Alex Jackson, Davinia, H. Tomlinson, Majestic and all its sports, Margaret Sargent, Plymouth, and Sam Crooks.

PLANT OUT WINTER GREENS

Winter green crops from early sowings, and particularly cauliflowers and Brussels sprouts sown in March (see March, First Week) should be planted outdoors in their permanent quarters at the first opportunity. Of course, they must be properly hardened off first, but it should be easy to accomplish this by early May. It is better to plant with a trowel rather than with a dibber, even though the work is done more rapidly with the latter tool. In most cases it is sufficient to plant 2 feet apart in rows 2½ feet apart, but these distances may need to be varied a little according to the size of the varieties you are growing. Seed packets usually give adequate information on these points.

Sow Dwarf French Beans

It should be safe to make a sowing of dwarf French beans in the open, if you were not able to raise any plants under glass last month. Sow the seeds singly about 6 inches apart in drills 2 inches deep. An economical method is to have two drills about 9 inches or 1 foot apart, then an alleyway about 2½ feet wide, then another couple of rows, and so on.

Sow Maincrop Beetroot

Early May is the time to sow the main crop of beetroot. For this you should choose a long-rooted or tankard beet rather than a globe variety, unless your ground happens to be very shallow. Sow the seeds in drills 2 inches deep and 18 inches apart. If you space the seeds, which are quite large, at about 2 inches apart it will be a very simple matter to thin the seedlings to about 6 inches later on.

Blanch Leeks

If you planted leeks in trenches during April (see April, Second Week) you must commence to blanch them as soon as they are well established and growing freely. The best method is to make tubes out of stiff brown paper, slip one of these over each plant, fastening it to a bamboo cane and drawing a little soil up around its base. The tubes should be about 6 inches in length and about 3 inches in diameter.

Commence to Cut Asparagus

From now onwards, for something like six weeks, you should be able to cut good asparagus from established beds. It is, however, a great mistake to cut any shoots at all until the roots are well established. I certainly do not advise you to cut a single shoot until the second year after planting, and it may even be worth waiting until the third year.

It is an excellent plan to give established asparagus beds a dressing of salt at the rate of 3 ounces per square yard. A second application can be given a fortnight later.

131

STRAW THE STRAWBERRY BEDS

Place clean straw around and between strawberry plants. The object of this is twofold: mainly to protect the fruits later on from mud splashings, but also to provide a mulch and so conserve soil moisture, a most important point in the cultivation of good strawberries.

RING UNFRUITFUL APPLES AND PEARS

Apple and pear trees that persistently refuse to blossom and bear fruit can often be made fruitful by checking the flow of food from the leaves to the roots. This is done by removing a

RINGING A FRUIT TREE.

A strip of bark ¼ inch wide is removed right round the main trunk of the tree or near the base of each of the main branches. A handy tool, made from a ¼-inch thick iron bar and two razor blades, is shown in the inset.

ring of bark around the main trunk or low down on each main branch. Now is the time to do it, and the method is to cut out a strip of bark, ¼ inch wide, down to the wood and right round the branch or trunk. You should understand, however, that ringing will only be of assistance if the trees are failing to flower as well as to fruit. If they bloom freely but yet bear no crop the cure must be sought elsewhere. It may be that the trees lack suitable " mates " for cross pollination, that the position is too exposed, or that the trees are under-nourished.

132

Spray Apple Trees against Scab

It is at just about this time that the expanding blossom buds on apple trees reach the point of development described by growers as "pink bud stage"—*i.e.*, the first trace of pink petal colouring can be seen. This is the ideal moment for applying a second application of lime sulphur wash at full winter strength as a preventative of scab disease. You must not delay beyond this stage or the spray may do considerable damage to flowers and leaves. The actual details of application are exactly the same as for the earlier spraying (see April, Second Week).

CUTTING THE RING.

The strip of bark around the fruit tree branch or trunk must be removed very carefully and without injury to the wood beneath.

SECOND WEEK

Plant Early-flowering Chrysanthemums

By this time early-flowering chrysanthemums raised from cuttings taken in February and March should be sufficiently hardened off to be planted outdoors in the beds in which they are to flower. Choose a good open place and well-manured, deeply cultivated ground if you want blooms of the highest quality. For cutting it is best to have the plants in beds by themselves, 15 inches apart in rows 2 to 2½ feet apart; but they can also be used to fill up spaces in the herbaceous border, in which case they should be spaced 15 inches apart each way. Plant with a trowel, taking care to make holes large enough to accommodate all roots without doubling or twisting. Make moderately firm and water freely if the soil is dry.

Plant out Seedlings of Hardy Perennials, etc.

If you were able to sow hardy perennials and alpines in a greenhouse or frame in March (see March, Second Week) you may now plant the seedlings outdoors. Place them in a nursery bed where they can grow on undisturbed throughout the summer. The soil should be good but not heavily manured—indeed, it is better that it should have no manure at all for alpines. Set the plants in lines about 1 foot apart leaving from 3 inches to 1 foot between the plants according to the nature of their growth.

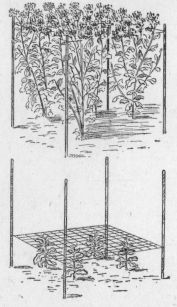

STAKING BORDER CHRYSANTHEMUMS.

This is a very handy method. A square of string netting is stretched between four canes arranged around the plants while they are still young. As they grow the shoots pass through the netting and get all the support they require.

Violas, primroses, and polyanthuses succeed best in a partially shaded place, but the other plants mentioned in my March notes prefer a reasonably sunny position. Similar remarks apply to herbs raised from seed and also to hardy perennials raised from root cuttings (see January, General Work).

STOP INCURVED CHRYSANTHEMUMS

Incurved chrysanthemums which should be stopped during this week in order to get flowers at the usual show period in November are Advancement, Progress, Mrs. H. L. Southam, and Bronze Progress.

REMOVE GREENHOUSE PLANTS TO FRAME

You can further clear the greenhouse by removing a good many of the winter- and spring-flowering plants to frames; but keep plenty of sacks at hand for use at night during the first week or so, as we often have treacherous weather about the middle of May. In addition to forced bulbs, shrubs, and bedding plants, about which I have already given advice (see April, General Work and Third Week), you can now clear out arum lilies, freesias, vallottas, and any perpetual-flowering carnations that have for the time being finished flowering. It is not worth keeping the various greenhouse primulas, cinerarias, and calceolarias for another year after they have finished flowering. All these should be raised annually from seed.

Greenhouse cyclamens, both seedlings raised last August (see August, Second Week) and old flowering plants, will also be better in a shady frame during the summer. The old corms must be kept practically dry from now onwards until the middle of August, but the seedling plants should be maintained in growth all the time, and that means an ample water supply.

PRICK OUT WINTER GREENS

It is a mistake to let winter green crops get overcrowded in the seed beds. Prick out all the seedlings from the April sowing (see April, Second Week) into a nursery bed in the open. This should be well broken down on the surface and fairly rich. Plant the seedlings 3 inches apart in lines 8 inches apart. Do the same to any seedlings left over from the March sowings, but give these rather more room.

PRICK OFF AND PLANT CELERY

Celery sown last month (see April, Second Week) will require to be pricked off into a frame. Give the seedlings plenty of space for they will be growing fast now. Plants 4 inches apart in rows 6 inches apart will not be overdoing it. Ventilate carefully at first but very freely after a week or so.

It will not be possible to keep the earliest celery (see February, Third Week) in boxes or frame beds any longer without risk of checking them severely in transplanting, so get them out into the trenches now (see April, General Work). There is still danger of frost sufficient to kill the plants, so you must keep some protection at hand. The simplest and best method is to draw up some soil to form a ridge on each side of the shallow trench and then to rest some ordinary frame lights on this, so converting the whole trench into a temporary frame. Set the plants 1 foot apart in a single line down the middle of the trench if it is a narrow one, or in two lines, one at each side of the trench, if it is a wide one. Water in really freely. Celery loves moisture and will fail if allowed to get dry.

SOW CHICORY

Chicory is often neglected by amateurs, but it is a most useful vegetable and a welcome change from seakale and endive in the winter and spring. It is blanched and eaten raw or cooked.

135

Sow seeds now in a sheltered place and on rich, deeply dug ground. Sow sparingly in drills ½ inch deep and 1 foot apart.

Plant Tomatoes in Unheated Greenhouses

When you have cleared the greenhouse sufficiently you can plant it with tomatoes for a late summer crop. Little or no artificial heat will be needed for these from now onwards if you are careful with ventilation and you have stout canvas blinds that can be lowered over the glass on frosty nights. The tomatoes can be grown in pots as advised for the early crops (see March, Second Week), or you can have them in boxes, on a bed of soil made up on the staging, or in a border on the floor. In any case the plants should be at least 1 foot apart in rows which should themselves be quite 2½ feet apart. An alternative method, which certainly makes working easy, is to have two rows quite close together (say 15 inches apart) and then an alleyway 3 feet wide. Make the soil very firm around the roots. The best compost is good fibrous loam, with a little well-rotted manure, leaf-mould, bonemeal, etc. (see the mixture recommended for potting, March, Second Week). Water the plants in freely after planting or potting, and provide each with a small bamboo cane for support.

A BED FOR TOMATOES.

This sectional impression of a tomato bed shows the method employed when the staging is of the open lath type. This is covered with galvanised iron sheets, which are in turn covered with a thick layer of coarse cinders or gravel for drainage before the soil is placed in position.

Spray Pear Trees

By this time most of the blossom will probably have fallen from pear trees, and it will be necessary to spray again with

Bordeaux mixture if there is much danger of scab attacking the trees during the summer. The ideal period is between a week and ten days after blossom can first be shaken from the topmost branches. The details of application are exactly the same as before flowering (see April, Second Week). If caterpillars have been troublesome in previous years, it is also an excellent plan to spray with a good insecticide, such as derris, or to mix derris powder at the rate of 2 ounces to 5 gallons of Bordeaux wash.

DUST STRAWBERRIES WITH FLOWERS OF SULPHUR

If you had any trouble last season with mildew on strawberries, now is the time to take preventive measures this year by dusting the leaves thoroughly with flowers of sulphur. You can either place the sulphur in a small muslin bag, hold this over the plants and hit it with a stick, or else pur-

HEELING IN TULIPS.

The plants have been removed from the flower garden to make room for summer bedding, and are being planted temporarily in an out-of-the-way border so that the bulbs may complete their growth and ripen properly.

chase a small powder blower from any dealer in horticultural sundries. This latter is a very handy implement to have about the place, for it can also be used to apply any of the dry powder insecticides and fungicides that have become so popular, particularly for use in greenhouses.

137

THIRD WEEK

CLEAR BEDS FOR SUMMER BEDDING

Next week it will be time to make a start at planting the summer bedding subjects and so some time this week you must clear the beds of their spring occupants. Lift daffodils, hyacinths, and tulips as carefully as possible and with all the roots that you can get and heel them in temporarily in any out of the way, but preferably sunny, place. Heeling in simply means making a trench about 6 inches deep, laying the bulbs in this with their leaves exposed to sun and air and covering the roots and bulbs with soil which should be made moderately firm. It is useless to take the bulbs up and dry them straight away, for they have not yet finished their growth and would be too weak to do any good another year, but if heeled in as described, some, at least, will give flowers next season.

REMOVING SIDE SHOOTS FROM A SWEET PEA.

The tendrils should also be nipped back, as indicated by the black line, so that the whole strength of the plant is concentrated on a single stem. This method of training is not necessary for garden display, but only when big flowers are required.

REMOVE SIDE SHOOTS FROM SWEET PEAS

Early sweet peas that are being grown on the single stem (cordon) system will need regular attention from now on in the way of removal of all side

138

shoots and tendrils. Be careful not to pinch out flowering stems by mistake; it is quite easy to tell these, as the flower buds are evident even at an early stage.

The later peas will be in need of staking and tying in (see April, Third Week).

STOP EARLY-FLOWERING CHRYSANTHEMUMS

If early-flowering chrysanthemums required for specimen blooms and planted out last week are not showing a break bud—that is to say, a flower bud—at the extremity of the central growth, stop them now by pinching out the tip and first pair of leaves. Note well that this instruction applies only to plants that are being grown for large specimen blooms. If your object is to have a big number of comparatively small flowers, two stoppings are necessary, one in April (see April, General Work) and the other in June (see June, General Work).

POT LATE-FLOWERING CHRYSANTHEMUMS

It should now be possible to get most of the late-flowering chrysanthemums,

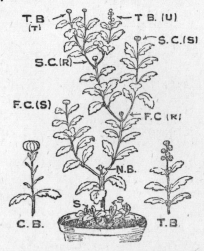

CHRYSANTHEMUM TERMINOLOGY.

The plant shown has every kind of shoot and bud that is referred to by special terms. S.: root suckers suitable for making into cuttings. N.B.: break bud rubbed out, resulting in a natural break. F.C.(R): first crown bud rubbed out to allow second crowns to form. F.C.(S): first crown bud saved or " taken." S.C.(S): second crown bud "taken." S.C.(R): second crown bud rubbed out to allow terminal buds to form. T.B.(T): terminal buds thinned out to one per stem. T.B.(U): terminal buds unthinned. The separate sketches show a typical crown bud and terminal buds in greater detail.

including Japanese exhibition varieties, incurves, decoratives, and singles, into their final flowering pots. Exception, of course, must be made in the case of late cuttings, some of which may as yet be barely rooted. Flowering pots for the early-rooted cuttings should be 8 or 9 inches in diameter according to the strength of the plants, while for late March cuttings 6-inch pots should prove

FINAL POTTING.

A chrysanthemum being placed in the pot in which it will flower. A stick is used to firm the soil around the plant.

adequate. Use a good coarse compost with about three parts fibrous loam, pulled apart by hand and not sifted, one part dried cow manure, one part coarse sand, and a 7-inch pot full of bonemeal added to each barrowload of compost. This soil must be made quite firm around the plants, and it is advisable to use a wooden rammer to force it down around the sides of the pots. After potting, remove the plants to a sheltered place in the open.

POT BEGONIAS, GLOXINIAS, ETC.

Begonias, gloxinias, and streptocarpuses from an early sowing (see January, Third Week) should be ready for removal to their flowering pots. Do not be in a hurry, however, if roots are not showing freely around the sides of the present balls of soil. Overpotting does no good—but then neither does overcrowding. The flowering pots should be 5 or 6 inches in diameter. Use the same soil mixture as before (see April, Second Week). Water freely, place in the greenhouse, and shade from direct sunshine.

SOW RUNNER BEANS OUTDOORS

It is now time to make a good sowing of runner beans in the open. Sow the seeds individually or in pairs about 8 inches apart in two lines 10 inches apart. If you require more than one double row, have an alley-way of at least 8 feet wide between each set. Cover the seeds with 2 inches of soil. If you sow the seeds in pairs and they all germinate you will need to single the seedlings out later on.

PLANT OUT CELERIAC

Celeriac raised from seed in March (see March, Fourth Week) may now be planted outdoors. Choose an open position and reasonably rich soil and plant 15 inches apart in rows 18 inches apart.

140

Plant Melons and Cucumbers in Frames

Melons raised in the greenhouse last month (see April, Third Week) may be planted in frames. Prepare a compost as described for cucumbers (see March, First Week) and allow one plant for each full-sized garden light (6 feet by 4 feet). Plant on a small mound of compost in the centre of the space covered by the light. Pinch out the point of each plant when it has made about five leaves.

Cucumbers raised from seed last month (see April, Third Week) for cultivation in unheated frames may also be planted in exactly the same way as melons (see above). Subsequent training is the same as for cucumbers in frames on hotbeds (see April, General Work).

Spray Raspberries, Loganberries, etc.

Raspberries and loganberries, and also to a smaller extent blackberries, sometimes suffer severely from a disease known as cane spot. Purplish patches of decayed tissue appear on the canes, gradually encircling them and cutting off the supply of sap. If you have had any of this trouble in former years, spray now with lime sulphur wash at twice the ordinary summer strength.

Commence to Pick Green Gooseberries

It is usually possible to get a first picking of green gooseberries at about this time. The fruits will still be very small and immature and it would be foolish to strip the branches as yet, but if you remove a few here and there where they are overcrowded it will give the remainder a chance to develop more fully and will give you the opportunity of enjoying an early gooseberry pie. This thinning can be repeated from time to time as the fruits increase in size until eventually they are spaced out evenly two or three inches apart for ripening.

FOURTH WEEK

Plant out Bedding Plants and Half-hardy Annuals

If the weather appears reasonably settled and you have followed out instructions regarding hardening off, now is the time to plant

141

LIFTING HALF-HARDY ANNUALS FOR
BEDDING OUT.

*It is important to keep as much soil as
possible around the roots when removing
plants from boxes.*

out the majority of bedding plants and half-hardy annuals. As I mentioned in the General Notes for this month, I make exception in the case of dahlias, heliotropes, scarlet salvias, and cannas, all of which are very susceptible to the cold and are better kept where they can be protected easily until the first week in June. Plant with a trowel, giving roots plenty of room and firming the soil thoroughly around them. Water in liberally if the soil is dry.

PLANT WINDOW BOXES, HANGING BASKETS, ETC.

This is also the time to fill window boxes, hanging baskets, and ornamental vases with their summer occupants. To hang over the edge you can have ivy-leaved pelargoniums, Lobelia tenuior, Campanula isophylla, Lysimachia nummularia aurea, and Asparagus Sprengeri, while good plants of erect habit for this purpose are zonal pelargoniums, marguerites, fuchsias, petunias, and bedding calceolarias. Give the plants a thorough watering after planting. The hanging baskets must be well lined with sphagnum moss to prevent the soil from washing through.

PLANT OUT CHRYSANTHEMUMS FOR LIFTING

It is possible to grow many of the late decorative chrysanthemums without keeping them in big pots all the summer. Plants from 4- or 5-inch pots are planted outdoors now exactly like the early border varieties (see Second Week) and are allowed to grow on in the open ground until September or early October, when they are lifted, carried into

PLANTING OUT SUMMER BEDDING.

*Make a hole of ample width with a
trowel and be certain to make the soil
really firm around the roots.*

the greenhouse, and either placed in big boxes or planted in beds of soil. One great advantage of this method is that plants do not need constant watering during the summer.

START LAST BATCH OF ACHIMENES

A last batch of achimenes (see February, First Week), started now, will carry the display of flowers well on into the autumn.

PRICK OFF PRIMULAS

Greenhouse primulas sown in April (see April, Fourth Week) will need to be pricked off in other boxes or seed pans by this time. Use the same compost as for seed sowing and space the seedlings about 1½ inches apart each way. Water them in well and then place them in a sheltered frame. The plants will be better in frames for the rest of the summer. Ventilate rather sparingly at first, but freely once the seedlings take hold of their new soil.

SOW VEGETABLE MARROWS AND RIDGE CUCUMBERS OUTDOORS

Vegetable marrows and ridge cucumbers can now be sown outdoors where the plants are to grow. Sow the seeds singly or in pairs about 3 feet apart, cover them with 1 inch of soil, and then invert flower pots over them as an additional protection. It is common practice to prepare vegetable marrow beds by building up a mound of turves, but in view of the fact that the plants can do with any amount of moisture, it is really much better to dig out a large hole and fill this with the chopped turves, or, better still, a mixture of turfy loam and manure. It is then a comparatively simple matter to flood the bed from time to time with water. Ridge cucumbers are better on low mounds of turf and dung, for they need all the sun they can get to make them grow rapidly. Still, do not build up the mounds too steeply or watering will be a problem.

PLANT OUT FRENCH BEANS

If you were able to raise some French beans in boxes last month (see April, Second Week), and have hardened the plants carefully in a frame, you may now plant them out with safety. Choose a reasonably sheltered place and be ready to cover the

143

PROTECTION FOR SEEDLING FRENCH BEANS.

The plants are liable to be injured by frosts, so if nights are cold it is advisable to give some protection, as shown.

plants at night with some sheets of brown paper should the weather turn suddenly frosty. Plant the beans 1 foot apart in rows 2 feet apart.

SPRAY APPLES AGAINST SCAB, CODLIN MOTH, ETC.

By this time the blossom will probably be falling freely from all save the latest-flowering apples. About ten days after it can first be shaken from the topmost branches is the ideal time to give yet one more spraying with lime sulphur wash as a protection against scab disease (see April, Second Week, and May, First Week). This time the wash should be used at the summer strength, which means that it must be diluted something like three and a third times more than for the pre-blossom applications. You should consult manufacturers' instructions on this point, for different brands may vary in strength. If you have any reason to suspect that caterpillars of the codlin moth or apple sawfly may attack your apples (these are the grubs that eat into the apples and cause maggotty fruits) mix derris with the lime sulphur, either ordinary derris powder at 2 ounces per 5 gallons or a proprietary brand of derris used according to manufacturers' instructions.

CODLIN MOTH.

A section of an apple attacked by the larva of this moth.

THIN OUT RASPBERRY CANES

Look over the raspberry plantation and reduce the number of new canes if these are very numerous. There is no

144

1. Forking strawy manure into the bottom of a hole prepared for a dahlia.
2. After planting the dahlia is covered each night with a pot until all
danger of frost is past. 3. Placing long stakes to runner beans. Slaked
lime has been scattered round the plants to keep slugs at bay. 4. Japanese
chrysanthemums in their summer quarters. The pots are being tapped to
find out from the ring whether the soil is wet or dry.

1. Propping peaches forward so that they catch the sun. 2. Tying in valuable young side growths on a peach tree. These will bear fruit the following year. 3. A cucumber lateral just starting into growth. This must be removed unless required to take the place of a vine that is worn out. 4. View in cucumber house showing method of growing the plants on mounds of compost.

point in having more than six canes per plant, and these should be quite close to the clump for preference. Raspberries have a habit of sending up suckers all over the bed, and unless you remove them from the alleyways it may be almost impossible to get between the canes to pick fruit later on.

FLOWERS, VEGETABLES, AND FRUITS IN SEASON DURING MAY

Hardy Herbaceous Plants.—Adonis *autumnalis*, Anchusa *myosotidiflora*, A. *officinalis*, Aquilegia *chrysantha*, A. *longissima*, A. *Skinneri*, A. *vulgaris vars.*, aquilegias (*long-spurred hybrids*), Aster *subcœruleus*, Baptisia *australis*, Barbarea *vulgaris plena*, Bellis *perennis vars.* (*daisy*), Centaurea *montana*, Cheiranthus *Allionii*, C. *Cheiri* (*wallflower*), Dicentra *eximia*, D. *spectabilis*, Doronicum *plantagineum*, Eremurus *Elwesii*, E. *robustus*, E. *himalaicus*, Euphorbia *cyparissias* (*spurge*), E. *pilosa major*, Galax *aphylla*, Geranium *armenum*, G. *Endressii*, G. *nepalense*, Geum *bulgaricum*, G. *coccineum hybrids*, Heuchera *tiarelloides*, Incarvillea *grandiflora*, Iris *florentina*, I. *germanica vars.* (*Flag, German iris*), I. *longipetala and vars.*, I. *susiana*, Lupinus *polyphyllus hybrids* (*lupins*), Meconopsis *cambrica and vars.*, Mertensia *virginica*, M. *lævigata*, M. *paniculata subcordata*, Myosotis *hybrids* (*forget-me-nots*), Nepeta *Mussini*, Pæonia *albiflora and vars.* (*Chinese pæony*), P. *officinalis and vars.* (*pæony*), P. *tenuifolia and vars.*, P. *Wittmanniana*, Papaver *orientale and vars.* (*Oriental poppy*), Phlox *divaricata vars.*, Polygonatum *multiflorum* (*Solomon's Seal*), Pyrethrum *hybrids*, Ranunculus *bullatus plenus*, Saxifraga *umbrosa* (*London Pride*), Smilacina *racemosum*, Trollius *europæus and vars.*, Verbascum *Thapsus*, Veronica *gentianoides*, violas (*bedding*), Viola *tricolor* (*pansy*).

Hardy Bulbs and Tubers.—Allium *albopilosum*, A. *cœruleum*, A. *giganteum*, A. *karataviense*, A. *Moly*, A. *neapolitanum*, A. *Ostrowskyanum*, A. *Rosenbachianum*, Anemone *coronaria and vars.*, Calochortus *albus*, C. *amabilis*, C. *Benthami*, C. *clavatus*, C. *Kennedyi*, C. *lilacinus*, C. *Maweanus*, C. *venustus*, C. *Weedii*, Camassia *Cusickii*, C. *esculenta*, C. *Leichtlinii*, C. *Quamash*, Convallaria *majalis* (*lily of the valley*), Cyclamen *repandum*, Erythronium *americanum*, E. *californicum*, E. *Dens-canis*, E. *grandiflorum and vars.*, E. *Hartwegii*, E. *Hendersonii*, E. *revolutum*, Fritillaria *camtschatensis*, F. *Imperialis and vars.*, F. *Meleagris vars.*, hyacinths (*large-flowered hybrids*), Iris *cristata*, I. *Hoogiana*, I. *Korolkowii*, I. *Lorteti*, I. *Sisyrinchium*, I. *stolonifera*, I. *tingitana*, Ixiolirion *montanum and vars.*, Leucojum *æstivum*, L. *pulchellum*, Muscari *comosum monstrosum*, M. *Heavenly Blue*, Narcissus *Jonquilla vars.*, N. *poeticus recurvus and Double White*, Romulea *rosea*, Scilla *amœna*, S. *hispanica and vars.* (*Spanish bluebell*), S. *nonscripta and vars.* (*bluebell*), Trillium *erectum*, T. *grandiflorum*, T. *ovatum*, T. *recurvatum*, T. *sessile and vars.*, T. *stylosum*, Tulipa *Batalini*, T. *Gesneriana*, T. *persica*, T. *saxatilis*, T. *Sprengeri*, T. *tubergeniana*, tulips (*Cottage, Darwin, Rembrandt, and Parrot*).

ROCK PLANTS.—Achillea *tomentosum*, Æthionema *coridifolium*, Æ. *grandiflorum*, Æ. *pulchellum*, Æ. *Warley Rose*, Alyssum *saxatile and vars.*, A. *spinosum*, Androsace *lactea*, A. *primuloides*, A. *sarmentosa and vars.*, A. *sempervivoides*, Anemone *sylvestris and vars.*, Antennaria *dioica and vars.*, Aquilegia *cœrulea*, A. *glandulosa*, A. *jucunda*, Arabis *albida and vars.*, A. *alpina*, A. *aubrietioides*, Arctostaphylos *Uva-ursi*, Arenaria *balearica*, A. *laricifolia*, A. *montana*, A. *purpurascens*, Armeria *cæspitosa*, A. *maritima and vars.*, Asperula *hirta*, Aster *alpinus and vars.*, A. *Forrestii*, Astilbe *simplicifolia*, Astragalus *tragacanthus,* Aubrietia *deltoidea and vars.*, Bellis *rotundifolia cœrulescens*, B. *sylvestris*, B. *bellidioides*, Calceolaria *polyrrhiza*, Campanula *alpestris*, C. *Aucheri*, C. *garganica and vars.*, C. *Poscharskyanum*,

AQUILEGIA CŒRULEA.

Cheiranthus *alpinus*, Codonopsis *ovata*, Cornus *canadensis*, Cortusa *Matthioli*, Corydalis *cheilanthifolia*, C. *nobilis*, C. *tuberosa*, Cotyledon *Purpusii*, C. *simplicifolia*, Cypripedium *calceolus*, Delphinium *nudicaule*, Daphne *Cneorum*, D. *retusa*, Dianthus *cæsius*, Eomecon *chionantha*, Epigæa *repens*, epimediums (*as April*), Erinacea *pungens*, Erinus *alpinus and vars.*, Erodium *chamædryoides*, E. *corsicum*, Gentiana *acaulis*, G. *verna*, Geranium *argenteum*, G. *cinereum*, G. *Pylzowianum*, Geum *Borisii*, G. *montanum*, Globularia *incanescens*, G. *vulgaris*, Haberlea *Ferdinandi-Coburgi*, H. *rhodopensis*, Helianthemum *alyssoides*, H. *lunulatum*, H. *Tuberaria*, H. *vulgare in var.* (*sun rose*), Houstonia *cœrulea*, H. *serpyllifolia*, Hutchinsia *alpina*, Iberis *correæfolia*, I. *gibraltarica*, I. *saxatilis*, I. *sempervirens*, Iris *chamæiris*, I. *flavissima*, I. *gracilipes*, I. *graminea*, I. *verna*, Isopyrum *thalictroides*, Leucocrinum *montanum*, Linaria *alpina*, L. *hepaticæfolia*, L. *pallida*, Linnæa *borealis*, Linum *arboreum*, L. *monogynum*, Lithospermum *prostratum and vars.*, Lychnis *alpina*, L. *Lagascæ*, Mazus *Pumilio*, M. *reptans*, Morisia *hypogæa*, Myosotis *rupicola*, Œnothera *cæspitosa*, Omphalodes *Luciliæ*, O. *verna*, Orobus *vernus*, Oxalis *adenophylla*, O. *corniculata*, O. *enneaphylla*, Pentstemon *Menziesii*, P. *Scouleri*, Phlox *divaricata Laphami*, P. *Douglasi*, P. *subulata and vars.*, Potentilla *ambigua*, P. *aurea*, P. *fragiformis*, P. *nitida*, Primula *Auricula and vars.*, P. *capitata*, P. *chrysopa*, P. *farinosa*, P. *frondosa*, P. *Juliæ*, P. *Mooreana*, P. *nutans*, P. *pubescens*, P. *Sieboldii*, P. *Veitchii*, Ramondia *pyrenaica and vars.*, R. *serbica*, Ranunculus *alpestris*, R. *gramineus*, Saponaria *ocymoides*, Saxifraga *Aizoon and vars.*, S. *Andrewsii*, S. *cochlearis*, S. *Cotyledon and vars.*, S. *decipiens vars. (mossy saxifrages)*, S. *hypnoides vars.*, *(mossy saxifrages)*, S. *granulata plena*, S. *lingulata and vars.*, S. *longifolia*, Schizocodon *soldanelloides*, Sedum *pilosum*, Shortia *uniflora*, Silene *acaulis*, Sisyrinchium *angustifolium*, S. *bermudianum*, S. *filifolium*, S. *striatum*, Stachys *corsica*, Tanakæa *radicans*, Tiarella *cordifolia*, Trollius *pumilus*, Veronica *Cataractæ*, V. *canescens*, V. *filiformis*, V. *fruticans*, V. *pectinata*, V. *rupestris*, Viola *biflora*, V. *bosniaca*, V. *calcarata*, V. *canadensis*, V. *cornuta and vars.*, V. *cucullata*, V. *gracilis and vars.*, V. *hederacea*, Wahlenbergia *graminifolium*, W. *Pumilio*, W. *serpyllifolia*.

HARDY AQUATICS AND BOG PLANTS.—Caltha *leptosepala*, C. *palustris and vars.*, C. *polypetala*, Cardamine *pratensis plena*, Dodecatheon *Hendersonii*, D. *Meadia*, D. *radicatum*, Geum *rivale*, Hottonia *palustris*, Iris *lævigata*, I. *ochroleuca*, I. *Pseudacorus*, Mimulus *cupreus*, M. *luteus and hybrids*, Myosotis *palustris*, Orchis *latifolia*, O. *maculata*, O. *palustris*, Primula *Beesiana*, P. *Bulleyana*, P. *chionantha*, P. *Cockburniana*, P. *helodoxa*, P. *japonica*, P. *littoniana*, P. *microdonta and vars.*, P. *pulverulenta and vars.*, P. *rosea*, P. *secundiflora*, P. *sikkimensis*, P. *vittata*, Ranunculus *aquatilis*, Villarsia *(Limnanthemum)*, *nymphæoides*.

ANNUALS.—Hardy vars. sown September (see list, September, First Week).

BEDDING PLANTS.—Cheiranthus *Allionii*, double daisies, forget-me-nots, wallflowers.

EVERGREEN SHRUBS.—Andromeda *polifolia*, Berberis *aquifolium*, B. *Darwini*, B. *empetrifolia*, B. *Gagnepainii*, B. *hakeoides*, B. *replicata*, B. *stenophylla*, B. *verruculosa*, Buddleia *globosa*, Ceanothus *dentatus*, C. *rigidus*, C. *thyrsiflorus*, C. *veitchianus*, Choisya *ternata*, Cotoneaster *Franchetii*, Erica *cinerea vars.*, E. *lusitanica*, E. *mediterranea*, Fabiana *imbricata*, Gaultheria *Shallon*, Jasminum *Giraldii*, Kalmia *glauca*, Ledum *latifolium*, L. *palustre*, Leiophyllum *buxifolium*, Leucothoe *Catesbæi*, Olearia *Gunniana*, O. *nitida*, Osmarea *Burkwoodi*, Photinia *serrulata*, Pieris *Forrestii*, P. *formosa*, Pyracantha *coccinea and vars.*, P. *Gibbsii*, P. *Rogersiana*, Rhododendron *argyrophyllum*, R. *calostrotum*, R. *cantabile*, R. *catawbiense*, R. *charitopes*, R. *chryseum*, R. *cinnabarinum*, R. *Falconeri*, R. *fastigiatum*, R. *Fortunei hybrids*, R. *glaucum*, R. *Griffithianum hybrids*, R. *hæmatodes*, R. *impeditum*, R. *intricatum*, R. *Keysii*, R. *lapponicum*, R. *Loderi*, R. *orbiculare*, R. *ponticum hybrids*, R. *racemosum*, R. *rubiginosum*, R. *repens*, R. *Sargentianum*, R. *sino-grande (shelter)*, R. *Soulei*, R. *Smirnowi*, R. *vernicosum*, R. *Wardii*, also many fine hybrid rhododen-

JUNE

GENERAL WORK

SPRAY AGAINST PESTS

GREENFLY is likely to become more of a nuisance this month unless you take appropriate measures to destroy it at the first sign of attack (see May, General Work). Caterpillars may also put in an appearance now. In most cases they can be poisoned before they have done much damage by spraying with derris, which, fortunately, is not poisonous either to human beings or domestic animals. Use 2 ounces of derris powder and 4 ounces of soft soap to 5 gallons of water, or else purchase one of the proprietary derris insecticides and mix it according to manufacturers' instructions. Continue to water the soil around lettuces, delphiniums, and other slug favourites with permanganate of potash on mild, damp evenings (see May, General Work).

TRIM HEDGES

You can trim evergreen hedges lightly at any time during the month. If you grow Berberis Darwini as a hedge, the best time to trim it is immediately the flowers fade. Cut the flowering shoots back sufficiently to give the hedge a neat appearance.

CONTINUE TO FEED PLANTS IN FULL GROWTH

Herbaceous plants and vegetables that are growing freely will be all the better for one or two more applications of a quick-acting fertiliser and some soakings with weak liquid manure (see May, General Work).

REMOVE RUNNERS FROM VIOLETS AND STRAWBERRIES

If left to their own devices, violets will make innumerable runners during the summer and early autumn. You should remove these from time to time, cutting them off close to the main clump, for if allowed to grow unchecked they will reduce the strength of the crowns and so make them less capable of producing winter flowers.

Similar remarks apply to the runners produced by strawberries, unless you require some of these for propagation (see July, First Week).

Disbud Roses for Exhibition

Hybrid tea, tea, and pernetiana roses will be forming their flower buds freely throughout the month, and if you want some big blooms for exhibition or cutting you must disbud them from time to time. This simply means that out of each cluster of buds

A Violet Clump Throwing Out Runners.

These long thin shoots, growing out in all directions from the centre of the plant, must be removed, or they will take strength from the flowering crowns.

only the big terminal one must be retained, all the side buds being nipped out at as early a stage as possible.

Stake and Disbud Border Carnations

Border carnations will be forming their flower stems and these must be staked as necessary. Beginners often go wrong over this. The natural habit of the border carnation is to arch its flower slightly and not hold it stiffly erect. This you must allow it to do, and any ties you make must be sufficiently low down the stem not to interfere with its natural arching habit. If you make ties all the way up to the bud, rain will collect in the expanding flower and spoil the petals and hot sun will complete the damage.

Make Successional Sowings

Successional sowings are almost precisely the same as those for last month (see May, General Work). Lettuces, endive, radishes, mustard and cress, turnips, should still be sown at intervals. It is too late to sow maincrop peas, but it is not a bad plan to make a sowing at the beginning of the month of an early variety. Choose a fully open place for this last crop, for late peas in the shade are certain to be ruined by mildew. All the salad vegetables, and also turnips, will be better in a rather shady place.

Plant Winter Greens

Throughout June you should miss no opportunity of planting out all manner of winter greens, including Brussels sprouts, broccoli, kale, and savoy. In most cases these should be planted about 2 feet apart in rows 2½ feet apart, but, as different varieties grow to varying sizes, you should consult the seedsman's notes on the seed packet regarding this. Make the soil really firm around the roots; none of the cabbage family does well in loose soil, and for this reason the beds should be well trodden before planting. Then after planting, run a hoe through the surface to leave a dust mulch.

A Blind Cauliflower.

All winter greens are liable to go " blind," losing their growing points (A). *Such plants are quite useless.*

Lift Autumn-sown Onions as Required

During June the bulbs of autumn-sown onions (see August, Fourth Week) will have attained sufficient size to be used. Do not lift the whole crop yet, however, for the bulbs will not be properly ripened. Simply dig up a few onions at a time as you require them.

Stake Culinary Peas

Peas sown last month must be staked in the same way as the earlier batches (see May, General Work).

Feed and Fumigate Tomatoes under Glass

The earliest tomatoes (see January, Second Week) will be ripening freely, while even the latest batches planted last month (see May, Second Week) will be setting fruits during the month. All must be watered freely—they will need supplies every day when the weather is warm—and should be fed regularly as I described in my notes for last month (see May, General Work). Plants in flower should be pollinated, as explained in the same place; while training, stopping at the apex of the house, and the

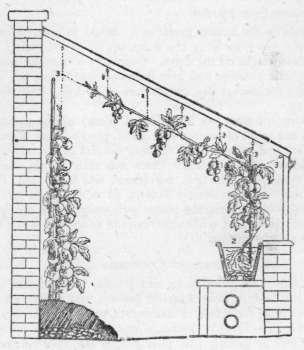

TRAINING TOMATOES IN A LEAN-TO HOUSE.
The back wall plants are shown planted in a bed, but they could equally well be grown in pots.

removal of all side shoots must proceed as before. A top dressing of well-rotted manure will help the later plants.

White fly may become a nuisance now. If it does, fumigate at once with one or other of the numerous proprietary white-fly vapours, sprinkling the specified quantity of fumigating liquid on the path in the evening and then keeping the house closely shut up until the morning. Repeat twice, at intervals of three

FIRST WEEK

PLANT TENDER BEDDING PLANTS

The few tender bedding plants that I advised you to omit from May planting (see May, Fourth Week) may now go outdoors into their flowering quarters. These plants include dahlias, begonias, scarlet salvias, heliotropes, and cannas, also a few choice foliage plants, such as abutilons, cordylines, ricinus, Zea mays, and Leucophyton Browni. Details for planting are exactly as for those plants put out in May.

SOW PERENNIALS AND BIENNIALS

Most perennials and biennials, if sown out of doors now, will make good sturdy plants for placing in flowering quarters in the autumn. I make exception only in the case of forget-me-nots and Brompton stocks, which I find are better sown rather later as they get too big if sown now, tending to flower before the winter; this is always a bad point. The most useful biennials are Canterbury bells, various verbascums, and Coreopsis grandiflora. Perennials which are almost invariably treated as biennials are wallflowers, Cheiranthus Allioni, foxgloves, Sweet Williams, double daisies, Iceland poppies, and Campanula pyramidalis. These may also be sown now. Amongst the easiest perennials to raise from seed are aquilegias, lupins, oriental poppies, hollyhocks, and delphiniums, also easy rock plants such as aubrietias, Alyssum saxatile, and Campanula carpatica; but there are many other things that you can try if you can obtain the seeds. Sow thinly in drills 6 or 8 inches apart and cover with from $\frac{1}{4}$ to 1 inch of soil, according to the

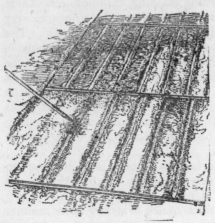

COVERING SEED DRILLS.

This can be done very conveniently with the back of a rake drawn along the drill, as shown.

size of the seeds. Violas, pansies, primroses, and polyanthuses may also be sown now outdoors, but it is preferable to choose a rather shady place for these.

Sow St. Brigid Anemones

Anemones of the St. Brigid and Du Caen types can also be raised quite readily from seed sown outdoors now and will flower next summer. Choose a sunny, sheltered position and sow the seed very thinly indeed in drills $\frac{1}{2}$ inch deep and 9 inches apart. The reason that I stress the importance of thin sowing is that then no transplanting will be necessary and the plants can grow on unchecked in the seed bed until they have flowered next year.

Plunge Pot Shrubs and Roses Outdoors

From this time until the end of September, all the shrubs and roses that have been grown in pots for early flowering, and are either still in the greenhouse or have been removed to shelters and frames, will be much better in a sunny but not too scorchingly hot position outdoors. This also applies to greenhouse heaths, Indian azaleas, camellias, and acacias. The ideal method is to prepare a deep bed of sifted boiler ashes or coarse sand, and to plunge the pots up to their rims in this. Watering will be considerably reduced by this means and the soil in the pots will be maintained at a more even temperature. Do not on any account choose a position that is exposed to cutting draughts, as, for example, near an alleyway between buildings. Syringe daily with clear water

An Outdoor Plunge Bed.

The planks, nailed on edge, serve to keep the plunging material from spreading about. Pot plants, plunged as shown, require much less watering than those which are stood in the open without any protection.

throughout the summer to ward off attacks by red spider. This is particularly necessary in the case of Indian azaleas.

PRICK OFF CINERARIAS

Cinerarias sown early in May must be pricked off 2 inches apart each way in seed boxes filled with the compost recommended for seed sowing. Stand in a frame and ventilate freely.

PLACE CHRYSANTHEMUMS IN SUMMER QUARTERS

Exhibition and decorative chrysanthemums grown in pots will also be better right out in the open from now onwards. If you have many of these plants I advise you to make a special standing

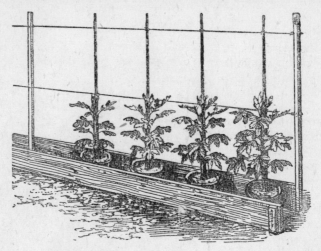

SUMMER QUARTERS FOR CHRYSANTHEMUMS.

The two boards on edge keep the pots in position. If desired, sand, ashes, or moss peat can be placed between them to form a small plunge bed.

ground for them in an out-of-the-way place. The soil should be well covered with sharp sifted boiler ashes or gravel to give good drainage. The plants are then arranged in straight rows at least 2½ feet apart, so that you can move between them easily for watering, tying, bud staking, etc. Drive a good strong stake into the ground at each end of each row, stretch a couple of wires between the pairs of stakes and then attach each bamboo cane to the wires. This is the ideal method with exhibition chrysanthemums grown to a single stem. With big decorative plants the horizontal wires get in the way, and one must rely on the canes alone to support the plants.

THIN OUT VEGETABLE SEEDLINGS

Various vegetable seedlings from April and May sowings will still be in need of thinning (see May, General Work).

PLANT OUTDOOR TOMATOES

Tomatoes that have been well hardened off in frames may be planted outdoors in a sunny, sheltered position. A border at the foot of a fence or wall with a southerly aspect is the best possible place for the plants, which should be 15 inches apart. If you have more than one row, space them 2½ feet apart and have them running north and south, so that all the plants get an equal share of sunshine. In the case of one row only it is better for it to run east and west. The soil should be in good condition, but not too richly manured, as it is wise to let tomatoes set a few fruits and then to feed regularly with any reliable tomato fertiliser. Be sure to plant really firmly.

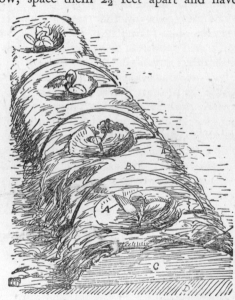

PLANT VEGETABLE MARROWS AND RIDGE CUCUMBERS

Vegetable marrows and ridge cucumbers raised under glass and properly hardened off may be planted out on a prepared bed (see

A BED FOR RIDGE CUCUMBERS.

The low mound of soil and manure (C) built above the normal level of the soil (D) exposes the plants to the sun without making watering too difficult. This task is assisted by the shallow depressions (A) in which each plant is set. The hoops (B) support temporary night shelter until danger of frost is passed.

L

May, Fourth Week). If the weather is cold and nights tend to be slightly frosty, keep some big flower pots at hand and invert one over each plant every evening, removing it in good time the next morning. The plants should be at least 3 feet apart each way in the beds. Pinch out the tip of each plant when it has made about six or seven leaves. Then train the laterals that form evenly around the plant to fill the bed and pinch the tip out of each as soon as it reaches the edge of the bed.

Plant Runner Beans

Runner beans that you raised in boxes under glass in April will be ready for planting out in double lines 10 inches apart, allowing 8 inches from plant to plant in the rows. If you have more than one row of beans they should be at least 8 feet apart, because when they grow up they cast a considerable amount of shade. For this same reason it is an advantage if all the rows can run north and south, as then each row does stand a chance to get some direct sunshine.

You must provide a stout stake for each plant. These stakes should be at least 8 feet long and must be thrust as firmly as possible into the ground. There are many ways of finishing the task, but none that is simpler than to cross the sticks at the top and then place other sticks horizontally in the forks so made. Bind all the sticks together where they meet and you will have a support for your beans that will stand any amount of wind.

If you cannot obtain stakes for all your runner beans you can grow some of them as bush plants by the simple proc of pinching out the growing points of the shoots from time to time. Quite a good crop of beans can be obtained in this manner, though, of course, it will not be so heavy, nor will the beans be quite so fine, as those from plants grown in the more usual way on stakes.

Plant Celery

You can also plant out celery with safety and without the necessity for any protection. Details of work are the same as for the earliest crop (see May, Second Week). Get out all plants that are 3 inches in height or more. Backward seedlings and those from late sowings may wait for a few weeks yet. Water in freely.

162

Pinch Broad Beans

The earliest broad beans should now have set about three clusters of pods each, and it is wise to stop them growing any taller by pinching out the tip of each plant. This may prevent an attack by black fly, because this pest invariably goes for the young growing tips, and if there is no soft growth it will seek food elsewhere. Incidentally, the stopping will hasten the development of the pods.

SECOND WEEK

Repot Auriculas

If you grow auriculas in pots now is the time to repot them. Shake the old soil from the roots and make certain that these have no woolly aphis upon them. This, by the way, is the same pest that causes the white woolly patches on apples, and is often known as American blight. If it should be present wash the roots in a solution of any good petroleum emulsion insecticide or sprinkle them with nicotine powder. Then repot either in 3½- or 4-inch pots, reducing the size of the plants if necessary and using a compost of four parts loam, one part dried cow manure, one part leaf-mould, and one part mixed sand and crushed oyster shell. Pot firmly, water freely, and place in a frame or a sheltered place outdoors. You can remove offsets with roots if you wish and pot them separately.

Divide Auriculas, Polyanthuses, etc.

Auriculas, polyanthuses, and coloured primroses growing in the open may be lifted and carefully divided if they are particularly good selected varieties. In the case of ordinary mixed strains, however, it is better to raise a new stock each year from seed, as the old plants tend to get weakened by attacks from greenfly, red spider, etc.

Lift Anemones in Frames

Anemones of the St. Brigid and Du Caen types, grown in frames for winter and spring flowering, will have completed their growth by this time and should be lifted. Shake the tubers clear of soil and place them in trays, surrounding them with a little dry peat moss. Then stand the trays in a cool, dry place. The corms will keep safely under these conditions until you wish to plant them again.

DIG EARLY POTATOES

The earliest potatoes planted at the end of February will probably be ready for digging. Lift one or two roots and see what kind of a crop there is. There is no point in waiting for the tubers to mature. So long as they are big enough to be used, lift them, but only as you actually require them for use. It is a great mistake to dig too many early potatoes at once for they lose quality rapidly when out of the ground.

THIN CHICORY

Chicory sown last month (see May, Second Week) will require thinning. Leave the seedlings 9 inches apart.

SOW SHORTHORN CARROTS

Make a last sowing of shorthorn carrots outdoors (see March, Third Week). These will come in at about the same time as the maincrop carrots and will be more tender and delicately flavoured for immediate use. The maincrop is principally of value for storing for winter use.

SOW PARSLEY FOR SUCCESSION

Make a third small sowing of parsley for succession (see February, Fourth Week, and April, Third Week).

PEARS READY FOR FINAL THINNING.

It is at this stage of development that the number of fruits must be reduced to one, or at most two, per cluster.

EXPOSE SHALLOT BULBS

Shallots will now be approaching their ripening period and you should draw the soil away from the bulbs a little in order to allow them to swell freely and get the full benefit of sunlight.

COMMENCE TO THIN APPLES AND PEARS

You will now be able to see how many fruits have been formed on your apple and pear trees. It is no use leaving too many, or they will only get misshapen, small, and poor in quality. Usually one per spur is enough, and two should be regarded as the maximum. If there are more than this the weakest or least satisfactory will have to be removed, and you can commence to do this now, but do not complete the work yet for there is usually a fairly heavy natural fall later in the month. Be content at the moment to thin the fruits

PEAR THINNING COMPLETED.

This drastic reduction in the number of fruits is amply justified if quality is the first consideration.

to about four per cluster, removing any that are noticeably poor, badly shaped, or spotted. You will find a pair of pointed vine scissors most serviceable for this work.

COMMENCE TO SUMMER PRUNE GOOSEBERRIES AND CURRANTS

You can save yourself a great deal of winter work, and incidentally improve the yield of your gooseberry and currant bushes by summer pruning. Start this now, but do not attempt to complete it all at once. The ideal is to spread the work over a period of about six weeks. Then the bushes will not suffer any check from sudden loss of foliage. Summer pruning, by the way, does not apply to black currants but only to the red and white kinds. It consists in cutting off the ends of all side shoots when they are 5 or 6 inches in length. Shorten them to about 3 inches.

THIRD WEEK

PRUNE FLOWERING SHRUBS

Any shrubs that flowered during May or early June can be pruned now, but this is not to say that pruning is always necessary. Much depends upon the purpose for which the shrub is being

165

grown and the amount of space that you can spare it. For example, evergreen ceanothuses must be pruned annually when grown against a wall, but there is no necessity to prune them at all if they are cultivated as bushes in the open. The method against walls is to cut back to within an inch or so of the main branches all laterals that are growing away from the wall. Brooms may get very straggly if they are not pruned annually. You must never cut back into very hard, old wood, but it is

SUMMER-PRUNING A GOOSEBERRY.

The older fruiting wood is marked A. *Current year's shoots, labelled* B, *must be shortened a few at a time, as indicated by the crosses, with the exception of shoots terminating branches, which are allowed to grow unchecked.*

quite safe to clip the bushes lightly now, shortening the young flowering shoots to within an inch or so of the older branches. Lilacs, rhododendrons, and azaleas need no regular pruning of a severe nature, but it is a great advantage to cut off the faded flower trusses and so prevent the formation of seed. Clematis montana may be cut back sufficiently to keep it within bounds. The popular Cydonia japonica must be pruned when grown against a wall, and the best method is to shorten laterals a few at a time, spreading the work over a period of several weeks.

Take Pink Pipings

Now is the time to propagate pinks by means of cuttings. Select healthy-looking, non-flowering shoots 4 or 5 inches in length and pull them out at a joint. This is known as taking a " piping." Insert these pipings firmly, 2 inches deep and about 4 inches apart each way, in sandy soil, preferably in a frame, but failing this in a shady border outdoors, and keep well watered. If in a frame shade from direct sunlight. They should be well rooted and ready for planting out by the end of September.

Cut back Aubrietias, etc.

Aubrietias, arabis, and perennial candytufts may be cut back quite considerably as soon as they have finished flowering if you wish to prevent the plants from spreading very far. In any case, it is a good plan to remove the faded flowers before seed pods form. The work can be done very quickly with a large pair of scissors, or, in the case of large clumps, with garden shears.

Pot Cyclamen into Flowering Pots

About this time cyclamen seedlings that were potted individually in April (see April, First Week) will be ready for their final potting into 5-inch pots. Use a similar compost to that mentioned before, but add a little well-rotted manure to it if possible. As before, be careful not to bury the corm. After potting, arrange the plants in an unheated frame and shade from sunshine for a few days. After this the plants may have more light, but should always be shaded from very hot sunshine and must be ventilated freely, indeed the lights may be removed altogether most of the time and only replaced when the weather is stormy or cold.

Sow Cinerarias and Primulas for Succession

To provide a succession of flowers after those from the May sowing (see May, First Week) you should now make a second sowing of cinerarias. The seeds are treated in exactly the same way as before, except that now no artificial heat will be needed to effect germination. You can even place the seed pans in a frame if you are short of space in the greenhouse.

It is also an excellent plan to make a second sowing of P. sinensis and its variety stellata to flower after the earliest plants (see April, Fourth Week). P. malacoides may be sown now for

167

the first time. It grows more rapidly than the others, and there is nothing to be gained by sowing earlier.

Sow Greenhouse Calceolarias

Sow the large hybrid greenhouse calceolarias now. Seed should be sown in well-drained seed boxes and given the lightest possible covering of fine sand, for it is very small. Cover the boxes with brown paper and place the seeds in a frame to germinate. This is better than a greenhouse as it can be ventilated more

SOWING SEEDS OF GREENHOUSE PLANTS.

The surface of the compost in the seed pot or pan must be pressed firm and level. The bottom of another pot can be used for this, as shown on the left. The seeds must then be scattered very thinly, and this can be done more easily if they are placed in a paper trough and tapped from it with finger or pencil.

freely. There is nothing more likely to harm greenhouse calceolarias than excessive heat.

Sow Coleworts

Coleworts are really small cabbages, and they are very useful as a catch crop. Sow a little seed broadcast now and you will be cutting useful heads all through the autumn and winter.

Sow French Beans

Make one more sowing of French beans in a sheltered place outdoors in exactly the same way as advised in the notes for

May, First Week. This will provide you with plants that will crop in September and continue until the first sharp frosts.

STOP CUTTING ASPARAGUS

It is most unwise to cut asparagus after the third week in June. Allow the plants to make foliage now so that new crowns may be formed for next year. Give the bed a small dressing of any good compound fertiliser. If you prefer to make your own mixtures, use three parts superphosphate of lime, two parts sulphate of ammonia and one part sulphate of potash at the rate of 2 ounces per square yard.

FOURTH WEEK

SOW BROMPTON STOCKS AND FORGET-ME-NOTS

This is a good time to sow Brompton stocks to stand the winter and flower outdoors next May and June. It is possible to germinate the seeds in the open, but I find it better to sow in boxes and place these in a frame. Here the seeds can be shaded from strong sunshine and protected from rain storms until they germinate. Cover the seeds very lightly with sandy soil and water moderately. Forget-me-nots may be sown at the same time, but these germinate freely enough in a shady place in the open. Sow in drills ½ inch deep and 6 inches apart.

DIVIDE MOSSY SAXIFRAGES

Old clumps of mossy saxifrage may be divided, and this is good policy if they are tending to get brown in the centre. Discard the brown pieces altogether, and replant the green clumps in a semi-shady place in soil that contains plenty of leaf-mould or moss peat. Water freely for a few weeks.

LIFT AND DIVIDE GERMAN IRISES

This is the ideal time for lifting and dividing all the May and June flowering flag irises, as most of the plants will be commencing to make new roots. Of course, it is not wise to lift and divide the clumps every year, but after four or five years they tend to get overcrowded and to exhaust the soil. Then you should dig them up carefully with a fork, cut off the old central portions of bare rhizome, discarding them altogether, and replant the healthy outer growths with 3 or 4 inches of rhizome attached to each. Plant in well-prepared soil which has been dusted with superphosphate of lime at the rate of 2 ounces per square yard. If you use animal manure, work it in rather

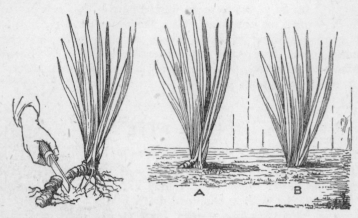

DIVIDING AND REPLANTING A GERMAN IRIS.

Old woody ends of rhizome unprovided with roots are best cut off cleanly with a sharp knife. The rhizomes should be kept well up near the surface (A) when replanting and must never be buried deeply (B).

deeply, so that it does not come in contact with the rhizomes. These, by the way, should only just be covered with soil.

COMMENCE TO BUD ROSES

It is usually possible to commence budding rose stocks at about this time, though much depends on the weather. If June is very dry, one may have to wait until well on into July, whereas if the weather is wet it is sometimes possible to start budding even earlier than this. The test is to make an incision in the stock and then attempt to lift the bark away from the wood. If it comes easily and cleanly budding can proceed at once, but if it drags away unwillingly it is better to wait awhile. The buds chosen should be from firm young shoots. A good test is to break off the thorns. If they come off easily, but leave moist-looking green scars, the wood is just right; if the scars are dry the wood is too ripe; but if the thorns refuse to break off easily, tearing instead, it is immature. Usually the tip of each shoot will have to be discarded as too young. There is no objection to using flowering stems.

POT CINERARIAS

The first batch of cinerarias, sown early in May, will do better singly in pots now. Use the compost described on page 62 and return the plants to a frame after potting. Ventilate very freely.

EXAMINE GRAFTED FRUIT TREES

It is a good plan to examine any fruit trees that you grafted in March or April to make quite sure that all is in order. If the stock appears to have swollen a good deal, remove the grafting wax and make quite sure that the raffia tie is not strangling the scion.

SPRAY RASPBERRIES WITH DERRIS

This is about the period to spray or dust raspberries with derris insecticide to kill the maggots that

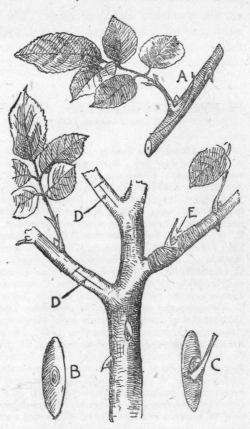

BUDDING A STANDARD ROSE.

A, *A suitable bud indicating the method of removal with a shield-shaped portion of bark.* B, *Inside view of the bud after the thin strip of wood contained within the shield-shaped portion of bark has been removed.* C, *Front view of the bud ready for insertion. Note that the leaf has been cut off, but the leaf stalk is retained to form a handle by which the bud can be held while it is being slipped into position beneath the bark of the stock.* D, *T-shaped incisions made in young growths from the stock.* E, *The bark is lifted with a scalpel and the bud is inserted and bound in place. Bush roses are budded just below ground level.*

171

coccinea and *vars.*, P. *Gibbsii*, P. *Rogersiana*, Phyllodoce *cœrulea*, Raphiolepis *japonica*, Rhododendron *azaleoides*, R. *catawbiense*, R. *discolor and hybrids*, R. *ferrugineum*, R. *Fortunei hybrids*, R. *Griersonianum* (*shelter*), R. *hirsutum*, R. *lapponicum*, R. *lepidotum*, R. *ponticum hybrids*, Salvia *Grahamii* (*shelter*), Sophora *tetraptera,* Stransvæsia *Davidiana*, S. *glaucescens*, Telopea *truncata*, Tricuspidaria *lanceolata* (*shelter*), Veronica *anomala*, V. *Balfouriana*, V. *buxifolia*, V. *cupressoides*, V. *Hectori*, V. *Hulkeana*, Viburnum *rhytidophyllum*, Vinca *major*, V. *minor,* Yucca *Whipplei*.

HARDY DECIDUOUS SHRUBS.—Abelia *triflora* (*shelter*), Abutilon *vitifolium*, Adenocarpus *decorticans*, Æsculus *Pavia,* Anthyllis *Hermanniæ*, Buddleia *alternifolia*, B. *Colvillei* (*shelter*), B. *globosa*, B. *paniculata*, Calycanthus *floridus*, C. *occidentalis* (*Allspice*), Carmichælia *grandiflora*, Ceratostigma *Willmottianum*, Chionanthus *retusa*, C. *virginica*, Colutea *arborescens*, Cornus *capitata* (*shelter*), C. *Kousa*, Cytisus *scoparius and vars.*, C. *sessilifolius*, Deutzia *corymbosa*, D. *crenata*, D. *discolor*, D. *longifolia*, D. *purpurascens*, D. *scabra and vars.*, D. *taiwanensis*, D. *Vilmorinæ*, D. *Wilsonii*, Diervilla *floribunda and vars.*, D. *florida and vars.* (*weigelia*), D. *grandiflora*, Diostea *juncea*, Dipelta *floribunda*, Discaria *serratifolia*, Fremontia *californica*, Gaylussacia *frondosa*, Genista *cinerea*, G. *dalmatica*, G. *germanica*, G. *hispanica*, G. *radiata*, G. *virgata*, Halimodendron *argenteum*, Hedysarum *multijugum*, Hydrangea *Bretschneideri*, H. *hortensis*, Indigofera *Potanini*, Jamesia *americana*, Kolkwitzia *amabilis*, Lonicera *chrysantha*, L. *Ferdinandi*, L. *hispida*, L. *Maackii*, L. *syringatha*, Magnolia *glauca*, M. *obovata*, M. *parviflora*, M. *sinensis*, M. *Wilsonii*, Meliosma *myriantha*, Menziesia *pilosa*, Neillea *bracteata*, N. *longiracemosa*, N. *opulifolia*, Notospartium *Carmichæliæ*, Paulownia *Fargesii*, Pettaria *ramentacea,* Philadelphus *coronarius*, P. *Delavayi*, P. *grandiflorus*, P. *inodorus*, P. *insignis*, P. *Lemoinei hybrids*, P. *microphyllus*, P. *purpurascens*, Plagianthus *Lyalli*, Potentilla *fruticosa*, Pterostyrax *hispidum*, Rhodotypos *kerrioides*, Robinia *hispida*, R. *Kelseyi*, Rosa *alba*, R. *alpina*, R. *bracteata*, R. *carolina*, R. *filipes*, R. *Helenæ*, R. *hugonis*, R. *macrantha*, R. *moschata*, R. *Moyesii*, R. *multibracteata*, R. *nitida*, R. *nutkana*, R. *omeiensis*, R. *rubiginosa* (*sweet briar*), R. *rugosa*, R. *sericea*, R. *Willmottiæ*, R. *xanthina*, hybrid roses (*tea, hybrid tea, hybrid perpetual, pernetiana, polyantha*), Rubus *deliciosus*, Sophora *viciifolia*, Spiræa *bracteata*, S. *canescens*, S. *discolor*, S. *Menziesii*, S. *Sargentiana*, S. *trichocarpa*, S. *Van Houttei*, S. *Veitchii*, Styrax *Wilsonii*, Syringa *chinensis*, S. *Emodi*, S. *japonica*, S. *villosa*, S. *vulgaris and vars.* (*lilac*), Vaccinium *stamineum*, Viburnum *cassinoides*, V. *dilatatum*, V. *pubescens*, V. *tomentosum and vars.*, Zenobia *speciosa*.

HARDY EVERGREEN TREES.—Prunus *lusitanica* (*Portugal laurel*).

HARDY DECIDUOUS TREES.—Æsculus *californica*, Æ. *carnea*, Æ. *indica*, Æ. *octandra*, Castanea *sativa* (*sweet chestnut*), Cratægo-mespilus *grandiflora*, Fraxinus *Mariesi*, F. *Ornus* (*flowering ash*), Laburnum *alpinum*, L. *vulgare*, L. *Vossii*, Magnolia *Fraseri*, M. *tripetala*, M. *Watsoni*, Paulownia *Fargesi*, Pyrus *Aria* (*Whitebeam*), P. *Aucuparia* (*mountain ash*), P. *coronaria*, P. *Hartwegi*, P. *hupehensis*, P. *ioensis*, Robinia *pseudacacia* (*false acacia*), Styrax *japonica*, S. *obassia*, Viburnum *Lantana* (*wayfaring tree*), V. *Lentago*.

HARDY CLIMBING PLANTS.—Aristolochia *californica*, A. *heterophylla*, A.

1. Cutting back the flowering stems of a broom after the flowers have faded.
2. Similar treatment applied to a mock orange (philadelphus). The long,
non-flowering stem in the centre will not be pruned. 3. Staking a border
carnation. The head of the flower stem is allowed to hang a little.
4. Removing the side buds from a border carnation. 5. Applying fertiliser
to a plant in the herbaceous border.

1. Removing a rose growth bud for budding. 2. The slip of wood removed with the rose bud is pulled out of the strip of bark.   3. The **T**-shaped incision made low down on a bush rose stock is opened ready to receive the bud.   4. The rose bud is bound in position with raffia.   5. The correct way to hold the shears when trimming the top of a hedge.   6. The opposite face of the shears is presented to the hedge when trimming the side.

moupinensis, A. *Sipho*, A. *tomentosa*, Bignonia *capreolata* (*shelter*), Berchemia *Giraldiana*, Clematis *azuræ hybrids*, C. *Durandii*, C. *florida and vars.*, C. *lanuginosa and vars.*, C. *montana rubens*, C. *patens vars.*, C. *Pitcheri*, Hydrangea *petiolaris*, Jasminum *officinale* (*jessamine*), J. *stephanense*, Lonicera *Brownii*, L. *caprifolium*, L. *Giraldii*, L. *glaucescens*, L. *Heckrotti*, L. *Henryi*, L. *japonica and vars.*, L. *Ledebourii*, L. *periclymenum belgica* (*early Dutch honeysuckle*), L. *plantierensis*, L. *Tellmanniana*, L. *tragophylla*, Passiflora *cœrulea* (*passion flower*), Periploca *sepium*, Rosa *arvensis* (*Ayrshire rose*), R. *Banksiæ* (*Banksian rose*), R. *cerasocarpa*, R. *lævigata*, hybrid roses (*climbing hybrid tea and tea, also Carmine Pillar*), Solanum *crispum*, S. *jasminoides*, Trachelospermum *divaricatum*, Wistaria *chinensis*, W. *formosa*, W. *frutescens*, W. *venusta*.

GREENHOUSE PLANTS.—Achimenes, Adenandra *fragrans*, A. *amœna*, Agapanthus *umbellatus*, annuals, hardy and half-hardy (*see February, Third Week, and March, First Week*), balsam, beaufortias, begonias (*tuberous-rooted*), boronias, bougainvilleas, callistemons, cannas, carnations (*perpetual-flowering and border*), celosias, Cestrum *elegans*, celsias, Clianthus *Dampieri*, C. *puniceus*, correas, Cuphea *ignea*, daturas, Epacris *longiflora*, Erica *Cavendishiana*, E. *Spenceriana*, E. *ventricosa*, eriostemons, Erythrina *Crista galli*, Francoa *ramosa* (*bridal wreath*), fuchsias, gloxinias, heliotrope, Hibbertia *dentata*, hippeastrums, hydrangeas, lantanas, Lapageria *rosea*, Lasiandra *macrantha*, lilies in var., Mandevilla *suaveolens*, marguerites, Mitraria *coccinea*, Oxalis *tetraphylla*, passifloras, pelargoniums (*regal, show, zonal, and ivy-leaved*), Plumbago *capensis*, Rehmannia *angulata*, streptocarpus (*old plants*), Streptosolon *Jamesonii*, tropæolums (*including double vars.*).

VEGETABLES IN STORE.—Onions, potatoes.

VEGETABLES IN THE GARDEN.—Asparagus, broad beans, broccoli (*late*), shorthorn carrots, cauliflowers (*sown September*), lettuces, mustard and cress, spring onions, onions (*sown August*), peas (*early vars.*), potatoes (*early vars.*), radishes, rhubarb, spinach, turnips (*sown March*).

VEGETABLES UNDER GLASS.—French beans, cucumbers, mushrooms (*cool cellars and sheds*), tomatoes.

FRUITS IN STORE.—Apples: *Allen's Everlasting* (D), *Annie Elizabeth* (C), *Encore* (C), *Sandling* (D), *Stark* (D), *Sturmer Pippin* (D), *Wagener* (C).

FRUITS OUTDOORS.—Cherries: *Early Rivers'* (D), *Guigne D'Annonay* (D), *May Duke* (D), *Olivet* (C), *Schrecken Bigarreau* (D), *Waterloo* (D). Gooseberries (*green*). Raspberries: *Red Cross, Lloyd George*. Strawberries: *Black Prince, George V., Royal Sovereign, Sir Joseph Paxton, The Duke, Western Queen*.

FRUITS UNDER GLASS.—Grapes, peaches, and nectarines (*early varieties started in January and forced steadily; see list, July, Fruits under Glass*).

JULY

GENERAL WORK

CUT OFF FADED FLOWERS, ETC.

FROM time to time during the month you should examine all the flowering plants in the garden and remove any blooms or flower spikes that are so faded as to be no longer decorative. This applies to roses, to early-flowering herbaceous plants, such as lupins, pyrethrums, delphiniums, oriental poppies, anchusas, campanulas, etc., and also to bedding plants and annuals, such as violas, pansies, antirrhinums, calendulas, and eschscholtzias. The object is to prevent seed formation, which weakens the plant unnecessarily. Exception to this rule may be made if one happens to want some seeds of any special thing, but then the best plan is to reserve one particular plant of this variety for seed bearing.

Continue to remove runners from violets (see June, General Work).

THIN AND DISBUD DAHLIAS, ETC.

If you want some extra fine dahlias for exhibition, you must thin out the plants and only allow them to bear a restricted number of flowers. A good strong plant of one of the large-flowered varieties may carry three stems, but no more. Remove others, keeping only the sturdiest. Then, when the flower buds appear, remove all except the central terminal one on each stem. Plants that are only grown for garden decoration do not need this drastic restriction and may be allowed to grow naturally. All will benefit from liberal soakings of weak liquid manure every few days.

It will also be necessary to continue the disbudding of roses as described in the notes for June, General Work.

CONTINUE TO TRIM HEDGES, ETC.

You can continue to trim evergreen hedges and topiary specimens as necessary to keep them neat and tidy.

Take Cuttings of Shrubs, Alpines, etc.

A great many hardy shrubs, and also shrubby alpines, such as helianthemums, pentstemons, etc., can be increased during July and August by cuttings prepared from firm young sideshoots and the ends of non-flowering stems. Select pieces from 1 inch to 4 inches in length, according to the nature of the plant. Prepare them by cutting the base of each cleanly through just below a joint and removing the lower leaves. Then insert them firmly in a suitable compost, burying them just sufficiently deep to keep them erect. If you can attend to the cuttings at any time during the day, use pure silver sand as the rooting medium; but if you are away from home most of the day, use a mixture of sharp sand, moss peat, and good loam in equal parts. The compost may either be placed in a frame or else prepared in the open and covered with a bell glass. If you can watch the cuttings frequently, no shading will be necessary;

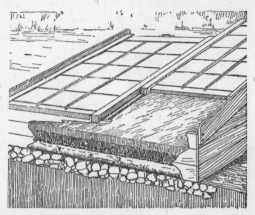

A Frame for Cuttings.

This sectional view of a frame shows a drainage layer of stones covered by sifted cinders, then turfy loam, with a bed of fine sandy soil on top for the cuttings.

but if they have to be left for hours on end, it is advisable to shade from strong direct sunlight. Cuttings unshaded and in pure sand may need watering every hour or so on a hot day, but those that are shaded and in compost are not likely to need water more than once in 2 days. Keep the frame or bell glass quite tight until the cuttings begin to grow, but then commence to admit a little air, increasing the amount daily.

Continue to Bud Rose Stocks

You can continue to bud rose stocks throughout the month so long as the bark parts readily from the wood of the stock (see

179

June, Fourth Week). Sometimes, if the weather gets very hot and dry, the stocks refuse to work properly and then the work should be discontinued for the time being.

CONTINUE TO SPRAY AGAINST FOES

Caterpillars, red spider, and thrips are still sources of danger in all departments of the garden, and there may still be some green-fly about, though this pest is not usually quite so abundant just after mid-summer. Take prompt measures to destroy these pests as soon as they put in an appearance (see June, General Work). Fungal diseases, such as mildew, rust, and black spot, are likely to be on the increase as the weather gets warmer. Occasional spraying with Bordeaux mixture or some other good fungicide is the only certain method of keeping them down. It is wise to spray roses every fortnight or so as a pre-cautionary measure, for it is much easier to pre-vent diseases than it is to cure them (see also note on potatoes, First Week).

ROSE BLACK SPOT DISEASE.

This is a very troublesome disease, but it can be checked by regular summer spraying with Bordeaux or Burgundy mixture.

CONTINUE TO FEED PLANTS IN GROWTH

You should continue to feed all plants that are making rapid growth as I advised in my notes for May and June (see May, General Work, and June, General Work). In the case of winter green crops planted during May and June, nitrate of soda may well be used in place of a compound fertiliser. Give two applications, each of $\frac{1}{2}$ ounce per square yard, at an interval of about 3 weeks.

180

Remove Grass Box from Lawn Mower

During this month and August, when the weather is likely to be hot, it is an excellent plan to remove the grass box from the lawn mower and let the tiny clippings fall on to the lawn. They will act as a mulch and will protect the roots from scorching.

General Greenhouse Management

There is really little to add to my remarks in the June notes on this subject. Fire heat for all ordinary greenhouse plants will now be quite unnecessary. Indeed, the problem in most cases will be to keep the house sufficiently cool by day. This is particularly the case in very small houses, which must, in consequence, be ventilated freely and shaded carefully. Shading for a few hours per day may even be necessary for such a sun-loving crop as tomatoes. Occasional damping down of paths and walls will also help matters, but the syringe must be used cautiously on plants themselves when the sun is shining brightly on them.

Pot on Zonal Pelargoniums, etc.

Spring-struck cuttings of zonal pelargoniums required for autumn flowering in the greenhouse are almost sure to need potting on into 6-inch pots during July. Similar remarks apply to other greenhouse plants raised from spring cuttings (see March, General Work), except that in some cases even bigger pots may be required. In this connection I refer you to my general remarks on potting in the notes for April, General Work, and would remind you that it is rarely wise to shift plants into pots more than two sizes larger than those in which they are already growing. Use the same compost as before but coarser in texture, and press it more firmly around the roots.

Continue to Thin Seedlings

Various vegetables sown last month for succession must be thinned out before they become overcrowded (see May, General Work).

Cut Globe Artichokes

From now onwards you can cut the heads of globe artichokes as they become available. On no account leave any on the plants so long that they commence to flower. The ideal time to cut them is when they are nice and plump, but before the scales begin to open out too much.

Continue to Plant Winter Greens

Continue to plant out all manner of winter green crops as you clear ground of early crops, such as dwarf peas, early potatoes, and the first sowings of turnips and salad vegetables. So far as possible, choose showery weather for this work, but do not delay long on this account. If July is persistently dry, push on with the planting and then water freely for a few days.

Plant March-sown Leeks

Leeks from the March sowing (see March, Third Week) may also be planted, as opportunity occurs, on similar ground to the winter greens. Plant with a large dibber in holes 9 inches deep, dropping the leeks right down into these, but not refilling the holes with soil. Simply water in thoroughly. This deep planting will blanch the stems without need for earthing up. The leeks should be 1 foot apart in rows 18 inches apart.

Continue to Blanch Leeks

The process of blanching leeks grown in trenches must be continued gradually, as explained in my notes for June, General Work.

Plant Celery for Succession

During the month you can make further plantings of celery as plants from late sowings become available. It is not wise to shift the plants to the trenches while they are very small. Wait until they are at least 3 inches in height and can be lifted with a nice ball of roots (see June, First Week).

Make Successional Sowings

These are in the main the same as for last month (see June, General Work). Sow turnips for the last time about the middle of the month. You can be rather more generous with the seed, as this crop will supply roots for storing. One more sowing each of lettuce, endive, and summer spinach should meet all requirements. It is still necessary to choose a shady place for all these crops, for heat and drought will make them run to seed prematurely. Mustard and cress and radishes can be sown as before, also in a cool position.

Feed, Train, and Fumigate Tomatoes

Outdoor tomatoes will be growing freely and forming their flower trusses. Keep each plant to a single stem and nip out all side shoots at the earliest opportunity. Water freely during dry weather and, as soon as the bottom truss is set and you can see the tiny fruits swelling, spread a 2-inch layer of well-rotted manure around the plants. From that time onwards feed every week with small doses of any good tomato fertiliser.

There is really nothing to add to my remarks on indoor tomatoes last month (see June, General Work). Cut back more foliage as you clear the lower trusses of fruit. Free ventilation, steady feeding, and ample watering are the all-important points to watch.

Feed and Train Cucumbers

Nor is there much to add to my notes on cucumbers in the same place. Plants in frames will now be tending to take the place of those in greenhouses, though even the latter may be kept going for a surprising time by frequent removal of all side growths that have ceased to bear and their replacement by young growth. Syringe and watering pot must be used constantly to keep up the necessary moisture in soil and air. Ventilate rather more freely, especially when the temperature shows signs of rising above 80 degs., but do not allow the air to get dry on this account or you are sure to have trouble with red spider and thrips. Heavier shading will help to keep the temperature down. Continue to stop and train the plants in frames and on outside ridges, and regulate growth in such a manner that the beds are never overcrowded but you are continually getting a new supply of laterals with flowers. Be very careful to cut the cucumbers directly they are fit to use. If a few hang and ripen, the plants will soon stop bearing.

TOMATO DEFOLIATION.

As the lower trusses ripen a few of the leaves can be shortened, as indicated, to let in more sunlight.

183

MANAGEMENT OF THE ORCHARD HOUSE

Peaches, nectarines, and apricots under glass must be treated according to their state of growth (see General Work, May and June). As trees are cleared of ripened fruits daily (or even twice daily) syringing should be recommenced, for there is no better way of keeping down that commonest of orchard house foes, the red spider. Ventilate freely by day, but do not let the temperature fall below 55 degs. at night. Even July nights can be chilly occasionally.

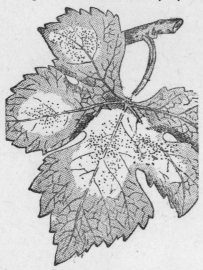

VINE MILDEW.

In outward appearance this disease is very similar to the mildew that attacks roses. It is encouraged by dry soil, a wet atmosphere, and overcrowded foliage.

PROTECT VINES FROM MILDEW

Thinning of the fruits will now become general with outdoor vines, and as the process is exactly the same as with indoor varieties I refer you to my earlier notes on that subject (see March, General Work). A thick mulch of well-rotted manure spread over the border will help the vines a lot at this season. Indoor vines in various stages of growth will also require treatment as before (see General Work for April, May, and June).

Mildew may become troublesome from now onwards, covering leaves and grapes with a white, mealy growth. If there is the slightest sign of this disease, give increased ventilation and dust foliage and fruits with flowers of sulphur. Make certain that the border is not short of water, for dry soil and damp, unventilated atmosphere are sure causes of mildew.

Shanking sometimes occurs at this time of the year. This is a physiological disorder which causes the footstalks of the berries to die, with the result that the berries themselves suddenly collapse. It is caused by poverty of soil or a cold, wet subsoil, and remaking of the border the following autumn is the best remedy.

FIRST WEEK

LIFT TULIPS, HYACINTHS, ETC.

Tulips and hyacinths will now have completed their growth and may be lifted and cleaned. Lay the bulbs in shallow trays and stand them in a dry, cool, airy place, but not in full sun. Dead tops can be removed and the bulbs sorted out into two sizes, the biggest for flowering again next year (though do not rely on them for the most important beds) and the smaller ones to be planted in good soil in an out-of-the-way place to grow on. If your garden is only small it will be best to throw these small bulbs away, for they will scarcely be worth the space they take up. Anemones of the St. Brigid and Du Caen types, and also turban ranunculuses are treated in much the same way, the corms being lifted as soon as foliage has died down. Store in a dry, cool place until planting time. Crocuses can also be lifted now, but only if they are overcrowded or you need the ground for something else. If you do have them out, get them replanted quite soon; they gain nothing from being out of the ground.

COMPLETE STOPPING OF CARNATIONS

By this time you should complete all the second stopping of perpetual-flowering carnations (see May, General Work). If the plants are stopped later than this they will not start to flower until well on in the new year, and carnations are much in demand at Christmas and even before. Roughly speaking, five months must elapse before a stopped growth can produce any flowers.

STAND OUT REGAL AND SHOW PELARGONIUMS

Show and regal pelargoniums will have practically finished flowering by this time and will be better out of the greenhouse. Stand them in the open in any sunny, fairly sheltered place and gradually decrease the water supply, practically witholding it for the last fortnight in July. If it rains a lot, lay the pots on their sides. The object is to check and ripen growth and give the plants a rest.

SOW CARROTS

A small sowing of shorthorn or intermediate carrots made now is often amply justified, especially if the season happens to be a bad one for carrot fly. This fly does all its damage early in the summer, and seedlings from a July sowing usually escape. In any case, young carrots in the autumn are very welcome.

Spray Potatoes with Bordeaux Mixture

Do not wait until disease attacks your potatoes, but spray them now with Bordeaux mixture. The potato late blight disease is so common that some of your plants are almost sure to get infected unless you take this precaution, and in any case spraying is repaid because it lengthens the season of growth and so indirectly increases the weight of the crop. You can purchase Bordeaux mixture in powder or paste form from any dealer in horticultural sundries and it is only necessary to dissolve this in water at the strength stated on the package. When spraying, be very careful to cover the under as well as the upper sides of the leaves.

Make an Outdoor Mushroom Bed

In sheds, pits, etc., mushrooms can be grown throughout the year, but unprotected outdoors they are only satisfactory in late summer and early autumn. Now is the time to make such a bed. First you will need to get a good quantity of fresh stable manure. This you must turn and shake with a fork two or three times, at intervals of a day or so, until the first heat of fermentation has died down and the manure is decaying steadily. Then build it up into a ridge-shaped heap in the open, or a more or less flat-topped bank against a wall. Beds made against a north wall at this time of the year are usually very satisfactory. Tread the manure firmly layer by layer as you build it up into the mound. When finished, the bed should be 2½ feet deep; it can be of any width, but 3 feet is usual and convenient. Plunge a soil thermometer into the bed and, when the temperature falls to 70 degs., insert sterilised mushroom spawn in small pieces at intervals of 10 inches all over the bed. Simply make a hole about 1 inch deep in the manure, push a piece of spawn in, and cover it with manure. Then cover the whole bed with a foot-thick layer of straw. You can purchase sterilised mushroom spawn in bottles. A quart bottle contains enough spawn to plant a bed from 30 to 40 square feet in area. After 2 or 3 weeks scrape away a little of the manure and see how things are getting on. If there are white filament-like growths penetrating the bed freely, the spawn is "running" and the bed is ready for casing.

This is done by covering the manure evenly with a 1-inch thick layer of loam, beaten smooth with the back of a spade. Then replace the clean dry straw to keep the bed at an even temperature. If the weather is dry, the bed must be watered occasionally with tepid water, but too much moisture is not desirable.

COMMENCE TO SUMMER-PRUNE CHERRIES AND PLUMS

You can now commence to summer-prune cherries and plums growing on walls. It is not worth while trying to apply this method of pruning to large bushes and standards, for these are better allowed to grow rather freely. With the one exception of the Morello cherry, the method is the same for all varieties. Side shoots which have been growing during May and June should be shortened by about one-third each, but leaders terminating main branches are left unpruned. Do not do all the work on any one tree at once,

SUMMER-PRUNING A SWEET CHERRY.

A typical fruiting lateral showing the way in which ends of laterals are removed (see black lines) to encourage production of further fruit buds.

but spread it over a period of about six weeks. In this way the trees will not suffer any check to growth. Morello cherries bear their best fruits on young wood, and so are disbudded just like peaches and nectarines. Side shoots growing on the fruiting

187

laterals are gradually rubbed off or pinched back a few at a time with the exception of two per lateral, one near its base and one at its tip. The former will replace it after the winter pruning, while the latters serves to maintain a good flow of sap to swell and ripen the fruits.

COMPLETE THINNING OF APPLES AND PEARS

It is now the time to complete the thinning of apples and pears (see June, Second Week). Reduce the fruits to one, or at most two, per spur.

BURN STRAW ON STRAWBERRY BEDS

If you have had any mildew or other disease on your strawberries or the plants have been badly attacked by greenfly, set fire to the straw on the beds as soon as you have gathered all the fruits. This will burn up all the foliage and leave the bed looking very bare and sad for a week or so, but the crowns themselves will not be damaged and will soon produce healthy new growth. Of course, you must not do this to any plants around which you intend to peg down runners (see below).

PEG DOWN STRAWBERRY RUNNERS

Strawberry plants tend to deteriorate after a few years, and so it is advisable to raise a few new plants every year to take the place of old, worn-out ones. To do this it is only necessary to peg down, at this time of the year, some of the plantlets that form on the runners. Each runner will form a number of plantlets if allowed to do so, but for propagation that nearest the parent plant is the best, and the tip of the runner may be pinched out beyond this. It is not usually wise to peg down more than three or four plantlets around each old plant. There are two methods of doing the work : one is simply to press the plantlet down on to the soil in the strawberry bed and hold it

PROPAGATING STRAWBERRIES.

Runners from the parent plant have been pegged down into pots sunk to their rims in the strawberry bed.

in position with a wooden or wire peg; and the other is to fill a 3-inch flower pot with a mixture of loam, leaf-mould, and sand, plunge this into the strawberry bed at any convenient point, and peg the plantlet into it. The second method is the better of the two because, when the rooted runners are severed from their parent plant later on and are removed to a new bed, there need be no serious root disturbance. The pot, complete with roots, is simply lifted from the strawberry bed and the ball of soil tapped out intact. But rooting in pots does mean a little more watering. If you can get all the runners you require now, so much the better, for early rooting gives the best results, but if there are not enough runners at the moment you can continue to peg down throughout the month.

Cut off any runners you do not need, because they only weaken the plant. Continue to do this throughout the summer.

SECOND WEEK

Prick out Perennials and Biennials

Perennials and biennials sown in June (see June, First Week) will be in need of pricking out into a nursery bed. This should be in an open position except for violas, pansies, primroses, and polyanthuses, which grow more quickly in partial shade. The ground must be well forked and reasonably rich, but not recently manured with dung. If it needs feeding, give a very light dressing of hop manure and fork this in. Get the seedlings up as carefully as possible (if the ground is dry it is a good plan to give it a thorough watering the day before you intend to move the seedlings) and replant them with a trowel. Plant in rows about 9 inches apart. The bigger growing plants, such as hollyhocks, delphiniums, and lupins, should be 9 inches apart in the rows, but 6 inches will be sufficient for wallflowers, double daisies, Cheiranthus Allioni, primroses, etc., while violas and pansies may be as close as 4 inches. Pinch out the tips of wallflowers and cheiranthuses to make them branch freely.

It is possible that Brompton stocks and forget-me-nots from the late June sowing may also be far enough advanced to prick out in the same manner. If not, do the work at the first favourable opportunity.

soil level and make an incision with a sharp knife through a joint near the base of each, as shown in the illustration. Then the slit portion of stem is covered with fine sandy soil and is held firmly in position with a wooden or wire peg. If the layers are kept well watered, roots will soon be formed from the sides of the cut. In late August or early September the rooted layers can be severed completely from the parent plant and be planted elsewhere or potted up.

SUMMER-PRUNE WISTARIAS

Wistarias that have filled their allotted space can be induced to flower freely year after year without making a lot of new growth by summer and winter pruning. Now is the time for the first of these operations. Shorten to about six leaves each all side growths formed on the main branches.

SUMMER-PRUNE ROSES

Bush and standard roses of the Hybrid Tea and Pernettiana types will pay for a light summer pruning now that the first flush of flowers is over. Cut back to about two leaves all stems that have flowered, but have no promising buds on them at the moment. Then give the beds a dusting of any good compound flower garden fertiliser and hoe this in.

PRICK OFF AND POT PRIMULAS, CALCEOLARIAS, AND CINERARIAS

Greenhouse primulas sown in mid-June will now need pricking off exactly like the earlier batch (see June, First Week). These first primulas will also in all probability require a shift. Do not let them get crowded in their boxes or pans, but move them on singly into 3-inch pots, using the compost described on page 24. Return to the frame after potting and give a little shade from strong, direct sunshine.

Calceolarias and cinerarias sown in June (see June, Third Week) are almost certain to be forward enough for pricking off in exactly the same manner as the primulas, except that the cinerarias should be spaced a good 2 inches apart each way.

SOW SPRING CABBAGE

This is the time to make a first sowing of cabbages for use in the spring and early summer. Do not sow all the seed now, however, but keep some for a further sowing during the second

1. Removing faded flowers from an eschscholtzia to prevent seed formation.
2. Disbudding a large flowered decorative dahlia. Only the central flower bud on each stem is retained. 3. Disbudding applied to a chrysanthemum. In this case it is surrounding shoots and not flower buds that are removed. 4. Summer pruning a red currant. 5. Pegging down a plantlet on a strawberry runner.

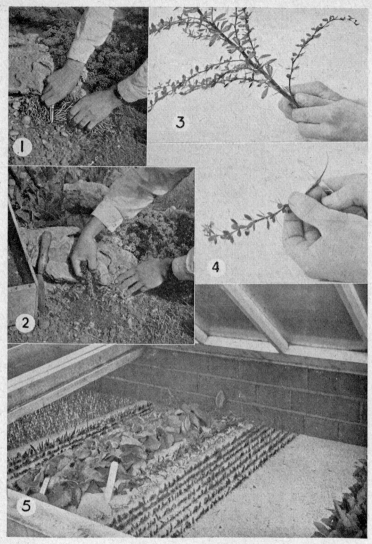

1. Cutting back a rock garden viola to encourage the formation of young shoots for cuttings. 2. The viola is top dressed with fine soil, leaf mould and sand with the same object. 3. Removing a shrub cutting with a " heel." 4. The slip of bark attached to the " heel" is removed. 5. A frame filled with summer shrub cuttings.

week in August, as sometimes the later seedlings do best in the long run. Choose a suitable variety, such as Ellam's Early Dwarf, Flower of Spring, or Harbinger. Scatter the seed thinly in a bed of finely broken soil and cover lightly. Water freely if the weather happens to be dry.

Lift and Store Autumn-sown Onions

Autumn-sown onions should now have completed their growth and ripened their bulbs, so you may just as well lift them and

A Pear Branch Ready for Summer-pruning.
The terminal shoot (leader) on the left will not be pruned during the summer, but the side shoots (laterals) must all be shortened by about one-third.

have the ground free for some other crop as, for example, winter greens. Lift the onions carefully with a fork and lay them out in a sunny place for a few days to dry off. Then shake the soil from them and store in shallow boxes in a cool dry place.

Commence to Summer-prune Apples and Pears

You can now start to shorten the laterals of apples and pears exactly as I described for cherries and plums earlier in the month (see First Week). The method is worth applying to all trained specimens, and also to small bushes, pyramids, and half standards, but involves too much labour in the case of full standards or very big bushes.

N

Start to Pick Apples and Pears

The earliest apples, such as Mr. Gladstone and Early Victoria, and also the pear Early Market, should be ripe by now, and you can commence to pick, but only as you actually require the fruits for use. These early varieties do not keep at all well off the tree, and no attempt must be made to store them. The test for ripeness in the case of apples is to lift a typical fruit without actually wrenching or twisting it off its branch. If it comes away easily with its stalk it is ready for picking, but if it parts unwillingly, tearing off part of the spur or breaking in the middle of its stalk, it is not yet ripe. With pears the best test is to press one or two of the fruits very gently near the stalk; if yielding they are ready.

A Ladder for Fruit Picking.

This special ladder, narrowing at the top, can be inserted between branches with much less risk of causing damage than the normal type.

FOURTH WEEK

Plant Madonna Lilies

This is the ideal time to plant Lilium candidum, the Madonna lily. It differs from almost all other lilies in making quite a lot of new growth in late summer, and it should be planted before this commences. Another peculiarity is that the bulbs grow practically on the surface. You should only cover them with 2 inches of soil.

194

After a while they will probably work themselves out until they show; make no attempt to cover them again. The bulbs should be 8 inches apart. This lily prefers a sunny position and reasonably good, but not freshly manured, ground.

PLANT COLCHICUMS, AUTUMN CROCUSES, ETC.

You should also plant colchicums, autumn-flowering crocuses, and sternbergias if you can obtain supplies. General bulb merchants rarely have them so early, but specialists will be able to supply. Plant the crocuses 3 inches deep and 3 inches apart; the colchicums and sternbergias 6 inches deep and 4 inches apart. All should be in well-drained soil and a rather sheltered but sunny position.

LIFT DAFFODILS AND BULBOUS IRISES

Daffodils and narcissi, also the various bulbous irises, will now have completed their growth and may be lifted and cleaned off if they are overgrown or you need the ground for something else. Otherwise leave them undisturbed for another year. They do not gain anything by annual lifting and drying, as do tulips and hyacinths. If you do lift them, get them replanted as soon as possible and certainly before the end of September.

CUT BACK HELIANTHEMUMS

Sun roses tend to get rather straggly if left to their own devices, but if cut back a little each year at about this time they can be kept quite neat and tidy. You can do the work with a large pair of scissors or even the garden shears.

COMMENCE TO FEED CHRYSANTHEMUMS

It is a mistake to commence to feed chrysanthemums of any type too early, but you can start now with safety. The more varied the " feed " the better. Give very small doses every five days or so mixed with plenty of water and used in place of the ordinary water. Liquid manure, made by steeping a small sack of cow, horse, or sheep droppings in a tub of water, can be varied with soot water and any good chemical fertiliser made especially for chrysanthemums and used strictly in accordance with manufacturers' instructions.

"Take" Early-flowering Chrysanthemum Buds

This term requires some explanation. It is virtually the chrysanthemum grower's equivalent to disbudding, for it means that the flower buds required for producing big blooms are retained, while all smaller buds or shoots surrounding or below them are rubbed out. It is only necessary to do this if you want big flowers borne singly on long stems. If your object is to have sprays of comparatively small flowers, let the plants grow on naturally. In any case you will not be able to complete all the disbudding at once, but look over the plants now, for some at least should be showing flower buds.

Sow Parsley for Autumn and Winter Use

Make a final sowing of parsley for autumn and winter use. If you sow the seeds in a very sheltered place, you can leave some of the plants undisturbed and keep on cutting from them as long as possible, but a portion of the seedlings will have to be transplanted into a frame in September if you wish to have a Christmas supply.

Sow Hardy Green Colewort

If you wish to have a really full supply of green vegetables right through the autumn months, make a small sowing of hardy green colewort now to supplement the supply of rosette colewort made last month (see June, Third Week). Details of sowing are exactly as before. This variety will be available after the rosette colewort is over.

Commence to Bud Fruit Stocks

Stocks of various fruit trees, such as apples, pears, plums, and cherries, can usually be budded at about this time. You can apply the same tests to the stocks as those suggested for rose stocks (see June, Fourth Week). Of course, there are no thorns by which you can test the shoots selected as scions, and as it is most important that they should be in just the right condition, you must examine them carefully. You should be able to peel the bark easily from the wood. If it tears, growth is either too young or too dry. The buds should be well developed and clearly visible. The actual details for budding are just the same as for roses,

196

except that instead of inserting them as low down on the dwarf stocks as possible, they should be put in about 8 inches above soil level. It is desirable that the union of rose stock and scion should be covered with soil, but this is not advisable in the case

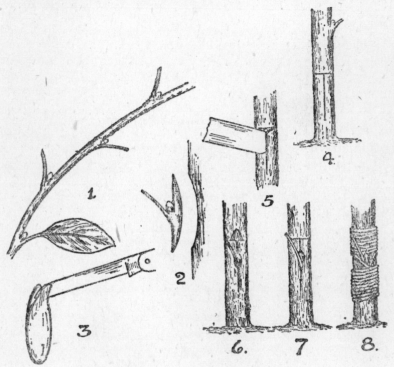

BUDDING A FRUIT TREE.

1, *A suitable young but firm growth from which to take buds.* 2, *A bud as cut from the stem.* 3, *Removing the strip of wood contained within the bark carrying the bud.* 4, *A T-shaped incision made in the bark of the stock.* 5, *The bark is raised carefully.* 6, *The shield-shaped piece of bark carrying the bud is slipped into position.* 7, *The top of the shield-shaped piece of bark is trimmed level with the top of the T-shaped incision.* 8, *The bud is bound firmly in position with soft twist.*

of fruit trees, for the scions might then make roots of their own, which would upset the particular effect, dwarfing or otherwise, of the stock chosen.

Buds can only be inserted into stocks that have thin, supple bark. Some form of grafting in spring (see March, Fourth Week) must be used in the case of old, hard-barked trees that are being reworked.

FLOWERS, VEGETABLES, AND FRUITS IN SEASON DURING JULY

HARDY HERBACEOUS PLANTS.—Acanthus *mollis*, Achillea *filipendulina*, A. *millefolium vars.*, A. *Ptarmica vars.*, A. *siberica*, Aconitum *Lycoctonum*, A. *Napellus vars.*, Adenophora *Bulleyana*, A. *latifolia*, Althæa *rosea vars.* (*hollyhock*), Alstrœmeria *aurantiaca*, A. *chilensis*, A. *hæmantha*, A. *Pelegrina*, A. *pulchella*, Anaphalis *margaritacea*, Anthemis *cupaniana*, A. *nobilis*, A. *Sancta-Johannis*, A. *tinctoria and vars.*, Anthericum *ramosum*, Armeria *latifolia and vars.*, Arnica *sachaliensis*, Artemisia *lactiflora*, Asclepias *tuberosa*, Asphodeline *lutea*, Asphodelus *ramosus*, Aster *ptarmicoides*, A. *subcœruleus vars.*, A. *Thomsonii*, Astilbe *Arendsii hybrids*, Astrantia *carniolica*, A. *major*, Baptisia *australis*, Bocconia *cordata*, B. *microcarpa*, Borago *laxiflora*, Calceolaria *John Innes*, Buphthalmum *salicifolium*, Campanula *alliaræfolia*, C. *glomerata dahurica*, C. *lactiflora*, C. *latifolia*, C. *persicifolia and vars.*, C. *pyramidalis*, C. *rapunculoides*, C. *rhomboidalis*, C. *Trachelium*, C. *Van Houttei*, Centaurea *babylonica*, C. *dealbata*, C. *macrocephala*, C. *montana*, C. *pulcherrima*, C. *ruthenica*, Centranthus *ruber*, Cephalaria *alpina*, C. *tartarica*, Chrysanthemum *leucanthemum vars.*, C. *maximum vars.*, Chicorium *Intybus vars.*, Cimicifuga *dahurica*, Clematis *integrifolia*, C. *recta*, Coreopsis *grandiflora vars.*, C. *lanceolata vars.*, Delphinium *Belladonna vars.*, D. *cardinale*, D. *formosum*, D. *sulphureum*, delphiniums in var. (*large-flowered hybrids*), Dianthus *Allwoodii*, D. *barbatus vars.* (*Sweet William*), D. *Caryophyllus vars.* (*border carnations*), D. *plumarius Cyclops*, Dicentra *eximea*, D. *spectabilis*, Dictamnus *Fraxinella*, Digitalis *ambigua*, D. *gloxinioides vars.* (*foxgloves*), D. *purpurea* (*wild foxglove*), Dracocephalum *Ruyschiana*, Echinacea *purpurea and vars.*, Echinops *banaticus*, E. *ritro*, E. *sphærocephalus*, Eremurus *Bungei and vars.*, Erigeron *aurantiacus*, E. *Mesa-grande*, E. *speciosus and vars.*, erigeron hybrids, Eryngium *alpinum*, E. *amethystinum*, E. *Bourgatii*, E. *giganteum*, E. *Oliverianum*, E. *planum*, E. *spinalba*, E. *Violetta*, Euphorbia *Myrsinites*, Filipendula *hexapetala plena*, Funkia *Fortunei*, F. *glauca*, F. *lancifolia*, F. *ovata*, gaillardia hybrids, Galega *officinalis and vars.*, Gaura *Lindheimeri*, Geranium *armenum*, G. *Endressii*, G. *eriostemon*, Geum *coccineum vars.*, G. *Heldreichii*, Gypsophila *paniculata and vars.*, Helenium *autumnale and vars.*, H. *Bigelovii and vars.*, Heliopsis *lævis*, H. *scabra*, Hemerocallis *aurantiaca*, H. *Forrestii*, H. *fulva*, H. *multiflora*, H. *Thunbergii*, hemerocallis hybrids, Heracleum *villosum*, Heuchera *brizoides*, H. *sanguinea and vars.*, Inula *glandulosa*, I. *Helenium*, I. *Oculus-Christii*, I. *Royleana*, Iris *dichotoma*, Isatis *glauca*, Kniphofia *caulescens*, K. *Macowanii*, K. *Nelsonii*, K. *rufa*, K. *Tuckii*, K. *Uvaria vars.*, Lavatera *Olbia*, Liatris *pycnostachya*, Linaria *dalmatica*, L. *purpurea*, Linum *narbonense*, L. *perenne*, Lychnis *chalcedonica*, L. *coronaria*, L. *Flos-jovis*,

L. *Haagiana*, L. *viscaria and vars.*, Lupinus *arboreus*, Lysimachia *clethroides*, L. *thyrsiflora*, Lythrum *Salicaria and vars.*, L. *virgatum vars.*, Malva *moschata*, Meconopsis *betonicifolia*, M. *cambrica and vars.*, M. *napaulensis*, M. *quintuplinerva*, M. *Regia*, Mertensia *sibirica*, Monarda *didyma and vars.*, Morina *longifolia*, Nepeta *grandiflora*, N. *Mussini*, Œnothera *biennis vars.*, Œ. *fruticosa and vars.*, Œ. *glauca*, Œ. *odorata*, Œ. *speciosa*, Papaver *nudicaule vars. (Iceland poppy)*, Pentstemon *barbatus*, P. *gentianoides hybrids (shelter in winter)*, P. *isophyllus*, Phlox *Arendsii hybrids*, P. *decussata hybrids*, P. *suffruticosa hybrids*, Phygelius *capensis*, Physostegia *virginiana and vars.*, Platycodon *grandiflorum*, Polemonium *carneum*, P. *cœruleum*, P. *humile*, P. *pauciflorum*, Polygonum *amplexicaule*, P. *bistorta vars.*, P. *campanula-*

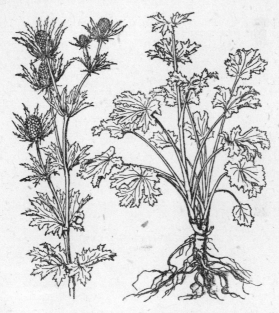

ERYNGIUM OLIVERIANUM.

tum, potentilla hybrids, Poterium *obtusum*, P. *tenuifolium*, Romneya *Coulteri*, R. *trichocalyx*, Rudbeckia *amplexicaule*, R. *californica*, R. *speciosa (Newmanii)*, R. *subtomentosa*, Salvia *argentea*, S. *Przewalskii*, S. *Sclarea and vars.*, S. *virgata*, Scabiosa *caucasica and vars.*, Sidalcea *candida*, S. *malvæflora and hybrids*, Solidago *Virgaurea præcox*, Spiræa *Aruncus*, S. *lobata*, S. *palmata*, Statica *bellidifolium*, S. *eximea*, S. *Gmelini*, S. *incana*, S. *latifolia*, Thalictrum *adiantifolium*, T. *dipterocarpum*, Tradescantia *virginica*, Trollius *Ledebourii and vars.*, Tropæolum *polyphyllum*, Verbascum *Chaixii*, V. *nigrum (vernale)*, V. *olympicum*, V. *phœniceum*, V. *thapsiforme (densiflorum)*, V. *Weidmannianum*, verbascum *hybrids*, Veronica *longifolia and vars.*, V. *spicata*, V. *subsessilis*, V. *virginica and vars.*

HARDY BULBS AND TUBERS.—Allium *azureum*, A. *Beesianum*, A. *sphæro-cephalum*, Anomatheca *cruenta*, Galtonia *candicans*, Gladiolus *Colvillei* *vars.*, Iris *xiphioides* (*English irises*), Lilium *amabile*, L. *Brownii*, L. *Burbankii*, L. *canadense*, L. *candidum* (*Madonna lily*), L. *cernuum*, L. *chalcedonicum*, L. *columbianum*, L. *concolor*, L. *croceum*, L. *Duchartrei*, L. *elegans* (*thunbergianum*), L. *giganteum*, L. *Grayi*, L. *Humboldtii*, L. *japonicum* (*Krameri*), L. *Martagon and vars.*, L. *Maxwill*, L. *monadelphum* *szovitzianum*, L. *pardalinum*, L. *parviflorum*, L. *parvum*, P. *philadelphicum*, L. *princeps and vars.*, L. *regale*, L. *superbum*, L. *sutchuenense*, L. *testaceum*, L. *Willmottiæ*, Ostrowskia *magnifica*, Tigridia *Pavonia*.

ROCK PLANTS.—Acantholimon *glumaceum*, Achillea *ageratifolia*, A. *argentea*, A. *Clavennæ*, A. *tomentosa and vars.*, Androsace *lanuginosa and vars.*, Antennaria *dioica and vars.*, Armeria *maritima and vars.*, Asperula *suberosa*, Astilbe *simplicifolia*, Calandrinia *umbellata*, Calceolaria *polyrrhiza*, Campanula *Allionii*, C. *barbata*, C. *carpatica and vars.*, C. *garganica and vars.*, C. *Portenschlagiana*, C. *Poscharskyana*, C. *pulla*, C. *pulloides*, C. *pusilla*, C. *Raddeana*, C. *Raineri*, C. *rotundifolia*, C. *sarmatica*, C. *Stans-fieldii*, C. *Tommasiniana*, C. *Wockii*, C. *Zoysii*, Chrysogonum *virginianum*, Conandron *ramondioides*, Convolvulus *althæoides*, C. *Cneorum*, C. *mauri-tanicus*, Coreopsis *rosea*, Crucianella *stylosa*, Dianthus *alpinus*, D. *cæsius*, D. *deltoides and vars.*, D. *Freynii*, D. *Knappii*, D. *neglectus*, D. *superbus*, Epilobium *Fleischeri*, Erodium *chamædryoides*, E. *chrysanthemum*, E. *corsicum*, E. *guttatum*, E. *macradenum*, E. *Manascavii*, E. *trichomanifolium*, Erythræa *Massoni*, Frankenia *lævis*, Genista *sagittalis*, G. *tinctoria plena*, Gentiana *Freyniana*, G. *lagodechiana*, G. *Purdomii*, G. *septemfida*, Geranium *argenteum*, G. *cinerium*, G. *Pylzowianum*, G. *sanguineum and vars.*, Geum *Borisii*, G. *montanum*, Globularia *cordifolia*, G. *nudicaulis*, Gypsophila *cerastioides*, G. *repens and vars.*, Helichrysum *bellidioides*, Hieracium *aurantiacum*, H. *villosum*, Hypericum *coris*, H. *fragile*, H. *nummularium*, H. *olympicum*, H. *repens*, H. *reptans*, Inula *acaulis*, I. *ensifolia*, Jasione *Jankæ*, J. *perenne*, Lavandula *vera nana*, Leontopodium *alpinum*, Lewisia *Columbiana*, L. *Cotyledon*, L. *Heckneri*, L. *Howellii*, Linaria *æquitriloba*, L. *alpina*, L. *hepaticæfolia*, L. *pallida*, Linum *alpinum*, L. *arboreum*, L. *flavum*, L. *monogynum*, L. *salsoloides*, Lychnis *Lagascæ*, Lysimachia *nummularia*, Matthiola *fenestralis,* Œnothera *acaulis*, Œ. *cæspitosa*, Œ. *missouriensis*, Œ. *riparia*, Onosma *albo-roseum*, O. *tauricum*, Othonopsis *cheirifolia*, Papaver *alpinum*, Parochetus *communis*, Pentstemon *Davidsonii*, P. *heterophyllus*, P. *Menziesii*, P. *Scouleri*, Phyteuma *comosum*, P. *Halleri*, P. *hemisphæricum*, P. *orbiculare*, P. *Scheuchzeri*, Potentilla *ambigua*, P. *aurea*, P. *fragiformis*, P. *nepalensis and vars.*, P. *nitida*, P. *Tonguei*, Primula *anisodora*, P. *capitata*, P. *Mooreana*, Prunella *incisa*, Ranunculus *alpestris*, R. *crenatus*, Rosa *Roulettii*, Scabiosa *graminifolia*, S. *Pterocephala*, Sedum *acre*, S. *album*, S. *anglicum*, S. *dasyphyllum*, S. *ellacombianum*, S. *Ewersii*, S. *hispanicum*, S. *kamtschaticum*, S. *Lydium*, S. *Middendorfianum*, S. *pulchellum*, S. *reflexum*, S. *rupestre*, S. *spathulifolium*, S. *spurium*, Semper-vivum *Allionii*, S. *arachnoideum and vars.*, S. *calcareum*, S. *Funkii*, S. *globiferum*, S. *Hookeri*, S. *montanum*, S. *tectorum*, S. *triste*, S. *violaceum*, Senecio *tyrolensis*, Silene *alpestris*, S. *Schafta*, Sisyrinchium *angustifolium*, Solidago *Buckleyi*, Stachys *corsica*, Statice *minuta*, Thymus *Serpyllum and vars.*, Tunica *Saxifraga*, Verbena *chamædryfolia*, Veronica *Bidwillii*, V.

carnosula, V. *Catarractæ*, V. *Hectori*, V. *pimeloides*, V. *pinquifolia*, Viola *bosniaca*, V. *cornuta and vars.*, V. *gracilis and vars.*, V. *hederacea*, Wahlenbergia *vincæflora*.

HARDY AQUATICS AND BOG PLANTS.—Acorus *Calamus*, Alisma *Plantago*, Anemone *rivularis*, Aponogeton *distachyon*, astilbes in var., Butomus *umbellatus*, Epipactis *palustris*, Iris *aurea*, I. *fulva*, I. *Kæmpferi and vars.*, I. *ochroleuca*, I. *sibirica and vars.*, Lysimachia *vulgaris*, Limnanthemum *nymphæoides*, Limnocharis *Humboldtii*, Menyanthes *trifoliata*, Mimulus *cardinalis*, M. *luteus and vars.*, M. *ringens*, Myosotis *palustris*, Nuphar *luteum*, nymphæas in var., Orchis *foliosa*, Parnassia *palustris*, Pontederia *cordata*, Primula *Beesiana*, P. *Bulleyana*, P. *Florindæ*, P. *Littoniana*, P. *microdonta and vars.*, P. *Poissonii*, Ranunculus *Lingua*, Rodgersia *æsculifolia*, R. *pinnata*, R. *podophylla*, R. *sambucifolia*, R. *tabularis*, Sagittaria *sagittifolia and vars.*, Senecio *Clivorum*, Spiræa *Ulmaria plena*, Stenanthium *robustum*, Stratiotes *aloides*, Typha *angustifolia*, T. *japonica*, T. *latifolia*, T. *Laxmannii*, T. *minima*.

ANNUALS.—Hardy vars. (*as June*); half-hardy vars. (*as list February, Third Week*).

BEDDING PLANTS.—*As June, but also* dahlias (*bedding and charm*) *and* begonias (*tuberous-rooted and sempcrflorens*).

HARDY EVERGREEN SHRUBS.—Abelia *grandiflora*, Bupleurum *fruticosum* (*seaside*), Calluna *vulgaris and vars.*, Carpenteria *californica* (*shelter*), Ceanothus *Burkwoodii*, cistus (*as June*), Cotoneaster *lactea*, C. *serotina*, Daboecia *polifolia*, Daphne *acutiloba*, Desfontainea *spinosa*, Erica *ciliaris and vars.*, E. *cinerea and vars.*, E. *Mackeyi*, E. *stricta and vars.*, E. *Tetralix*, E. *vagans and vars.*, E. *Watsonii*, Escallonia *exoniensis*, E. *floribunda* (*shelter*), E. *Ingramii*, E. *Iveyi*, E. *langleyensis*, E. *macrantha* (*shelter*), E. *pterocladon* (*shelter*), E. *punctata*, E. *rubra*, Hypericum *calycinum*, Jasminum *revolutum*, Kalmia *cuneata*, K. *latifolia*, Lavandula *Spica* (*English lavender*), L. *vera* (*Dutch lavender*), Leucothoe *Davisiæ*, Magnolia *glauca*, M. *grandiflora*, Myrtus *communis*, Olearia *Gunniana*, O. *Haastii*, O. *nummularifolia*, Osmanthus *fragrans*, Phlomis *fruticosa*, Salvia *Grahami* (*shelter*), Santolina *Chamæcyparissus*, Senecio *Greyi*, S. *laxifolius*, Teucrium *fruticans*, Ulex *nanus*, Veronica *angustifolia*, V. *anomala*, V. *Balfouriana*, V. *buxifolia*, V. *cupressoides*, V. *leiophylla*, V. *obovata*, V. *salicifolia*, V. *Traversii*, V. *vernicosa*, Vinca *major*, V. *minor*, Yucca *filamentosa*, Y. *gloriosa*.

HARDY DECIDUOUS SHRUBS.—Abelia *Schumanni*, Abutilon *vitifolium*, Æsculus *parviflora*, Amorpha *canescens*, Buddleia *alternifolia*, B. *variabilis and vars.*, Calycanthus *floridus*, Caragana *decorticans*, Carmichælia *grandiflora*, Ceanothus *americanus*, C. *azureus and hybrids*, Ceratostigma *Willmottianum*, Clerodendron *trichotomum*, Celtlra *alnifolia*, Colutea *arborescens*, Cytisus *leucanthus*, C. *nigricans*, C. *purpureus*, C. *virgata*, Deutzia *corymbosa*, D. *crenata and vars.*, D. *scabra and vars.*, D. *taiwanensis*, Escallonia *Phillipiana*, Fremontia *californica* (*shelter*), Fuchsia *macrostemma and vars.*, F. *Riccartonii*, Gaylussacia *frondosa*, Genista *ætnensis*, G. *cinerea*, G. *dalmatica*, Halimodendron *argenteum*, Hedysarum *multijugum*, Hydrangea *arborescens grandiflora*, H. *Bretschneideri*, H. *hortensis vars.*, Hypericum *patulum and vars.*, Indigofera *Gerardiana*, Iteà *virginica*, Jamesia *americana*, Leycesteria *formosa*, Lupinus *arboreus*, Lyonia *ligustrina*,

Magnolia *parviflora*, Meleosma *cuneifolia*, M. *myriantha*, Nandina *domestica*, Notospartium *cerasiformis*, Philadelphus *grandiflorus*, P. *incanus*, P. *insignis*, P. *microphyllus*, P. *Satsumi*, Plagianthus *Lyallii*, Potentilla *fruticosa*, Rhodotypos *kerrioides*, Rhus *Cotinus*, Robinia *Hartwegii*, Rosa *alba*, R. *anemonæflora*, R. *Beggeriana*, R. *bracteata*, R. *carolina Nuttaliana*, R. *filipes*, R. *Moyesii*, R. *multibracteata*, R. *rugosa*, hybrid roses (*tea, hybrid tea, hybrid perpetual, pernettiana, polyantha*), Rubus *odoratus*, R. *thyrsoideus plenus*, R. *ulmifolius bellidiflorus*, Spartium *junceum*, Spiræa *Aitchisonii*, S. *arborea*, S. *assurgens*, S. *discolor*, S. *japonica and vars.*, S. *Margaritæ*, S. *Menziesi and vars.*, S. *sorbifolia*, S. *Veitchii*, Stewartia *pentagyna*, S. *pseudocamellia*, Tamarix *pentandra*, Zenobia *speciosa*.

CISTUS PURPUREUS.

HARDY EVERGREEN TREES.—Eucryphia *pinnatifolia*, Koelreuteria *paniculata*.

HARDY DECIDUOUS TREES.—Æsculus *californica*, Castanea *sativa*, Catalpa *bignonioides*, Cladrastis *sinensis*, Lagestrœmia *indica* (*shelter*), Oxydendrum *arboreum*, Tilia *cordata*, T. *euchlora*, T. *petiolaris*, T. *platyphyllos*, T. *tomentosa*, T. *vulgaris* (*common lime*).

HARDY CLIMBING PLANTS.—Berberidopsis *corallina* (*shelter*), Clematis *Durandii*, C. *Fargesii*, C. *florida and vars.*, C. *Hendersonii*, C. *Jackmannii and vars.*, C. *lanuginosa and vars.*, C. *montana Wilsoni*, C. *Pitcheri*, C. *viticella and vars.*, Jasminum *officinale* (*jessamine*), J. *stephanense*, Lathyrus *latifolius and vars.* (*everlasting pea*), Lonicera *caprifolium*, L. *etrusca*, L. *Heckrottii*, L. *japonica and vars.*, L. *periclymenum and vars.* (*honeysuckle*),

JULY: SEASONABLE FLOWERS, ETC.

L. *plantierensis*, L. *tragophylla*, Passiflora *cœrulea*, Periploca *græca*, P. *sepium*, Polygonum *baldschuanicum*, hybrid roses (*climbing hybrid tea, tea, pernettiana, and polyantha, also multiflora, wichuraiana, noisette, hybrid bracteata, and hybrid rugosa*), Schizophragma *hydrangeoides*, Solanum *crispum*, S. *jasminoides*, Trachelospermum *divaricatum*, Tropæolum *speciosum*, Wistaria *frutescens*, W. *japonica*, W. *macrostachya*.

GREENHOUSE PLANTS.—Achimenes, Agapanthus *umbellatus*, annuals (*as June*), Asclepias *curassavica*, balsam, begonias (*tuberous-rooted*), boronias, bougainvilleas, Campanula *pyramidalis*, cannas, carnations (*perpetual-flowering and border*), Cassia *corymbosa*, celosias, celsias, Cestrum *elegans*, Clianthus *Dampieri*, C. *puniceus*, Cobæa *scandens*, correas, Crassula *coccinea*, crinums, Cuphea *ignea*, daturas, Didiscus *cœruleus*, Diplacus *glutinosus*, Erica *insignis*, E. *præstans rosea*, E. *ventricosa*, Erythrina *Crista galli*, Francoa *ramosa*, fuchsias, gloxinias, heliotrope, Hibbertia *dentata*, Hoya *carnosa*, Humea *elegans*, lantanas, Lagerstrœmia *indica*, Lapageria *rosea*, Lasiandra *macrantha*, Lilium *auratum*, L. *longiflorum*, L. *speciosum*, Mandevilla *suaveolens*, marguerites, Maurandya *Barclayana*, Mitraria *coccinea*, Nerium *Oleander*, pancratiums, passifloras, zonal pelargoniums, Plumbago *capensis*, Rehmannia *angulata*, Rhyncospermum *jasminoides*, streptocarpus (*old plants*), Streptosolon *Jamesonii*, swainsonias, tacsonias, tecomas, tropæolums (*including double vars.*).

VEGETABLES IN THE GARDEN.—Globe artichokes, broad beans, French beans, runner beans, shorthorn carrots, cauliflowers, lettuces, vegetable marrows, mustard and cress, onions, peas, potatoes (*early vars.*), radishes, spinach, turnips.

VEGETABLES UNDER GLASS.—Cucumbers, mushrooms (*cool cellars and sheds*), tomatoes.

FRUITS OUTDOORS.—Apples: *Early Crimson* (D), *Early Victoria or Emneth Early* (C), *Gladstone* (D), *White Transparent* (C). Blackberry: *Bedford Giant*. Cherries: *Archduke* (D), *Bedford Prolific* (D), *Blackheart* (D), *Black Tartarian* (D), *Early Amber* (D), *Elton* (D), *Flemish Red* (C), *Frogmore Bigarreau* (D), *Governor Wood* (D), *Kentish Bigarreau* (D), *Kentish Red* (C), *Knight's Early Black* (D), *Ludwig's Bigarreau* (D), *Peggy Rivers* (D), *Schrecken Bigarreau* (D), *Ursula Rivers* (D), *Whiteheart* (D), Currants, Red: *Earliest of Fourlands, Cherry, Fay's Prolific, Laxton's No. 1, Laxton's Perfection, The Comet*. Currants, White: *White Dutch, White Versailles*. Gooseberries: *Careless, Golden Drop, Early Sulphur, Keepsake, Leveller, Langley Gage, Lancashire Lad, Whinham's Industry, Whitesmith*. Loganberry. Pears: *Doyenne d'Ete* (D), *Early Market* (D). Phenomenal Berry. Plums: *Black Prince* (C), *Early Laxton* (C), *Rivers' Early Prolific* (C), Raspberries: *Lloyd George, Pyne's Imperial, Pyne's Royal, Red Cross, Yellow Antwerp*. Strawberries: *Givon's Late Prolific, Laxton's Latest, Tardive de Leopold, White Pine, Waterloo*. Veitchberry.

FRUITS UNDER GLASS.—Apricots: *Early Moor Park, Frogmore Early, Luizet, New Large Early, Precoce de Boulbon*. Grapes: *Buckland's Sweetwater, Foster's Seedling, Royal Muscadine*. Nectarines: *Cardinal, Early Rivers, Joan Rivers*. Peaches: *Duke of York, Amsden's June, Hale's Early, Waterloo*.

AUGUST

GENERAL WORK

Take Geranium Cuttings

YOU can take cuttings of both zonal and ivy-leaved bedding geraniums (pelargoniums) at any time during the month. Choose shoots, 4 or 5 inches long, that are not carrying flowers. Sever them cleanly just below a joint and insert the cuttings around the edge of well-drained 4- or 5-inch flower pots filled with sandy compost. The cuttings will root most rapidly if you stand them in a frame and shade them from direct sunshine, but they can also be rooted in any reasonably sheltered place indoors or out. Water moderately until the cuttings commence to grow, after which they will need increasing supplies.

If you want a batch of greenhouse zonal pelargoniums for late spring and summer flowering, take a batch of cuttings now and treat them in exactly the same way as the bedding varieties.

Continue to Bud Fruit and Rose Stocks

You can continue to bud both fruit and rose stocks throughout the month providing the stocks work well (see note on Rose Budding, July, General Work). As a rule, however, it is wise to complete rose budding as early in the month as possible, as late buds do not give such good results.

Examine the early buds put in during June and July and loosen any ties that are cutting into the bark. It is advisable to replace such ties with new ones, as the buds may not have made a very secure union yet.

Continue to Remove Faded Flowers, Runners, etc.

Throughout the month continue to remove faded flowers from roses, bedding plants, etc.; also runners from violets. Disbud roses and dahlias if you require some big flowers (see June and July, General Work).

Complete Trimming of Hedges, etc.

Evergreen shrubs grown as hedges or topiary specimens can still be trimmed during August, but it is wise to complete the

204

work for the season at the end of the month. Late trimming may result in soft autumn growth which will get damaged by frost.

CONTINUE TO SECURE SHRUB CUTTINGS

You can continue to take shrub cuttings during the month, as described in my notes for July (see July, General Work). Hydrangeas usually root very freely during this month, and do

HOW TO PROPAGATE A HYDRANGEA.

In order to obtain strong young plants each carrying a fine truss of bloom such as that shown on the right, cuttings of young growth trimmed just below a joint (inset) should be inserted singly in sandy soil in small pots and be kept in a shaded frame.

best if inserted singly in 2½-inch pots, so that there need be no subsequent root disturbance. They must be kept in a shaded frame without ventilation until rooted and should be watered very freely.

Keep an eye on the cuttings of shrubs, etc., taken last month, and as soon as these commence to grow remove them very carefully from the frames or bell glasses and pot them up separately in 2½-inch pots, using the usual compost (see page 43). Keep them in a frame or cool greenhouse for the time being, shading them from strong, direct sunshine and syringing them with tepid water every day, but as they get hardened and root out into the new soil, accustom them to outdoor conditions, and eventually, after a few weeks, remove them to a plunge bed in a sheltered place outdoors. Plant them in a sheltered nursery bed in October or March.

KEEP DOWN FOES

Most of my July notes on the subject of pests and diseases (see July, General Work) apply with equal force to August. One foe that is likely to be on the increase is the earwig. Sprays are not effective against this, but a reliable poison bait can be made by thinning 1 pint of black treacle with a little water, adding ½ lb. sodium fluoride dissolved in a small quantity of water, and then mixing with about 4 lb. of bran to form a moist but not wet mash. Another method of ridding the garden of earwigs is to trap them in small flower pots, filled with hay and inverted on sticks amongst dahlias, chrysanthemums, and other plants commonly attacked. Examine the traps every morning. Earwigs will hide in them by day, for they dislike the light.

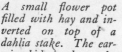

EARWIG TRAP.

A small flower pot filled with hay and inverted on top of a dahlia stake. The earwigs hide in the pot by day and can be collected and destroyed.

"TAKE" CHRYSANTHEMUM BUDS

Continue to "take" early-flowering chrysanthemum buds—*i.e.*, to secure the good buds you need for flowering and to remove all shoots and buds below them, as I explained in my notes for July, Fourth Week. A little later in the month exactly the same process must be applied to late-flowering chrysanthemums that are being grown for large blooms. Exhibition varieties are usually needed about the middle of November, and it is desirable that they should show their buds from the middle to the end of August. However, if some do show up early you must keep them (or "take" them, as the chrysanthemum grower confusingly puts it) now, for it is too late to remove them and wait for the next lot. Sometimes early buds can be retarded quite a bit by leaving the side shoots to grow up around them for a week or so before pinching them out, but you must not overdo this, or you may starve the bud too much.

GENERAL GREENHOUSE MANAGEMENT

All the remarks in the June and July notes on this subject still apply with as much force as ever. Ventilation will be needed both day and night: top and side

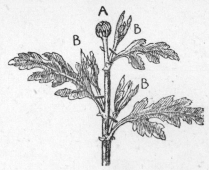

TAKING A CHRYSANTHEMUM BUD.

This means that the flower bud (A) is retained and all small side growths (B) lower down the stem are rubbed out.

most days, but top only at night unless conditions are exceptional. Always be ready with shading at the first sign of scorched foliage, and damp down paths, stages, and walls with increased freedom if red spider or thrips put in an appearance. August is generally the peak month for these drought-loving pests.

The earliest batches of achimenes, begonias, and gloxinias will have finished flowering by this time, and their water supply should be very gradually reduced so that they ripen their growth and go to rest. Similar remarks apply to early hippeastrums, which will also be coming towards the close of their season of growth.

MAKE SUCCESSIONAL SOWINGS

There are still a few successional sowings to be made. Mustard and cress and also radishes should be sown as before. A small sowing of shorthorn carrots made early in the month in a very sheltered place will continue the supply of young roots well into the autumn, while endive and lettuce sown about the middle of the month, also in a sheltered border, will provide you with seedlings some of which can be left to grow on undisturbed, while others are transferred to a frame.

START TO BLANCH ENDIVE

By this month endive from the first sowing (see April, Fourth Week) should be ready for blanching. Only do a few plants at a time, however, as blanching stops growth. There are several ways of accomplishing this task, but none, I think, better than the very simple plan of covering each plant with an inverted flower pot or a saucer. If you use flower pots, you must be careful to cover the hole in the bottom of each to secure perfect blanching. It usually takes about a fortnight to get a complete blanch.

Continue to Blanch Leeks

This work must be continued as I have already described (see June, General Work) until a sufficient length of blanched stem—usually about a foot—is obtained.

Lift Second Early Potatoes as Required

When you come to the end of the first early potatoes make a start on the second early or mid-season varieties such as Catriona and Arran Banner, but only lift a few roots at a time as you require them.

Plant Coleworts

You can continue to plant coleworts as ground becomes available (see July, General Work), but other winter greens should all be planted by this time.

Thin Vegetable Seedlings

Do not neglect to thin out seedlings of lettuce, spinach, etc., made last month. Do the work as soon as you can conveniently handle the seedlings and water those you leave if the soil is dry.

Feed and Train Tomatoes

In the main, treatment of tomatoes this month is exactly the same as during July (see July, General Work). As soon as the outdoor plants have made four trusses of flowers, stop them from growing further by pinching out the tips of the main stems.

Clear out Spent Cucumbers

It is probable that the early cucumbers will not be worth keeping any longer, especially if you have a good supply of plants in frames. Clear them out when they cease to bear freely, and take the opportunity to give the house a thorough clean out and scrub down. If you have been troubled with thrips and red spider, fumigate with naphthalene or sulphur while the house is empty. Use one of the lamps specially manufactured for vaporising these chemicals. They can be purchased from any dealer in horticultural sundries.

KILL AMERICAN BLIGHT ON APPLES

This is a suitable time to take steps to destroy American blight (also known as woolly aphis) on apples. This is an insect pest which infests cracks in the branches and twigs and protects itself

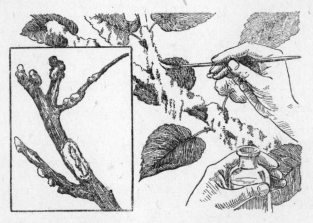

DESTROYING AMERICAN BLIGHT.

This pest is really a species of aphis which protects itself with a white, cotton-wool-like covering. It attacks the bark and eventually causes cracks and wounds (inset). The best remedy is to brush methylated spirits into the woolly patches.

with a white, cottonwool-like covering. Sprays are not very effective. Go over the trees carefully and brush methylated spirits into the woolly patches with a stiff paintbrush.

PICK AND SUMMER-PRUNE APPLES AND PEARS

During this month and also throughout September you should continue to pick apples and pears as they ripen, applying the tests already described (see July, Third Week). You should also continue to summer-prune the trees (see July, Third Week), but strive to complete the work by the end of the month.

Management of the Orchard House

There is nothing to add to my remarks on this subject in the notes for July, General Work, except that ventilation can be even freer and syringing of cleared trees more thorough than before.

Treat Vines according to Growth

Vines, both indoors and out, will be in various stages of growth, according in part to the time at which they were started and in part to the variety. Regarding actual treatment, there is nothing to be added to my former remarks (see notes on General Work, May, June, and July). Early vines from which you have gathered the crop should be ventilated freely and syringed fairly frequently if there is any sign of red spider on the leaves.

FIRST WEEK

Sow Stocks and Mignonette for the Greenhouse

Make sowings of both Beauty of Nice and Brompton stocks for flowering in pots in the greenhouse. The former will bloom from Christmas until February or March, while the Brompton stocks will follow on in late spring. Sow all very thinly in well-drained pans or boxes filled with the usual compost (see page 24), and germinate in a frame, shading until the seedlings appear, but thereafter giving full light and free ventilation. Prick off or pot separately in $2\frac{1}{2}$-inch pots as soon as the seedlings have two true leaves each.

Pot Freesias for Early Flowering

Providing the corms are properly ripened, the earlier freesias can be potted the better. The beginning of August is usually about as soon as one can purchase the corms, so if you want a supply of flowers for Christmas, pot up some now in 5- or 6-inch pots. You can place six corms in a 5-inch pot or ten in a 6-inch pot. Use a compost of three parts loam, one part moss peat, and one part dry cow manure and sand in about equal proportions. Bury the corms 1 inch deep in this and then stand the pots in a frame. Water moderately and shade from direct sunshine, but do not use the lights as yet. Old corms from last year that have been resting during the summer (see May, General Work) should also be shaken out and repotted now.

Pot Lachenalias

Lachenalias for winter flowering in the greenhouse should also be potted or be placed in hanging baskets (a very delightful method of growing these beautiful South African bulbs). The method of culture in pots is exactly the same as for freesias (see above). If to be grown in hanging baskets, the latter must be well lined with moss and then some of the bulbs should be placed at the bottom and around the sides of the basket, as well as on top. Use the same compost as for freesias in pots and cover the top bulbs to a depth of 1 inch. Hang the baskets up in a cool place for the time being and water moderately until growth commences. Purchase new corms now, or shake the old ones out of the dry soil in which they have been resting (see May, General Work).

Repot and Start Arum Lilies

The arum lilies that have been resting during the summer (see May, General Work) should now be started into growth. If they have been more than one year in their present pots, repot them first. Shake the old compost off the tubers and place them in 6-, 8-, or 10-inch pots, according to their size. If they have made any sturdy offsets, these can be detached and potted separately. Use a compost of three parts loam, one part dried cow manure, and one part sharp sand, with a sprinkling of bonemeal. Stand the pots in a sheltered place in the open and water very moderately at first, but gradually give more as growth proceeds.

AN ARUM LILY OFFSET.
A sturdy young growth detached from a large root and potted on its own.

Ripen off Onions

Onions from the January and March sowings will now be approaching ripeness, and you can hasten this by bending over the leaves just above the neck of each bulb.

Pot Winter-flowering Begonias

If you were able to root cuttings of winter-flowering begonias in late winter (see April, General Work), the plants should now be about ready for potting on into their flowering pots. These should be 5 or 6 inches in diameter. Use a compost of three

211

parts loam, one part moss peat, one part sharp sand, and one part dried cow manure and wood ashes, or, failing this, the general compost recommended on page 62. Place the plants on a shelf in the greenhouse and shade from direct sunshine.

Sow Tomatoes and Cucumbers for Winter

This is the time to sow both tomatoes and cucumbers for cropping during the winter months. I do not recommend either crop to the amateur, however, for the tomatoes must have an average temperature of 65 degs. and the cucumbers nearer 75 degs. if they are to be satisfactory. That means more artificial heat than most amateur gardeners have at command. In addition there is the difficulty of maintaining growth and getting the tomatoes to ripen when the days are short and light is poor. However, if you do decide to have a shot at either or both these crops, sow the seeds at once and follow the directions given for the early crops under glass.

SECOND WEEK

Cut Back Violas and Pansies for Propagation

It is an excellent plan to cut back a few plants of any good violas and pansies one may have with a view to encouraging basal growth which will provide cuttings next month. Scissor off the present flowering shoots to within 1 inch of the roots. Then scatter a little fine soil mixed with sand and sifted leaf-mould over the plants.

Pot Greenhouse Calceolarias and Cinerarias

As soon as greenhouse calceolarias begin to touch in the boxes in which they were pricked off last month (see July, Third Week) they must be pricked off a second time, leaving 3 inches from plant to plant, or, alternatively, potted up singly in 2½-inch pots. In either case use the general potting compost (see page 62) and return the plants to the frame, treating them as before and being very careful to keep them cool by free ventilation and shading. Also, keep a sharp eye on cinerarias in frames. The first batch sown in May (see May, First Week) is likely to require a move on into 5-inch pots, while the later batch, pricked off last month (see July, Third Week), will certainly very soon require first potting into 3-inch pots. This I have already described in the notes for June, Fourth Week. Syringe the plants daily with clear water.

Sow Cyclamen

It is possible to raise cyclamen from seed sown very early in the year and flower the plants the following winter, but very much better results are obtained by sowing about the middle of

ENCOURAGING THE FORMATION OF VIOLA CUTTINGS.

This old plant has been cut back and is being top-dressed with a light compost. Later on an abundance of young growths will be produced, many of which may be pulled out with a few white rootlets (inset).

August and keeping the seedlings growing steadily, but slowly, throughout the following autumn, winter, spring, and summer so that they make fine big corms for flowering the following autumn and winter. Sow in well-drained pans in the usual seed compost (see page 24), and space the seeds individually $\frac{1}{2}$ inch apart each way. Cover with $\frac{1}{4}$ inch of the same soil and then with a pane of glass and a sheet of brown paper, and germinate in any frame or greenhouse in which you can maintain a steady

213

temperature of 60 degs. or rather more. Very high temperatures are not necessary or advisable.

RESTART OLD CYCLAMEN CORMS

Old cyclamen corms that have been resting in a shady frame since May (see May, Second Week) may now be repotted and started into growth. Clean off all the old foliage, shake most of the soil off the roots and repot in the smallest pots that will accommodate the roots comfortably, without any doubling up. Use the same compost as for the final potting of seedlings (see

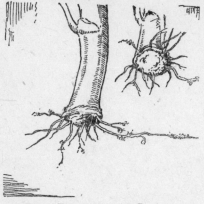

p. 167). Return the plants to a shady frame for a few weeks, ventilate rather sparingly, water very moderately at first, but syringe the corms daily with tepid water to encourage them to make new growth.

CUT BACK PELARGONIUMS AND INSERT CUTTINGS

Show and regal pelargoniums that were stood outdoors last month (see July, First Week) should now be cut back. Shorten all growths to about 1 inch and then commence to spray the plants daily with tepid water, continuing this daily throughout the month. The shoots that you cut off can be inserted as cuttings if you need some more plants. The method of preparing and rooting cuttings is exactly the same as for bedding geraniums (see General Work).

ROOT FORMATION AT BASE OF GERANIUM CUTTING.

The illustration shows the importance of trimming cuttings just below a joint, for it is from this that all the roots are formed.

SOW SPRING AND PICKLING CABBAGES

Make a second sowing of spring cabbages now in exactly the same way as I described in my notes for July, Third Week. The reason for this is that in some seasons the earlier seedlings grow thin and spindly and eventually run to seed instead of forming hearts.

If you also want to have some big red cabbages for pickling next year, sow a few seeds in exactly the same manner as for ordinary spring cabbages (see above).

LIFT EARLY BEETROOT

Beetroots do not improve by getting very big, so lift the early globe varieties rather before they average the size of tennis balls —which will probably be about this time. Twist off the tops without injuring the skin of the beetroot in any way (bleeding is very easily caused and, if severe, may spoil the colour of the roots) and store them in any cool shed, cellar, or room. They will keep all the better if surrounded by sand that is just moist.

PRUNE SUMMER-FRUITING RASPBERRIES

By this time the summer-fruiting raspberries will have quite finished cropping, and the sooner they are pruned the better. Cut out, right to ground level, all the canes that have just fruited, and train in the young canes in their place. This treatment will also suit the variety Lloyd George, for though this raspberry is sometimes described as perpetual-fruiting, any late summer or autumn fruits it may carry will be on the current year's canes, not on last year's canes.

THIRD WEEK

START NERINES

Give a little water to nerines that have been resting all the summer and increase the amount as soon as growth appears. The pots should stand on the staging in a sunny greenhouse. Ventilate freely and do not shade at all.

SOW SCHIZANTHUS FOR SPRING FLOWERING

In order to have really large plants of schizanthus in 7- or 8-inch pots for spring decorations in greenhouse and conservatory you should sow now. Sow seeds thinly in well-drained seed boxes, using the usual compost (see page 24), and germinate in a frame. Keep the lights on and the frame shaded until the seedlings appear, then remove the shading and begin to give a little ventilation, increasing this until after a week or so the lights are only used to keep off heavy rain. The cooler the condition under which

215

the plants are grown the better, for schizanthus get drawn very easily.

Sow Winter Spinach and Spinach Beet

Choose a fairly sheltered place and make a sowing of prickly-seeded spinach to stand the winter. Sow the seed thinly in drills 1 inch deep and 1 foot apart.

You can also make a sowing of spinach beet now for use in winter and spring. This useful variety of beetroot is grown solely for its leaves, which are used as a substitute for spinach. Sow the seeds in small groups 8 inches apart, in drills 1 inch deep, and make the drills 15 inches apart. Later, you can single out the clusters of seedlings.

Commence to Gather Mushrooms from Outdoor Beds

If you were able to make a mushroom bed in the open early in July (see July, First Week) you should examine it now for the first mushrooms. Gather the "buttons" as they form. The bed should continue in bearing well on into the autumn.

Make New Strawberry Plantations

Strawberry runners that were pegged down early last month (see July, First Week) should now have made good roots and can be severed from their parent plants. A few days later you can lift them carefully and plant them in new beds. Choose a good open position and soil that has been deeply dug and well manured. Plant the strawberries 1 foot apart in rows 2 feet apart. After the first year alternate plants can be removed if overcrowded.

If you want to grow some early strawberries in the greenhouse, pot up a few of the strongest young plants

A Sturdy Strawberry Plant.

This is the type of plant that can be obtained by rooting runners in pots.

216

in 6-inch pots, using a compost of three parts loam, one part dried manure, and one part sharp sand, with a sprinkling of wood ashes. Stand the pots in a frame or sheltered place outdoors, but do not cover with any lights as yet.

FOURTH WEEK

Prune Hydrangeas

Most hydrangeas will have finished flowering and will benefit from a little pruning. Cut off each faded flower truss as far back as the first plump-looking growth bud, and remove any thin, weakly looking stems. Of course, if some of the branches are still producing good blooms leave these unpruned.

Lift Spring-sown Onions

Onions sown in January under glass and in March outdoors should now have completed their growth, and there is no point in leaving them in the ground any longer. Lift them carefully with a fork and spread them out on the surface to dry. After a few days you can shake any soil from the bulbs and store them, either on shelves and in shallow boxes in a dry, frost-proof shed or room, or else strung together in ropes after the French fashion.

Sow Onions

This is the time to sow onions, both for use small as salading in the spring and also to provide early bulbs before the spring-sown crop. For the former purpose White Lisbon is the best variety as it is very mild in flavour, but for bulb-making choose one of the Tripoli varieties or Giant Rocca. Select a fairly sheltered place and ground that has been well cultivated but not recently manured. Sow the seeds thinly in drills $\frac{1}{2}$ inch deep and 9 inches apart.

Commence to Earth up Maincrop Celery

It is now time to begin to earth up the maincrop celery. The process is exactly as described for early celery (see July, Second Week) except that with these bigger plants more soil will be required. It is quite a good plan to draw the stems together with raffia ties before starting to earth up, so that one can have both hands free for working the soil around the plants.

217

FLOWERS, VEGETABLES, AND FRUITS IN SEASON
DURING AUGUST

HARDY HERBACEOUS PLANTS.—Acanthus *mollis*, Achillea *filipendulina*, A. *millefolium vars.*, A. *Ptarmica and vars.*, A. *sibirica*, Aconitum *Lycoctonum*, A. *Napellus vars.*, Adenophora *Bulleyana*, A. *latifolia*, A. *Potanini*, Althæa *rosea vars.* (*hollyhocks*), alstromerias (*as July*), Anaphalis *margaritacea*, Anemone *japonica and vars.*, Anthemis *cupaniana*, A. *Sancta-Johannis*, A. *tinctoria and vars.*, Artemisia *lactiflora*, Asclepias *incarnata*, A. *tuberosa*,

FUNKIA SIEBOLDIANA.

Aster *acris*, A. *Amellus and vars.*, A. *Frikartii*, A. *luteus*, A. *linosyris*, A. *ptarmicoides*, A. *Thomsonii*, Astilbe *Arendsii hybrids*, Boltonia *asteroides*, Buphthalmum *salicifolium*, Campanula *alliariæfolia*, C. *lactiflora*, C. *latifolia vars.*, C. *pyramidalis and vars.*, C. *sarmatica*, C. *Van Houttei*, Catananche *cœrulea and vars.*, Centaurea *montana and vars.*, C. *ruthenicus*, Chelone *Lyonii*, C. *obliqua*, Chrysanthemum *erubescens*, C. *macrophyllum*, C. *maximum vars.* (*Shasta daisies*), chrysanthemums (*early-flowering hybrids*), Cimicifuga *dahurica*, C. *japonica*, C. *racemosa*, Clematis *heracleæfolia and vars.*, C. *integrifolia*, C. *recta*, Coreopsis *grandiflora and vars.*, C. *lanceolata and vars.*, Dianthus *Alwoodii vars.*, D. *Caryophyllus vars.* (*border carna-*

tions), D. *plumarius* Cyclops, Dierama *pulcherrima*, Dracocephalum *Ruyschiana*, Echinacea *purpurea and vars.*, Echinops *bannaticus*, E. *ritro*, E. *sphærocephalus*, Erigeron Mesa-grande, E. *speciosus and vars.*, eryngiums (*as July*), Filipendula *hexapetala*, Funkia Fortunei, F. *lancifolia and vars.*, F. *ovata*, F. *Sieboldiana*, F. *subcordata*, gaillardias (*hybrids*), Galega *officinalis and vars.*, Gaura Lindheimeri, Gentiana *asclepiadea*, Geum *bulgaricum*, G. *coccineum vars.*, G. *Heldreichii*, Gypsophila *paniculata and vars.*, Helenium *autumnale and vars.*, Helianthus *multiflorus and vars.* (*sunflower*), H. *rigidus and vars.* (*sunflower*), H. *tomentosus*, Heliopsis *lævis*, H. *scabra and vars.*, Hemerocallis *aurantiaca*, H. *Forrestii*, H. *fulva rosea*, H. *minor*, H. *multiflora*, H. *Thunbergii*, hemerocallis *hybrids*, Heuchera *brizoides*, H. *sanguineum and vars.*, Inula *glandulosa*, I. *Helenium*, I. *macrocephala*, I. *Oculus-Christii*, I. *Royleana*, Kniphofia *erecta*, K. *Galpini*, K. *Macowanii*, K. *Nelsonii*, K. *rufa*, K. *Uvaria and vars.* (*red-hot poker*), Lactuca *Bourgæi*, Lavatera *Olbia*, Liatris *pycnostachya*, L. *spicata*, Linaria *dalmatica*, Linum *narbonense*, L. *perenne*, Lobelia *cardinalis*, L. *fulgens and vars.*, L. *syphilitica and hybrids*, Lychnis *chalcedonica*, L. *coronaria*, Lysimachia *ciliata*, L. *thyrsiflora*, Lythrum *virgatum vars.*, Malva *Alcea vars.*, M. *setosa hybrids*, Meconopsis *Wallichii*, Monarda *didyma and vars.*, Nepeta *grandiflora*, N. *macrantha*, N. *Mussini*, Œnothera *biennis vars.* (*evening primrose*), Œ. *fruticosa*, Œ. *glauca*, Œ. *odorata*, Œ. *speciosa*, Papaver *nudicaule and vars.* (*Iceland poppies*), Pentstemon *barbatus*, P. *gentianoides hybrids* (*shelter in winter*), P. *isophyllus*, Phlox *decussata hybrids*, Phygelius *capensis*, Physostegia *virginiana and vars.*, Phytolacca *decandra* (*fruits*), Platycodon *grandiflorum and vars.*, Polygonum *amplexicaule*, P. *bistorta vars.*, P. *campanulatum*, Potentilla *hybrids*, Poterium *canadense*, P. *obtusum*, P. *tenuifolium*, Romneya *Coulteri*, R. *trichocalyx*, Rudbeckia *californica*, R. *laciniata and vars.*, R. *maxima*, R. *nitida vars.*, R. *speciosa* (*Newmanii*), rudbeckias (*hybrids*), Salvia *azurea grandiflora*, S. *Przewalskii*, S. *Sclarea and vars.*, S. *uliginosa*, S. *virgata*, Saponaria *officinalis plena*, Scabiosa *caucasica and vars.*, Sedum *maximum*, Senecio *pulcher*, S. *tanguticus*, S. *Veitchii*, sidalceas (*hybrids*), Silphium *perfoliatum*, S. *scaberrimum*, Solidago *Ballardii*, S. *cæsia*, S. *serotina*, S. *Virgaurea and vars.* (*golden rod*), Spiræa *kamtschatica*, S. *lobata*, S. *palmata*, statices (*as July*), Stokesia *cyanea*, Thalictrum *dipterocarpum*, Tradescantia *virginiana*, Tropæolum *polyphyllum*, Veratrum *album*, V. *nigrum*, V. *viride*, verbascums (*as July*), Verbena *bonariensis*, V. *tenera Mahonetii*, V. *venosa*, Veronica *exaltata*, V. *longifolia and vars.*, V. *spicata and vars.*, V. *subsessilis*, V. *virginica and vars.*

HARDY BULBS AND TUBERS.—Allium *Beesianum*, Amaryllis *Belladonna vars.*, Anomatheca *cruenta* (*shelter*), Antholyza *æthiopica*, A. *crocosmioides*, A. *paniculata*, Crinum *longifolium and vars.*, C. *Powellii and vars.*, Cyclamen *europæum*, gladioli (*large-flowered and primulinus vars.*), Lilium *auratum*, L. *Batemanniæ*, L. *Bolanderi*, L. *cordifolium*, L. *Henryi*, L. *princeps*, L. *speciosum*, L. *superbum*, L. *tigrinum*, L. *Wardii*, L. *Willmottiæ*, montbretias (*hybrids*), Tigridia *Pavonia and vars.*

ROCK PLANTS.—Achillea *argentea*, A. *Clavennæ*, A. *tomentosa and vars.*, Androsace *lanuginosa and vars.*, Antirrhinum *Asarina*, A. *glutinosum*, Arnica *sachalinensis*, Astilbe *simplicifolia*, Calamintha *alpina*, Calystegia *japonica*, Calandrinia *umbellata*, Campanula *carpatica and vars.*, C. *coch-*

trope, Hibbertia *dentata*, Hoya *carnosa*, Humea *elegans*, Lagerstrœmia *indica*, Lapageria *rosea*, Lilium *longiflorum*, L. *speciosum and vars.*, Lasiandra *macrantha*, Mandevilla *suaveolens*, marguerites, Maurandya *Barclayana*, Nerium *Oleander*, Oxalis *Bowiei*, pancratiums, passifloras, Plumbago *capensis*, Rehmannia *angulata*, Rhyncospermum *jasminoides*, Saintpaulia *ionantha*, streptocarpus (*sown Jan.*), swainsonias, tacsonias, tecomas, Trachelium *cæruleum*, tropæolums (*including double vars.*), Vallota *purpurea*.

VEGETABLES IN STORE.—Onions, shallots.

VEGETABLES OUTDOORS.—Globe artichokes, broad beans, French beans, runner beans, globe beetroot, cabbage (*sown March*), carrots, cauliflowers, celery, ridge cucumbers, endive, kohl-rabi, lettuce, vegetable marrows, mustard and cress, mushrooms, onions, peas, potatoes, radishes, spinach, tomatoes, turnips.

VEGETABLES UNDER GLASS.—Cucumbers, mushrooms (*cool cellars and outhouses*), tomatoes.

FRUITS OUTDOORS.—Apples: *Advance* (D), *Beauty of Bath* (D), *Devonshire Quarrendon* (D), *Early Peach* (D), *Early Victoria* (C), *Ecklinville Seedling* (C), *Gladstone* (D), *Grenadier* (C), *Irish Peach* (D), *Keswick Codlin* (C), *Lady Sudeley* (D), *Langley Pippin* (D), *Leader* (D), *Lord Grosvenor* (C), *Lord Suffield* (C), *Maidstone Favourite* (D), *St. Everard* (D), *White Transparent* (C). Blackberries: *Bedford Giant, Himalaya Giant, John Innes, Parsley Leaved.* Cherries: *Emperor Francis Bigarreau* (D), *Florence* (D), *Geant d'Hedelfingen* (D), *Morello* (C), *Napoleon Bigarreau* (D), *Tradescant's Heart or Noble* (D), *Turkey Black Heart* (D). Currants, Red: *Fay's Prolific, Knight's Sweet Red, Laxton's No. 1, Laxton's Perfection, New Red Dutch, Raby Castle, Prince Albert, Rivers' Late Red.* Currants, White: *White Dutch, White Versailles.* Currants, Black: *Baldwin, Boskoop Giant, Daniel's September, Davison's Eight, Seabrook's Black, Tinker.* Gooseberries: *Careless, Cousen's Seedling, Keepsake, Lancer, Leveller, Langley Gage, Lancashire Lad, Warrington, Whinham's Industry, Whitesmith.* Loganberry. Lowberry. Melons. Mulberry. Pears: *Clapp's Favourite* (D), *Early Market* (D), *Jargonelle* (D), *Superb* (D). Phenomenal Berry. Plums: *Belgian Purple* (CD), *Belle de Louvain* (C), *Blackbird* (CD), *Blue Rock* (D), *Blue Tit* (D), *Bountiful* (D), *Cambridge Greengage* (D), *Czar* (CD), *Denniston's Superb* (D), *Early Laxton* (C), *Early Transparent Gage* (D) *Evesham Wonder* (C), *Gisborne's Prolific* (C), *Green Gage* (D), *Jubilee* (D), *Laxton's Gage* (D), *Miarbelle* (C), *Oullin's Golden Gage* (CD), *Prosperity* (C), *Purple Pershore* (C), *River's Early Damson* (C), *Supreme* (D), *Utility* (D), *Victoria* (CD), *Yellow Pershore* (C). Raspberries: *Lloyd George.* Veitchberry.

FRUITS UNDER GLASS.—Apricots: *Breda, Grosse Pêche, Hemskirk, Kaisha, Luizet, Moorpark, Oullin's Early Peach, Royal, Shipley or Blenheim.* Figs. Grapes: *Black Hamburg, Buckland's Sweetwater, Foster's Seedling, Madresfield Court, Royal Muscadine.* Melons. Nectarines: *Dryden, Elruge, Hardwick, Humboldt, Lord Napier, Violette Hative.* Peaches: *Advance, Crimson Galande, Early Grosse Mignonne, Goshawk, Hale's Early, Kestrel, Peregrine, Rivers' Early York.*

SEPTEMBER

GENERAL WORK

Plant Narcissi, Lilies, Bulbous Irises, etc.

Narcissi (including the trumpet daffodils), crocuses, Spanish, English, and Dutch irises, snowdrops, muscaris, scillas, and also all lilies—with the exception of Lilium candidum (see July, Fourth Week)—can be planted with fair success at any time during the autumn, but the best results are obtained by early planting. If you can complete this work before September is out, so much the better. Tulips and hyacinths, however, may with advantage wait a little longer (see October, Fourth Week). All bulbs should be planted on fairly rich, well-worked soil, but preferably not ground that has been recently dressed with animal manure. Artificials of the right type are quite a different matter. A dusting of bonemeal, at 4 ounces per square yard, makes an excellent finish to the preparation of any bulb bed. The actual depth of planting should vary a little according to the nature of the soil, being rather deeper on light than on heavy land, but a fair average is as follows: narcissi,

PLANTING BULBS IN GRASS.

A special bulb trowel with an extra broad blade is being used. It is equally suitable for planting bulbs in beds. Inset is a special tool made for planting in grassland. It extracts a wad of turf, which can then be replaced on top of the bulb.

5 inches deep, 8 inches apart; hyacinths, 6 inches deep, 8 inches apart; chionodoxa, 2½ inches deep, 3 inches apart; Crown Imperial, 6 inches deep, 1 foot apart; crocuses, 2 inches deep, 3 inches apart; dog's-tooth violets, 2 inches deep, 6 inches apart; Spanish, English, and Dutch irises, 4 inches deep, 6 inches apart; snowdrops, 3 inches deep, 3 inches apart; muscaris, 3 inches deep, 4 inches apart; Scilla sibirica, 2½ inches deep, 2 inches apart; Scilla campanulata, 4 inches deep, 4 inches apart; lilies (stem rooting), 8 inches deep, 12 inches apart; lilies (not stem rooting), 6 inches deep, 12 inches apart. In all cases depths refer to the hole prepared and not to the soil actually covering the top of the bulb. On the important point of whether a lily is or is not stem rooting, the catalogue of any specialist will give you full information and is usually obtainable free for the asking. The list is too long to be printed here (see also note on pot lilies, page 226).

Do all the planting with a trowel or spade rather than a dibber. The last-named tends to make a pointed hole in which the bulb hangs suspended, with a hole beneath it.

Sow Grass Seed

Grass seed will germinate well enough at any time during September, though, other things being suitable, the sooner it can be sown the better, for then it will be well established before the winter. Details are exactly the same as for spring sowing (see April, First Week).

Take Cuttings of Evergreen Shrubs, etc.

Many hardy evergreen shrubs can be propagated quite readily from cuttings taken during Sep-

To Provide Cuttings.
A typical growth from an evergreen shrub with side shoots, each of which would make an ideal cutting.

1. A lifted chrysanthemum being replanted in the greenhouse for flowering.
2. Chrysanthemum crown buds. All side shoots have been removed so that the whole strength of each stem goes into the flower. 3. Preparing to fumigate with nicotine. The lamp is being lit, while the cowl and dish to hold the liquid are held in the left hand. 4. Blocking up a crack beneath the greenhouse door to prevent escape of fumes during fumigation.

1. Applying a dry fungicide with the aid of a special powder blower.
2. Spraying a rose with nicotine insecticide to destroy greenfly. 3. An
espalier-trained apple tree after correct summer pruning. 4. Cutting out
the old canes from a summer-fruiting raspberry. 5. The raspberry after
correct pruning and training.

tember and rooted in a frame or even a sheltered border. The process is similar to that which I have described for summer cuttings (see July, General Work), except that, on the whole, larger shoots are selected. They may be from 6 to 9 inches in length and should be pulled off with a " heel " or cut closely beneath a joint. Insert them firmly 2 or 3 inches deep in very sandy soil. If in a frame keep the light on, but only shade from very strong direct sunshine. Water sufficiently to keep the soil moist but not sodden. Privet, Lonicera nitida, laurel, aucuba, rosemary, and lavender will all root readily in this way, and so will some herbs, such as thyme and sage.

Take Cuttings of Bedding Plants, etc.

Throughout September you can take cuttings of a variety of plants, notably bedding calceolarias and pentstemons, verbenas, mesembryanthemums, violas and pansies (cut back last month), zonal geraniums (including the bedding varieties), antirrhinums, and violets. With all except violets, violas and pansies the method is to prepare cuttings 3 or 4 inches in length from firm, non-flowering shoots. Violet cuttings are prepared from the ends of the runners; pieces about 3 inches in length are ideal. Viola and pansy cuttings are made from young, non-flowering shoots coming from the base of the plant or directly from the roots. Frequently

VIOLA CUTTINGS.

Left: a young shoot that can be pulled up with rootlets attached. Right: an ordinary cutting correctly inserted. In both cases the dotted line indicates soil level.

these can be pulled out with a few young, white rootlets attached. Zonal pelargonium cuttings should be rooted in pots, as I have already described (see August, General Work), and must be accommodated in a frost-proof greenhouse from late September onwards, but the others are better inserted directly into a bed of sandy soil prepared in a frame. Dibble them in a few inches apart, water freely, and keep the lights on and shaded until the cuttings are rooted. Then ventilate freely throughout the winter, only keeping the frames closed when frost threatens and removing the lights altogether when the weather is mild.

P

Prevent Mildew

The foe most to be feared during this month is mildew. It may appear on roses, culinary peas, delphiniums, chrysanthemums, gooseberries, plums, and a variety of other plants and fruits. In all cases it covers leaves and stems with a whitish powdery outgrowth. At the first sign of this disease spray plants with weak lime-sulphur (summer strength), Bordeaux mixture, or, best of all, one of the new colloidal sulphur sprays.

General Greenhouse Management

Nights now begin to get much colder and one must be watchful with ventilation. The aim should still be an average day temperature of close on 60 degs., with a night minimum not much below 50 degs. Side ventilators are not likely to be needed, and even the top ventilators should be closed early in the afternoon if the weather is cold. Shading can be washed off the glass about the middle of the month for all except the most shade-loving plants—some ferns, for example. Syringing and damping down should also be discontinued gradually. There will soon be too much moisture in the air for most greenhouse plants.

Continue the ripening of early hippeastrums, achimenes, begonias, and gloxinias (see August, General Work). Some of the later batches will also need less water if they have finished flowering.

Pot Lilies for the Greenhouse

I have separated lilies from the other bulbs for the greenhouse because their treatment is rather different and also because it is not so essential to pot early. If you can buy all the bulbs you need early in September, by all means get them potted, because lilies gain nothing by being out of the ground. But a good many bulbs come from abroad—some from the Far East—and these do not usually arrive until later, so you may have to wait awhile if you need any of these (see January, General Work).

Lilies are best grown singly, in pots 6 or 7 inches in diameter according to the size of the bulbs. Set the stem-rooting kinds (see page 224) well down in the pots and only just cover them with soil now. Then, later on, as the stem grows, you can add top dressings of soil until the pot is almost full. Non-stem-rooting bulbs are potted nearer the surface and are not top dressed. Use the compost described on page 62, but be careful to use lime-free loam. The pots are not plunged under ashes like narcissi, etc., but are stood in an unheated frame or greenhouse to form roots. Do not use any artificial heat until top growth is several inches in length.

PLACE BULBS IN ORNAMENTAL BOWLS

Hyacinths and narcissi that are to be grown in undrained ornamental bowls should be obtained as soon as possible. Special bulb fibre containing oyster shell and charcoal must be used for these. Put a few good lumps of charcoal in the bottom of the bowl, then spread a little fibre over it, set the bulbs firmly in position, allowing a clear inch between each, and just cover with more fibre. Water freely and stand in a cool, dark place (a cupboard will serve admirably) until the shoots are about 1 inch in length, when the bowls must be arranged in as light a place as possible. Keep the fibre moist throughout.

MAKE SUCCESSIONAL SOWINGS

These can no longer be made outdoors as in former months— or at any rate outdoor sowings are only likely to be successful in the mildest districts—but it is a good plan to make yet another sowing of lettuce and endive in unheated frames and also to sow radishes and mustard and cress in the same way.

PLANT SPRING CABBAGES

Cabbages from the July sowing (see July, Third Week) will be ready for removal early in the month to the plot in which they will mature. You could not do better than follow them on after onions that have just been lifted or place them on the ground that has recently been cleared of potatoes. Rake it clean, give it a dusting of old soot, and plant the cabbages about 1 foot apart in rows 18 inches apart. Later in the month the seedlings from the August sowing (see August, Second Week) should be treated in the same way. Coleworts may also still be planted on any available ground. They will come into use late in the autumn.

CONTINUE TO EARTH UP CELERY AND LEEKS

From time to time during the month continue to draw more soil around celery plants and leeks, as described in the notes for May, First Week, July, Second Week, and August, Fourth Week.

Continue to Blanch Endive

During the month you should continue to blanch a few endives as they reach a fair size (see August, General Work).

Treat Vines according to Growth

The same remarks as those I made in last month's notes still apply with equal force (see August, General Work).

Ripen Growth in the Orchard House

Late peaches and nectarines may still be carrying fruits, in which case the treatment recommended in earlier months must still be carried out, but the main effort during September is likely to be directed towards the thorough ripening of growth. This means plenty of ventilation when possible without lowering the temperature too much (55 degs. should be the day minimum, and it is as well that the thermometer should not fall more than a further 5 degs. at night), the discontinuance of ordinary feeding, and a gradual diminution of water supply. If growth tends to be excessive, give a dressing of sulphate of potash at 1 ounce per square yard.

Ripen off Melons in Frames

Melons in the greenhouse are likely to be finished, or nearly so, by this time, but plants in frames should be ripening their fruits and the atmosphere must be kept dry. Do not syringe the leaves at all and reduce the water supply to the roots, giving only sufficient to keep the leaves from flagging. Stand each fruit on an inverted flower pot to expose it to the sun as much as possible, and cover the frames at night with sacks or mats.

Continue to Pick Apples and Pears

Keep a sharp eye on apples and pears and continue to pick them as soon as they are ripe. In the case of certain varieties of pear, such as Beurre Hardy, Jersey Gratioli, Dr. Jules Guyot, and Williams, it is even advisable to pick a little before they are ripe and to complete the ripening process in a dry, fairly warm shed or room.

Complete Planting of Strawberries

There is still time to plant rooted strawberry runners in their fruiting quarters, as I explained last month (see August, Third

Week), but the sooner the work is completed the better. If for some reason you cannot get it all done in September, leave the rest of the plants undisturbed until March (see March, First Week).

FIRST WEEK

Sow Hardy Annuals

A number of hardy annuals may be sown outdoors now to stand the winter and flower in May and June next year. Sow them thinly where they are to flower and cover lightly with soil. Thin the seedlings out to 3 or 4 inches apart as soon as they can be handled, but leave any further thinning until March or April. Amongst the best varieties for sowing in this manner are annual alyssum, calendula, candytuft, clarkia, annual coreopsis, cornflower, godetia, larkspur, nigella, Shirley and Cardinal poppies, annual scabious, and viscaria. Antirrhinums can also be sown now, but unless your garden is fairly sheltered, I advise you to make this sowing in a frame. Give free ventilation, but use the lights to protect the seedlings against frost.

Sow Annuals for the Greenhouse

As I have already explained (see March, First Week), many annuals make first-rate pot plants for the cool greenhouse. If sown now they will commence to flower in early spring and continue until May. Sow thinly in well-drained seed boxes or pans and germinate in a frame or unheated greenhouse. Shade until the seedlings appear, but subsequently giving them plenty of light and air.

Plant Anemones

Make a first planting of anemones of the St. Brigid and Du Caen types. If these are put in in successional batches, it is possible to extend the flowering season. The tubers should be planted 3 inches deep and 6 inches apart. If you wish you can also make a similar planting in a frame, as by this means you can get even earlier blooms—with a bit of luck by January. Place the lights in position, but ventilate moderately when the weather is mild.

Pot and Box Bulbs for Early Flowering

Lose no time in potting or boxing all the hyacinths, early tulips, narcissi (including early trumpet daffodils), ixias, gladioli of the Colvillei type, and bulbous-rooted irises, particularly I. tingitana, that you require for flowering in the greenhouse during the winter and spring. It is true that this work can be done at almost any time until the end of October, but there is no comparison between the results obtained from early and late potting. Also there is nothing to be gained by spreading the work over a long period. A succession of flowers can be obtained partly by choosing different varieties, some early and some late, and partly by keeping all the bulbs in cool quarters until they are needed and then bringing them into a warm greenhouse a few at a time. It does not much matter what size receptacles you use, but perhaps the best are pots 4 to 6 inches in diameter and boxes about 18 inches by 12 inches and 4 inches deep. Use a compost of loam three parts, moss peat one part, and sharp sand one part, and set the bulbs in this with a clear inch between them. Just cover them with the compost. Then stand all the pots and boxes outdoors in any fairly sheltered place, give them a good soaking, and cover all except ixias, gladioli, and irises with 3 inches of old sifted ashes, moss peat, coconut fibre, or sand. The object is to keep them cool, moist, and dark and so encourage the formation of plenty of roots before top growth starts. The bulbs must remain in this plunge bed for at least 8 weeks before they are brought into the greenhouse.

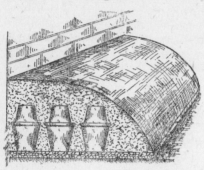

BULBS IN A PLUNGING BED.

In this case each pot of bulbs has been covered with an empty inverted pot, a plan which, though not essential, certainly makes for cleanliness.

Pot More Freesias

Make a further potting of freesia corms as described in the notes for August, First Week. If these are placed in a frame, and are protected from frost with lights but no attempt is made to force them, they can be introduced to the warm greenhouse a few at a time from November onwards and will supply a succession of flowers in winter and early spring.

Pot on Primulas and Calceolarias

There may be quite a lot of potting on to be done if growth during August has been fairly good. Greenhouse primulas from the April sowing (see April, Fourth Week) should be about ready for their final pots, 5 inches in diameter, while the June-sown primulas (see June, Third Week) are also likely to need potting singly into 3-inch pots. In both cases the compost already mentioned so many times (see page 62) should be used. After potting, the plants can go back into the frame for a few weeks, but will not need much shading now, and they must be ventilated more sparingly.

Greenhouse calceolarias which were given more space in August (see August, Second Week) must also be moved along before they get starved. They can now go into $3\frac{1}{2}$-inch pots, other particulars being the same as for the primulas.

Sow Cauliflowers

In a sheltered place make a small sowing of cauliflowers. Scatter the seed thinly, broadcast, and cover with $\frac{1}{2}$ inch of fine soil.

Make a Mushroom Bed under Cover

As I explained in the July notes (see July, First Week), mushrooms can be grown at any time of the year but are easier to manage at certain seasons. Just as July is the ideal time for making outdoor beds, so early September is the best for beds in frames, outhouses, etc. These beds will commence to crop about the middle of October, just as the outdoor mushrooms are coming to an end, and with a little care will continue well into the winter. The method of forming the beds is exactly the same as before, except that in the case of frames the whole area is covered with manure to a depth of 2 feet. Also it is particularly import-

SPAWNING A MUSHROOM BED.

Small pieces of the spawn are pushed into the bed of prepared manure.

231

ant to cover frame beds with an extra thick layer of straw. The frame lights may also be covered with thick mats or sacking, for mushrooms do best in the dark, and the extra covering will help to keep the bed at an even temperature.

SECOND WEEK

PRUNE RAMBLER ROSES

Most rambler roses will have finished flowering and may be pruned. If they have made a great deal of new growth, much of it from near ground level, you can cut out all the old canes that have just borne flowers, but if there is not much young wood you will have to keep the best of the old and simply remove that which is obviously worn out or diseased. In this latter case you must be careful to cut back all faded flower trusses, together with any hips they may be bearing. Weeping standard roses are pruned at the same time and in a similar manner. After pruning, train the long shoots round the umbrella-shaped training frames, which should be securely fastened to the stakes supporting the plants.

LIFT MAINCROP CARROTS

Lift the maincrop carrots sown in April (see April, Second Week). If they are left in the ground any longer the roots are liable to crack. Dig them up carefully with a fork, cut off the tops and store the roots in a heap in any shed, cellar, or other frost-proof place. They will keep better and be less likely to shrivel if they are covered with sand or sifted ashes.

LIFT MAINCROP BEETROOT

The main crop of long beetroot sown in May should also be lifted and stored at about this time (and, in any case, before the roots get old and coarse) as I described for early beet in the notes for August, Second Week.

FIX GREASE BANDS

Now is the time to fix grease bands around fruit trees. They are particularly serviceable on apples, but it is advisable to have them on all the bigger fruits just for safety. These grease bands

232

are actually strips of grease-proof paper tied round the trunk or main branches, and also any stakes, at least a couple of feet above ground level and covered with a tacky substance. You can buy both paper strips and tacky compound from your local dealer in horticultural sundries. Keep the bands sticky until next March. They will catch all manner of insects that try to crawl over them, and are particularly serviceable against the winter moth, March moth, and woolly aphis (American blight).

PRUNE LOGANBERRIES

By this time loganberries will have finished fruiting and they should be pruned as soon as possible. Simply cut out to the base of the plant all canes that have just borne fruit and train the young canes in their place.

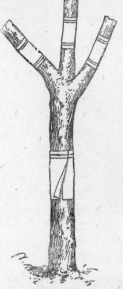

GREASE BANDS.

A double line of defence has been prepared on this tree. Any insects that crawl over the lower band will be caught on those further up the tree. The bottom strip of greaseproof paper has not yet been fully fixed and has been partially rolled back to make the illustrations more plain.

THIRD WEEK

COMMENCE TO PLANT EVERGREEN SHRUBS

From now until about the second week in October is usually the ideal time for planting hardy evergreen shrubs. Of course, you cannot do this work if the weather happens to be hot or the ground is dry, but neither condition is likely to continue for long at this time of the year. Plant very firmly and stake all big specimens at once. Later on, if winds are very cold and drying, erect temporary shelters of hurdles, evergreen boughs, or sacking strained between stakes to protect the shrubs, at any rate on north and east.

PLANT VIOLETS IN FRAMES

Violets that have been growing outdoors since April (see April, Second Week) should now be removed to frames for winter flowering. The frames must stand in a sunny and fairly sheltered

233

position and be filled with good loamy soil to within 8 inches of the glass. Plant the violet clumps almost touching one another. Water them in freely, but do not close the frames as yet. Later on, if frost threatens, put the lights on; but throughout the winter give the plants free ventilation whenever the weather is mild.

PLANT ROOTED CARNATION LAYERS

Carnation layers pegged down towards the end of July (see July, Third Week) should be well rooted by this time. Scrape away a little of the soil and see how things are. If there are plenty of fibrous roots around the cut area sever the layers from

the parent plants and, a few days later, lift them—each with a good ball of soil—and transfer them to their flowering quarters or, alternatively, pot them in 4- or 5-inch pots, place them in a frame, and plant them out in March (see March, Fourth Week). In either case the soil should be good and loamy, with a liberal addition of crushed mortar rubble and a sprinkling of bonemeal.

A CARNATION LAYER.
Roots have formed and the layer has been detached.

PRICK OFF SCHIZANTHUS

Schizanthus seedling month's sowing (see August, Third Week) will be in need of pricking off. This should be done at the earliest possible moment, because if there is one thing the schizanthus will not stand it is getting drawn up through overcrowding. Prick off the seedlings 2 inches apart each way into deep, well-drained seed trays filled with the same compost as that used for seed sowing.

PICK ALL TOMATOES

Outdoor tomatoes are not likely to ripen any more on the plants now, so it is as well to pick all the fruits that are showing some trace of colour and stand them in a sunny window to ripen. Absolutely green fruits can be made into tomato chutney. The summer crop of tomatoes under glass will also be coming to an end and, in view of the fact that every inch of greenhouse space is likely to be required in the next few weeks, it will be as well to clear these also, treating them in the same way as the outdoor fruits.

Lift Potatoes for Storing

The exact date at which maincrop and late potatoes should be fit for storing cannot be decided entirely by the calendar as it depends to some extent upon disease and also the weather. If much disease appears, it is wise to lift the tubers at once, before they get badly affected. Similarly, if August is very dry at first and then wet later tubers may begin to make second growth and must be lifted before they have dissipated themselves in a multiplicity of small potatoes. But, given average weather and freedom from disease, lifting commonly becomes general about this time. There is no necessity to wait until haulm dies down if the tubers are a good size and the skin holds really firmly to them. You can easily satisfy yourself on these two points by lifting a sample root. If you decide to lift the whole crop, put aside any damaged tubers for immediate use and store the rest in a frost-proof shed or cellar. An alternative is to make a clamp in the open. This is done by placing a layer of dry straw on the ground, heaping the potatoes on it in a steep-sided bank, covering with more straw and then a good coating of soil beaten down with the back of a spade. It is a wise precaution to draw a few wisps of straw through the soil at intervals along the ridge to allow warm, damp air to escape.

Thin out Vegetable Seedlings

Spinach beet, winter spinach, lettuce, and endive, from the sowings made last month (see August, Third Week and General Work), will need thinning out. Leave the plants of spinach beet about 15 inches apart and the spinach itself about 4 inches apart. The lettuces should be from 8 to 12 inches apart, according to variety, and the endive 12 inches apart. The seedlings of endive and lettuce can be transplanted carefully, either to a very sheltered border or, better still, to a frame. Water them in freely and they will provide a succession to those plants left undisturbed. An alternative method with endive is to thin out the plants now to about 4 inches apart and then lift the bigger plants at the end of October and transfer to a frame. They stand transplanting much better than lettuce, and by means of this late shifting one can

235

sometimes make use of a frame that is filled with cucumbers or melons at the moment.

Prick out Red Cabbage

If you sowed pickling cabbage last month, prick out the seedlings now, 6 inches apart each way, in any fairly sheltered place. The plants will remain in this nursery bed until March, when they should go into their final quarters.

FOURTH WEEK

Pot Cyclamen Seedlings

Cyclamen seedlings from the sowing made in August (see August, Second Week) should be ready for pricking off or potting. Often the seed germinates very irregularly, so, if some of the seedlings are too backward for potting at the moment, leave them in the seed pans, lifting the more forward ones with a sharpened wooden tally. The ideal time for potting is when the seedlings have two or three leaves each. Pot singly in 2-inch pots, using the compost described on page 62. Keep the tiny corms well up on the surface of the soil. After potting, stand the pots on a shelf or staging in the greenhouse, giving them a good light place but shading them for a while from any very strong direct sunshine. Maintain an average day temperature of 55 degs. and 45 degs. at night. Similar remarks apply if you decide to prick off in boxes instead of potting singly.

House Late-flowering Chrysanthemums

It is wise to bring all chrysanthemums that are to flower in the greenhouse into its protection now before frost damages their tender buds. Pot plants should be carried in and set on a hard bottom of ashes or gravel, or be arranged on staging, while plants that have been grown outdoors for lifting (see May, Fourth Week) must be dug up with as much soil as possible and either be planted in the greenhouse borders or else be dropped into suitable boxes and tubs. In all cases give the plants sufficient room for air to circulate between them and light reach their leaves, otherwise you are certain to have trouble with mildew. Ventilate very freely while the weather is mild, but at any threat of frost close the house early in the afternoon and even use a little artificial heat if necessary.

SHELTER TENDER PLANTS

It will also be necessary to give some shelter to all tender greenhouse plants that have been outdoors during the summer months. This includes pelargoniums of various kinds (not forgetting the cuttings that have been rooted in pots), marguerites, perennial mesembryanthemums, fuchsias, double tropæolums, hydrangeas, heliotropes, Indian azaleas, camellias, genistas, arum lilies, and agapanthus (blue Kaffir lily). Any of these that have been used for summer bedding should also be lifted and potted if you wish to save them for another year. Scarlet salvias may be treated in the same way, unless you intend to raise new plants annually from seed, and similar remarks apply to any particularly choice forms of bedding lobelia or ageratum which you wish to raise from cuttings in the spring. The blue Salvia patens, also dahlias and begonias used for bedding may be left outdoors until frost first blackens their foliage. If you have not room for the other bedding plants as they are, you can cut back growth severely so that they do not take up so much space.

A good frame will provide sufficient protection for all these plants for a while if you cover the lights with sacks on frosty nights, but by the end of October it will be safer to have most of them inside the greenhouse, where you can use a little artificial heat to exclude frost.

Perpetual-flowering carnations that have been stood out for the summer should also be brought into shelter before they are injured by frost. Stand them in a light greenhouse with plenty of ventilation and just enough artificial heat to keep out frost and prevent the atmosphere from getting damp and stagnant.

TRANSPLANT PARSLEY TO FRAME

Lift some of the parsley seedlings from the July sowing (see July, Fourth Week) and transplant them carefully into a frame filled with good soil with which you have mixed some leaf-mould and a little old manure. Set the plants about 6 inches apart each way and water them in freely. They will provide a crop throughout the winter if you use the lights just for frost protection.

YOUR GARDEN WEEK BY WEEK

alpina, L. *pallida,* Lippia *repens,* Lithospermum *prostratum and vars.,* Nertera *depressa (fruits),* Œnothera *cæspitosa,* Œ. *missouriensis,* Œ. *riparia,* Œ. *taraxacifolia,* Origanum *Dictamnus,* Pentstemon *heterophyllus,* Polygonum *affine,* P. *vaccinifolium,* Potentilla *ambigua,* P. *fragiformis,* P. *nepalensis and vars.,* P. *Tonguei,* Pyrola *rotundifolia,* Scabiosa *graminifolia,* S. *pterocephala,* Sedum *Ewersii homophyllum,* S. *Sieboldii,* Silene *Schafta,* Solidago *brachystachys,* S. *Buckleyi,* Spiræa *digitata nana,* Statice *minuta,* Talinum *calycinum,* Tunica *Saxifraga,* Verbena *chamædryfolia,* Viola *canadensis,* V. *cornuta and vars.,* Zauschneria *californica.*

HARDY AQUATICS AND BOG PLANTS.—Gentiana *Pneumonanthe,* Kirengeshoma *palmata,* Lythrum *Salicaria and vars.,* mimulus *(as July),* Phragmites *communis,* Parnassia *palustris,* Sagittaria *sagittifolia and vars.,* Polygonum *Cookii,* P. *sachalinense,* Senecio *Clivorum,* Stenanthium *robustum,* Typha *angustifolia,* T. *japonica,* T. *latifolia (reed mace).*

ANNUALS.—Hardy vars. *(as June, but sown in May),* half-hardy vars. *(as July).*

BEDDING PLANTS.—*As July.*

HARDY EVERGREEN SHRUBS.—Abelia *grandiflora (shelter),* Aplopappus *ericoides (shelter),* Berberis *stenophylla semperflorens,* Bigelowia *graveolens,* Buddleia *auriculata,* Bupleurum *fruticosum (seaside),* Ceanothus *Burkwoodii,* Daboecia *polifolia,* Erica *ciliaris and vars.,* E. *cinerea and vars.,* E. *Mackayi,* E. *stricta,* E. *Stuartii,* E. *Tetralix and vars.,* E. *vagans and vars.,* E. *Watsoni,* Escallonia *exoniensis,* E. *Iveyi,* E. *floribunda (shelter),* E. *montevidensis,* E. *rubra,* escallonia hybrids, Hypericum *calycinum,* H. *galioides,* H. *Moserianum,* Osmanthus *Aquifolium,* O. *Fortunei,* Parasyringa *sempervirens,* Phormium *Colensoi,* P. *tenax,* Rhododendron *serotinum,* Teucrium *fruticans,* Ulex *Gallii,* U. *nanus,* Vaccinium *ovatum,* Veronica *angustifolia,* V. *salicifolia,* V. *speciosa and vars.,* Viburnum *coriaceum,* Vinca *major,* V. *minor,* Yucca *gloriosa,* Y. *recurvifolia.*

HARDY DECIDUOUS SHRUBS.—Abelia *chinensis,* A. *Schumannii,* Amorpha *canescens,* Buddleia *paniculata,* B. *variabilis and vars.,* Calycanthus *occidentalis,* Caryopteris *Mastacanthus,* Cassia *marylandica,* Ceanothus *azureus and hybrids,* Ceratostigma *Willmottianum,* Clerodendron *Fargesii,* C. *trichotomum,* Clethra *alnifolia,* Colletia *armata,* C. *cruciata,* Colquhounia *coccinea,* Coluta *arborescens,* C. *orientalis,* Cyrilla *racemiflora,* Desfontainea *spinosa (shelter),* Desmodium *spicatum,* Fuchsia *macrostemma and vars.,* F. *Riccartonii,* Hedysarum *multijugum,* Hibiscus *syriacus and vars.,* Hydrangea *arborescens grandiflora,* H. *hortensis and vars.,* H. *paniculata grandiflora,* Hypericum *hircinum,* H. *Hookerianum,* H. *patulum and vars.,* Indigofera *amblyantha,* I. *Dielsiana,* I. *Gerardiana,* I. *hebepetala,* I. *pendula,* Itea *virginica,* Leptodermis *oblonga,* Leycesteria *formosa,* Oxydendron *arboreum,* Perowskia *atriplicifolia,* Polygonum *vaccinifolium,* Potentilla *fruticosa and vars.,* Rubus *thyrsoideus plenus,* R. *ulmifolius bellidiflorus,* Spartium *junceum,* Spiræa *Menziesii and vars.,* Tamarix *pentandra,* Tripetaleia *bracteata,* Vitex *Agnus-castus (shelter).*

HARDY EVERGREEN TREES.—Arbutus Unedo *(strawberry tree),* Magnolia *grandiflora and vars.*

HARDY DECIDUOUS TREES.—Alnus *maritima,* A. *nepalensis,* A. *nitida,* Aralia *chinensis,* Laburnum *alpinum autumnale,* L. *caramanicum,* L. *vulgare semperflorens,* Lagerstrœmia *indica,* Sophora *japonica.*

240

1, 2 and 3. Cutting back and potting a bedding geranium before there is danger of frost. 4. Potting hyacinths for forcing. The bulbs will be just covered with soil. 5. A crop of mushrooms in a frame. Note the thick covering of straw to exclude light and keep the bed at an even temperature. 6. Violets planted in a frame for winter flowering. 7. Greasebands around a standard fruit tree.

1. Lifting a dahlia root after the leaves have been blackened by frost.
2. Boxing border chrysanthemum roots at the end of the season. 3. Young cauliflowers pricked out in a frame for the winter. 4. Schizanthus seedlings after their first potting. The plant on the left has been pinched to encourage branching. 5. Gladioli lifted and ready for drying off.

HARDY CLIMBING PLANTS.—Berberidopsis *corallina* (*shelter*), Clematis *æthusifolia*, C. *calycina*, C. *coccinea*, C. *connata*, C. *Durandii and vars.*, C. *flammula*, C. *Hendersonii*, C. *Jackmannii and vars.*, C. *Jouiniana*, C. *lanuginosa and vars.*, C. *orientalis*, C. *paniculata*, C. *Pitcheri*, C. *Rehderiana*, C. *tangutica*, C. *viticella and vars.*, Jasminum *officinale* (*jessamine*), Lonicera *alseuosmoides*, L. *Brownii*, L. *etrusca*, L. *Heckrottii*, L. *japonica and vars.*, L. *periclymenum serotina* (*late Dutch honeysuckle*), L. *tragophylla*, Pilostegia *viburnoides*, Polygonum *baldschuanicum*, Rosa *bracteata and hybrids*, hybrid roses (*climbing teas, hybrid teas and pernetianas, and hybrid musks*), Solanum *crispum autumnalis*, S. *jasminoides*, Tecoma *grandiflora Thunbergi*, T. *radicans*, Tropæolum *speciosum*.

FRUITING TREES, SHRUBS, AND CLIMBERS.—Berberis *acuminata*, B. *Aquifolium*, B. *aristata*, B. *brevipaniculata*, B. *concinna*, B. *Darwinii*, B. *dictyophylla*, B. *Gagnepainii*, B. *Hookeri*, B. *Lycium*, B. *polyantha*, B. *Prattii*, B. *pruinosa*, B. *rubrostilla*, B. *Sieboldii*, B. *sinensis*, B. *Thunbergi*, B. *vulgaris*, B. *Wilsonæ*, B. *yunnanensis*, Coriaria *japonica*, C. *terminalis*, Cotoneaster *adpressa*, C. *amœna*, C. *bullata*, C. *buxifolia*, C. *congesta*, C. *Dielsiana*, C. *divaricata*, C. *Francheti*, C. *frigida*, C. *Henryana*, C. *horizontalis*, C. *humifusa*, C. *lucida*, C. *microphylla*, C. *rotundifolia*, C. *salicifolia and vars.*, C. *Simonsii*, C. *thymæfolia*, Cratægus *altaica*, C. *aprica*, C. *brachyacantha*, C. *Carrierei*, C. *coccinea*, C. *cordata*, C. *Crusgalli*, C. *durobrivensis*, C. *heterophylla*, C. *Korolkowi*, C. *macrantha*, C. *mollis*, C. *monogyna* (*hawthorn*), C. *orientalis*, C. *oxyacantha* (*hawthorn*), C. *prunifolia*, C. *punctata*, Euonymus *alatus*, E. *europæus* (*spindle-berry*), E. *latifolius*, Hippophæ *rhamnoides* (*unisexual*), Lycium *chinense and vars.*, Pernettya *mucronata*, Pyracantha *angustifolia*, P. *coccinea and vars.*, P. *Gibbsii*, P. *Rogersiana*, Pyrus *alnifolia*, P. *Aria* (*whitebeam*), P. *Aucuparia* (*mountain ash*), P. *baccata* (*Siberian crab*), P. *Eleyi*, P. *Malus vars.* (*crab apple*), P. *munda*, P. *Niedzwetzkyana*, P. *prunifolia*, P. *ringo*, P. *toringoides*, P. *Vilmorini*, Rhaphithamnus *cyanocarpus*, Rosa *alpina*, R. *altaica*, R. *Fargesii*, R. *macrophylla*, R. *microphylla*, R. *Moyesii*, R. *nutkana*, R. *omeiensis*, R. *pomifera*, R. *rugosa and hybrids*, R. *setipoda*, R. *Soulieana*, R. *tomentosa*, R. *Webbiana*, Sambucus *glauca*, S. *nigra and vars.* (*elderberry*), S. *pubens*, Skimmia *Fortunei*, S. *japonica* (*unisexual*), Viburnum *betulifolium*, V. *Davidii*, V. *Henryi*, V. *Lantana* (*wayfaring tree*), V. *molle*, V. *Opulus* (*guelder rose*), V. *prunifolium*, V. *rhytidophyllum*, Vitis *heterophylla*, V. *vinifera purpurea*.

GREENHOUSE PLANTS.—Achimenes, Agapanthus *umbellatus*, Asclepias *curassavica*, begonias (*tuberous-rooted*), Bignonia *venusta*, bougainvilleas, bouvardias, Browallia *speciosa major* (*sown March*), Campanula *isophylla*, C. *pyramidalis*, cannas, carnations (*perpetual-flowering*), Cassia *corymbosa*, celsias, Cobæa *scandens*, daturas, Erica *insignis*, Francoa *ramosa*, fuchsias, gloxinias, heliotropes, Hibbertia *dentata*, Humea *elegans*, Lagerstrœmia *indica*, lantanas, Lilium *longiflorum*, L. *speciosum and vars.*, Luculia *gratissima*, marguerites, Maurandya *Barclayana*, nerines, Oxalis *variabilis*, petunias, Saintpaulia *ionantha*, streptocarpus, Trachelium *cæruleum*, Vallota *purpurea*.

VEGETABLES IN STORE.—Beetroot, onions, shallots.

VEGETABLES OUTDOORS.—Globe artichokes, French beans, runner beans, beetroot, broccoli, cabbage (*sown April*), carrots, cauliflowers, celeriac, celery, ridge cucumbers, endive, kohl-rabi, leeks, lettuce, vegetable marrows, mushrooms, mustard and cress, parsnips, peas, potatoes, radishes, spinach, tomatoes, turnips.

VEGETABLES UNDER GLASS.—Cucumbers, mushrooms (*cool cellars and out-houses*).

FRUITS OUTDOORS.—Apples: *Devonshire Quarrendon (D), Ecklinville Seedling (C), Epicure (D), Exquisite (D), Fortune (D), Gascoyne's Scarlet (D), Golden Spire (C), Grenadier (C), James Grieve (D), Keswick Codlin (C), Lady Sudeley (D), Langley Pippin (D), Lord Grosvenor (C), Lord Suffield (C), Maidstone Favourite (D), Peasgood's Nonsuch (CD), St. Edmund's Russet (D), St. Everard (CD), Stirling Castle (C), Thomas Rivers (C), Worcester Pearmain (D).* Apricots: *Breda, Hemskirk.* Black-berries: *Himalaya Giant, John Innes, Parsley-leaved.* Cherries: *Morello (C) (north wall).* Currants, black: *Baldwin, Daniel's September.* Figs. Grapes: *Brant, Early Black July, Miller's Burgundy, Royal Muscadine, Reine Olga.* Melons. Nectarines: *Early Rivers, John Rivers, Lord Napier.* Peaches: *Hale's Early, Peregrine.* Pears: *Beurré d'Amanlis (D), Clapp's Favourite (D), Colmar d'Été (D), Directeur Hardy (D), Docteur Jules Guyot (D), Fertility (D), Magnate (D), Marguerite Marillat (D), Marquis (D), Michaelmas (D), Souvenir de Congrès (D), Triomphe de Vienne (D), Williams' Bon Chrétien (D).* Plums: *Belle de Louvain (C), Bradley's King (Damson) (CD), Bryanston Gage (D), Coe's Golden Drop (D), Comte d'Althan's Gage (D), Cox's Emperor (CD), Cropper (CD), Damascene (CD), Diamond (C), Farleigh's Prolific Damson (Cluster or Crittenden), Giant Prune (C), Goldfinch (D), Green Gage (D), Jefferson's Gage (D), Kirke's Blue (D), Late Transparent Gage (D), Merryweather (Damson), Monarch (CD), Pond's Seedling (C), Reine Claude de Bavay Gage (D), Shropshire Prune Damson (CD), Victoria (CD), White Bullace (CD), White Magnum Bonum (D).* Raspberries: *Hailsham, Lloyd George, October Yellow, October Red, November Abundance.*

FRUITS UNDER GLASS.—Apricots: *Grosse Pêche, Moorpark.* Figs. Grapes: *Black Hamburg, Black Prince, Foster's Seedling, Madresfield Court, Royal Muscadine.* Melons. Nectarines: *Darwin, Newton, Pine Apple, Rivers' Orange, Stanwick Elruge, Spenser, Victoria.* Peaches: *Alexandra Noblesse, Barrington, Bellegarde, Dymond, Gladstone, Goshawk, Grosse Mignonne, Lady Palmerston, Late Devonian, Prince of Wales, Princess of Wales, Royal George, Sea Eagle, Salwey, Stirling Castle, Thomas Rivers, Violette Hâtive, Walburton Admirable.*

OCTOBER

GENERAL WORK

USE SLOW-ACTING FERTILISERS

OCTOBER is a good month during which to use such slow-acting fertilisers as basic slag, bonemeal, and kainit. The first supplies phosphates and lime, the second mainly phosphates, and the third mainly potash. Most fruit trees will benefit from a top-dressing of basic slag and kainit applied now, the former at 6 and the latter at 3 ounces per square yard. The herbaceous border may have bonemeal at 4 ounces per square yard, and this will also do a lot of good to bulb beds and to bulbs that are naturalised in grass. Lime can also be applied now. All parts of the vegetable garden can do with a dose every third or fourth year, unless the ground happens to be naturally impregnated with lime or chalk. Use about ½ pound per square yard of hydrated (air-slaked) lime. On light sandy soils ground chalk is really better, but must be given more freely—about 2 pounds per square yard. In all cases the fertilisers or lime need only be scattered over the ground. Rain will wash them in, and if the ground is to be dug or forked later on this will further incorporate them with the soil.

GATHER FALLEN LEAVES, ETC.

Be careful to sweep up all fallen leaves from time to time during the month. They are a particular source of danger in the rock garden, for if they lie thickly upon the plants they may kill them. All healthy leaves can be built up into a heap in some out-of-the-way corner and left to rot. Similar remarks also apply to any other soft refuse—old pea and potato haulm for example, and the tops of carrots, beetroots, etc. But if there has been any disease in the plants from which leaves or refuse have come, do not keep them in this way but burn them without delay.

TURF AND REPAIR LAWNS

This is an excellent time to lay new lawns from turf or to repair worn patches in old ones. Cut out the turf from the worn places with an edging tool and lift with a sharp spade or special turf-lifting tool, making all sides straight. It is a well-nigh impossible task to fit a patch neatly into a curved hole. When laying a number of turves side by side, stagger them like the bricks in a wall so that all the joints do not come together in both directions. This will give a better " bind " until such time as the turves have rooted into their new quarters (see March, General Work, for further particulars).

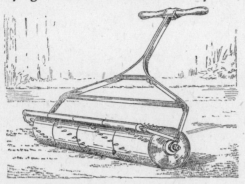

A SPIKED ROLLER FOR THE LAWN.

The purpose of this is to perforate hard turf and so let in air and permit dressings of sharp sand and peat to penetrate.

If your lawn has been used a lot for games during the summer, it will also benefit from a thorough aeration, either with a spiked roller or a fork thrust in at frequent intervals. Then mowing will not be necessary anything like so frequently from early October onwards. An occasional raking with a spring-toothed grass rake will remove moss, and you should also use a birch broom frequently to distribute worm casts. If these are allowed to lie on the grass, they will kill it in small patches.

PREPARE ROSE BEDS, FRUIT SITES, ETC.

You should get all new rose beds, also the site for new fruit trees and deciduous trees and shrubs of all kinds, prepared as early in October as possible. The ideal time for planting all these things is in November (see November, General Work), and it is all to the good if the ground can have a few weeks in which to settle between digging and planting. Dig the ground at least 2 feet deep, and, unless it is already very rich, work in plenty of well-rotted animal manure or decayed vegetable refuse in the second spit, but keep it away from the surface for it will do no good to freshly planted roots. Finish off with a surface dusting of basic slag at the rate of 6 ounces per square yard. This is most useful, for it sweetens the soil and also adds phosphates to it. If you can also dig or trench any other vacant ground during October so much the better, for, though this work can be done at any time

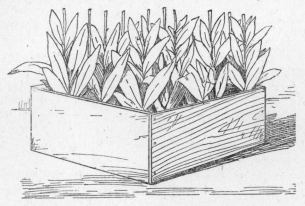

A Box of Canna Roots.

These plants were lifted before their growth had been killed by frost, so they have been placed in a box to ripen off.

during the autumn or winter when the ground is not very sticky, considerable advantage is gained by early soil cultivation. Leave the surface quite rough so that a large area is exposed to the weather.

Lift Begonias, Dahlias, etc.

Begonias, dahlias, cannas, and Salvia patens that have been growing out of doors during the summer months must be removed to a frost-proof store just as soon as their foliage is blackened by frost. Precisely when this will happen no one can say. Very often it is early in October, but there have been seasons when these plants have continued unharmed until November. So keep a sharp look-out and be ready to dig

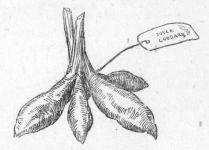

A Dahlia Root.

Lifted, shaken free of soil, clearly labelled, and ready for storing.

245

the tubers up as soon as frost puts a stop to their display. Cut off the dead growth just above the tubers and store the latter in trays and boxes according to their size. It is a good plan to pack them round with dry moss peat or coconut fibre, as this is a protection and keeps them from drying out too much. Do not water at all, but place the boxes in any dry, fairly cool, but frost-proof place. A good outhouse will do well—or a cupboard, so long as it is not alongside a fireplace.

Plant Spring Bedding

As soon as you are able to clear beds of their temporary summer occupants, such as geraniums, marguerites, scarlet salvias, begonias, dahlias, etc. (see September, Fourth Week, and also notes on begonias, dahlias, etc., above), and have cleared out all annuals that have finished flowering, lose no time in planting the spring occupants of the beds. These may include wallflowers, Cheiranthus Allioni, forget-me-nots, double daisies, polyanthuses, and coloured primroses, together with various bulbs, particularly tulips and hyacinths. May-flowering tulips can be planted together with forget-me-nots or wallflowers, but the early-flowering tulips and hyacinths are not sufficiently tall to stand above these and so, if you wish to have a groundwork beneath them, use double daisies, arabis, or aubrietias. Wallflowers and cheiranthuses should be planted from 9 to 12 inches apart, according to the size of the plants; forget-me-nots, double daisies, polyanthuses, etc., 6 to 8 inches apart. I have given distances for bulbs by themselves on pages 223, 22, and 255, but if they are planted with a groundwork of other plants they may be spaced out more: 12 to 15 inches apart will be a good average. The only preparation that the ground will need is a dressing of hop manure at the rate of a double handful per square yard, well forked in, and a top-dressing of bonemeal at 4 ounces per square yard.

Plant Herbaceous Perennials

On light, well-drained soils, October is quite a good month for planting most herbaceous perennials, but it is better to do the work in spring (see March, General Work) on all heavy or wet soils. Details of planting are exactly the same in either case. Perennials and biennials raised from seed in June (see June, First Week) may also be planted now.

INSERT HARD-WOODED CUTTINGS

Many shrubby plants, both ornamental and useful, including gooseberries, currants, and rambler roses, can be increased at this time of the year by means of what the gardener calls "hard-wooded cuttings." These differ from summer cuttings (see July, General Work) in being prepared from much riper and firmer wood. Select shoots of the current year's growth from 6 inches to 1 foot in length according to the nature of the plant. They can either be cut immediately below a joint, exactly like the summer cuttings, or else may be pulled off the parent plant with a thin strip of older wood (gardeners call these heel cuttings, but most amateurs refer to them as slips). If you adopt the latter method, and it is a good one, trim off the thin piece of bark close to the knob of wood at the base of the cutting (actually what the gardener means by "heel"). In the case of gooseberries, nick out all the lower growth buds to prevent sucker shoots from being formed below the soil. Insert the cuttings to a depth of 3 or 4 inches in sandy soil, in a sheltered place outdoors. These hard-wooded cuttings root slowly and will not be ready for removal to their permanent quarters until the following autumn.

HARD-WOODED CUTTINGS.

The long black line indicates soil level when the cuttings are correctly inserted, while the short lines show where the cuttings should be trimmed. Buds are left below ground level (left) if sucker shoots are not a disadvantage, but in many cases it is better to remove these lower buds (right).

GENERAL GREENHOUSE MANAGEMENT

Nights are now likely to be sufficiently cold to necessitate the use of artificial heat for the majority of favourite greenhouse plants. The ideal temperatures to be aimed at are about 55 degs. by day, rising to 65 or 70 with direct sun heat and never falling below 45 degs. even on the chilliest nights. Damping down and syringing are not likely to be needed, except for hothouse plants in temperatures over 65 degs. Supply water to plants in growth in sufficient quantity to keep the soil moist right through, but avoid splashing unnecessarily and be careful to keep water off the leaves and crowns of primulas. Air should be admitted through top ventilators rather than those at the side, and it is unlikely that any ventilation will be needed at night for most of the plants. Chrysanthemums, however, must be kept as hardy as possible or they may contract mildew. If this disease does appear, dust the leaves with flowers of sulphur, space the plants out as much as possible to let in light and air, and use a little artificial heat to dry the atmosphere—but in normal seasons it is inadvisable to use the heating apparatus regularly for chrysanthemums until the end of the month.

Rest Begonias, Gloxinias, etc.

Tuberous-rooted begonias, gloxinias, achimenes, and hippeastrums will be more than ever going to rest and can be finally dried off during this month, after which the begonias may be shaken out of their soil and stored in dry coconut fibre or peat moss. Gloxinias are sometimes treated in the same way, but are really better in the soil in which they have been growing. Tap the dry balls of compost out of the pots, heap them together, and cover them with sacks. Of course, both these and the begonias must be in a dry, frostproof place, but a high temperature is not desirable. Something around 50 degs. is ideal.

Hippeastrums are allowed to get dry in their pots, after which they can be stood in any out-of-the-way place—piled up on their sides if that is more convenient. Similar remarks apply to cannas which are grown in pots.

Vallotas are never dried off to quite this extent, but their water supply is greatly reduced during the winter. It is quite sufficient to keep the soil just slightly moist. Reduce the temperature to about 45 degs. if possible. Similar remarks apply to clivias. This is a good time to purchase and pot new bulbs of both these plants. Use the ordinary potting compost and the smallest pots that will hold the bulbs comfortably.

Pot Hardy Plants for the Greenhouse

Several hardy perennial plants commonly grown out of doors also make good pot plants for the greenhouse. They include herbaceous astilbes in a great number of varieties, Solomon's Seal and Dielytra spectabilis. Pot these now in the smallest pots that will accommodate the roots and then stand them in a frame or plunge them in ashes or sand in a sheltered place outdoors until you need them. They can be brought into the greenhouse in successive batches from January onwards, and if kept in a temperature of about 60 degs. will grow rapidly and soon come into flower.

Disbud Perpetual-flowering Carnations

Young plants of perpetual-flowering carnations rooted as cuttings in the winter should now be forming flower buds, and to get the best results these must be thinned out. Leave only the central terminal bud on each flower stem and remove all others at as early a stage of development as possible. See that the long, slender stems are properly staked. There is nothing better for this purpose than the circular galvanised wire supports made specially for the purpose.

Protect Cauliflowers

The white hearts (curds) of cauliflowers are liable to be damaged by frost, so look over the bed occasionally and bend some of the outer leaves over any hearts that are forming. This will give them all the protection they need.

Continue to Blanch Endive

Similar instructions to those given in my August and September General notes still apply.

Ripen Growth in Orchard House and Vinery

Your aim should still be to ripen any soft green growth that remains on peaches, nectarines, and apricots in the orchard house. Keep the air as dry as possible by free ventilation and, if possible, the occasional use of artificial heat if the air outside is very damp and stagnant; do not syringe at all unless red spider is still about, and maintain a temperature of 45 to 50 degs.

Similar remarks apply to vines. In the case of late vines that are still carrying bunches it is a good plan to remove some of the foliage so that berries are exposed to the light and relieved from the danger of drips of water falling from the leaves.

249

FIRST WEEK

PROTECT OUTDOOOR CHRYSANTHEMUMS

If any of the early-flowering border chrysanthemums are still flowering well, it will be advisable to rig up some kind of temporary shelter over them. Quite an effective method is to drive a few stout stakes, about 5 feet in length, into the bed at convenient points, join them across the top with a few horizontal

A TEMPORARY SHELTER FOR OUTDOOR CHRYSANTHEMUMS.
Strips of canvas are stretched over a light wooden framework when frost threatens.

bars nailed or tied in position, and then throw some sacking over them on frosty nights, making it secure at the corners with string. It does not take much to keep off the light frosts that are quite capable of ruining all the chrysanthemum flowers and buds.

POT ON CINERARIAS AND STOCKS

Cinerarias sown during the third week in June are likely to be in need of a shift into roomier quarters. Give them 5-inch pots and the same compost as before, but rather coarser in texture.

250

You can still keep them in a frame for a few weeks if you are very careful to close it up early in the afternoon and cover with sacks on cold nights, but they will soon have to go into the greenhouse.

Precisely similar remarks apply to stocks intended for winter flowering (see August, First Week).

Pot a Last Batch of Freesias

This is the time to make a last potting of freesias to flower in the spring. Details are as before (see August, First Week), except that now you will have to use the lights considerably more, especially at night, for there will be danger of frost.

Bring Early Arums, Freesias, and Lachenalias into the Greenhouse

If you want to have some arums to cut for Christmas, you must bring a batch of plants into the greenhouse now. Arrange them in a light place not too far removed from the glass and maintain a night temperature of 55 degs., rising about 10 degs. by day. Water freely.

You may also bring in the first batch of freesias (see August, First Week). Arrange them on the staging and maintain a temperature 5 degs. or so lower than for the arums. Lachenalias in pots and boxes (see August, First Week) may also be brought into the greenhouse now. There is no need to hurry them at all unless you want early flowers. Any temperature above freezing point will serve for them.

Plant Spring Cabbage

Plant as many as possible of the spring cabbages from the August sowing (see August, Second Week). Any seedlings that remain in the seed beds after the middle of the month are best left undisturbed until February (see February, Second Week).

Complete Earthing up of Late Celery and Leeks

Complete all earthing up of celery as soon as possible. I have already given full particulars in the notes for July, Second Week, and August, Fourth Week. Sometimes rust appears on the leaves at this time of the year. Prompt removal of affected plants, followed by immediate spraying with Bordeaux mixture, will check it.

251

Leeks should also be earthed up for the last time. The longer the length of fully blanched stem obtained, the better.

SECOND WEEK

Sow Sweet Peas

The best exhibition sweet peas are obtained from sowings made at this time of the year. Some growers sow outdoors where the plants are to bloom, but a far better method in most districts is to sow in pots—about five seeds in a 3-inch pot—and to germinate them in an unheated frame. Once the seedlings are up they can be ventilated very freely—indeed, the lights will only be needed in very frosty or windy weather. The great advantage of this method is that the seedlings are much more under control and can be protected from excessive cold or wet if necessary.

Prick off Cauliflowers

Cauliflowers sown last month (see September, First Week) must now be transferred to a frame. Prepare a bed of finely broken soil in this and dibble the seedlings straight into it 3 inches apart each way. Ventilate freely and only use the lights when there is danger of frost.

Gather all Remaining Apples and Pears

At this time it is wise to complete the gathering of all apples and pears. It is not advisable to let them hang once the weather gets really wintry. Bring all into store. Apples keep very well if carefully packed in boxes deep enough to hold three or four layers. These should be stood in a cool but frostproof place preferably with a slightly moist atmosphere. A shed with an earthen floor is ideal, because there is usually a little moisture arising from the floor. Pears, however, keep more satisfactorily in a rather dry atmosphere; indeed, with them it is really a slow ripening process rather than keeping. Lay them out thinly in a room or cellar with an average temperature of about 50 degs. Never pile them one on top of the other.

THIRD WEEK

Lift Gladioli and Montbretias

All gladioli corms will be better out of the ground now. Dig them up carefully with a fork, shake the soil from the roots, tie them up in small bundles by their stems, and hang them up to dry in any frostproof place. They will do well enough in a shed or garage so long as you can keep frost out. Later on, when the foliage has withered up, you should cut it off just above the

A GLADIOLUS PLANT AS LIFTED.

*Only the tops have been trimmed off. The old, withered corm still adheres
to the bases of the two new corms formed during the summer.*

corms and place the latter in shallow boxes, in which they can be stored under the same conditions as before. Remove any small corms and keep these for growing on in a reserve bed. They may not flower next year, but they can be fattened up for the following season. Tiny cormels (spawn) can also be kept and grown on, but this is more of a specialist's job, and is only worth the candle with new and expensive kinds. Pull off and throw away the old, shrivelled corms that adhere to the bottoms of the new ones.

Choice montbretias are also better out of the ground for the

253

winter, but there is no need to move the old common kinds, for these are hardy enough to look after themselves. Some people store the choice varieties exactly like gladioli, but I prefer to replant them, close together, in a frame and keep them nearly but not quite dry until early March, when they can be started into growth once more. The lights can be kept on most of the time, but it is a good plan to remove them occasionally for a few hours on mild days, just to give the frame an airing.

A GLADIOLUS CORM AFTER CLEANING.

The old corm has been broken away, leaving a clean scar.

STOP FEEDING CHRYSANTHEMUMS

It is rarely wise to continue the feeding of exhibition chrysanthemums after this date. Experience proves that, if feeding is carried on too long, buds tend to decay in the centre. From now on supply with plain water only.

LIFT AND STORE TURNIPS

Lift a good supply of turnips of reasonable size and store them in a frostproof place for the winter. They will keep quite well in a heap in any dry shed or outhouse, but are all the better for a light covering of dry sand or ashes. Cut off the tops first. If you leave some of the roots in the ground, they will supply a useful crop of turnip tops in late winter and spring.

CUT BACK ASPARAGUS AND GLOBE ARTICHOKES

The growth of asparagus will have turned yellow and the sooner it is removed the better. Do this with a pair of garden shears and cut off all the tops close to the soil. All rubbish should then be raked together and burned.

The yellowing leaves and stems of globe artichokes should also be cut down. Then fork between the plants lightly and cover the crowns with some sharp dry ashes or a thin layer of leaves as a protection against frost.

FOURTH WEEK

Plant Tulips and Hyacinths

Unlike many other hardy bulbs, tulips and hyacinths do benefit from a thorough drying off and ripening out of the ground, and there is nothing to be gained by planting before late October. This is also convenient, because they can then be planted in the beds just cleared of summer bedding plants and annuals. Give the soil a dusting of bonemeal at the rate of 4 ounces per square yard, fork this in, and then plant the bulbs: the hyacinths 6 inches deep and 8 inches apart, early tulips 3 inches deep and 8 inches apart, May-flowering tulips 4 inches deep and 8 inches apart.

Pot on Greenhouse Plants

Right at the end of October it is a good plan to finish off any greenhouse potting there may be to do before getting really busy with outdoor planting. It is probable that June-sown primulas and calceolarias will be ready for a move into 4- or 5-inch pots, while the early cinerarias, sown at the beginning of May, will require their last shift into the 7- or 8-inch pots in which they will flower. In all cases the general potting compost will do admirably, but may be rather coarser in texture for the cinerarias than for the other plants. It is no longer really safe to have any of these plants in frames, and you should remove them to a light, airy greenhouse in which you can maintain an average temperature of 55 degs.

Roses and deciduous pot shrubs such as lilacs, deutzias, forsythias, and cherries, that are to be flowered early in the greenhouse, may also be repotted now if they need it; but do this work with as little root disturbance as possible. Simply transfer the unbroken pot-ball to a larger receptacle and work some fresh compost around it. After this treatment return the plants to a frame or to a plunge bed in a sheltered position outdoors.

Pot Annuals for the Greenhouse

Annuals sown in September for flowering in the greenhouse in spring should now be ready for potting singly in 3-inch pots. Use the usual compost (see page 62), and after potting arrange

255

the plants in a frame or cool greenhouse. In either case water moderately and ventilate freely whenever the weather is mild, but be careful to exclude all frost. Pinch out the points of clarkias to make the plants branch.

Precisely similar remarks apply to schizanthus seedlings pricked off in September (see September, Third Week). Pinch out the growing tip of each plant, as advised for clarkias.

In the case of a few annuals grown for greenhouse display, a better effect is obtained by placing three or four plants in a pot than by potting singly. Examples are leptosyne, limnanthes, mignonette, nemophila, phlox, and saponaria.

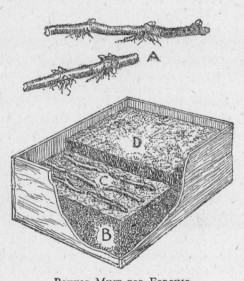

BOXING MINT FOR FORCING.

Short lengths of root (A and C) are laid in soil in a deep seed box (B) and are covered with a little more fine soil (D).

LIFT AND BOX MINT

A supply of young mint shoots are usually very welcome at Christmas and after, and can be obtained very easily by lifting a few roots now, laying them thinly on any fairly light compost spread in deep seed trays, covering them with a further inch of the same compost and bringing them into a warm greenhouse. Any temperature over 50 degs. will secure growth—the higher it is the quicker the roots will grow, that is all. Keep just moist at first, but when shoots begin to appear, water more freely.

MAKE LILY-OF-THE-VALLEY BEDS

This is a good time at which to make new lily-of-the-valley beds. Choose a cool, semi-shady place and good rich soil with plenty of humus. Plant the crowns separately, 3 inches apart in

1. While a hole is being prepared for a rose bush the roots of the plant are protected with a sack.   2. The rose bush placed in the hole with a stake to hold it in position, while soil is worked around and between the roots. 3. Planting a climber well away from the base of a wall so that its roots get plenty of moisture.   4. Planting a fruit tree.   Note the way in which its roots have been spread out.

1. A bush gooseberry before winter pruning. 2. The same bush after rather drastic thinning out and shortening. 3. A fan-trained peach after winter pruning and training. 4. A young bush apple tree before winter pruning. 5. The same tree after correct pruning, designed to build up a good framework of growth and encourage spur formation.

rows 6 inches apart. The simplest method is to nick out shallow trenches with a spade, lay the roots in these, and just cover the crowns.

FLOWERS, VEGETABLES, AND FRUITS IN SEASON DURING OCTOBER

HARDY HERBACEOUS PERENNIALS.—Aconitum *autumnale*, A. *Fischeri*, A. *Wilsonii*, Anemone *japonica and vars.*, Aster *cordifolius and vars.*, A. *ericoides and vars.*, A. *grandiflorus*, A. *Novæ-Angliæ vars.*, A. *Novi-Belgii vars.* (Michaelmas daisy), A. *ptarmicoides*, Boltonia *asteroides*, gaillardias, geums, Helianthus *multiflorus vars.*, H. *orgyalis*, H. *rigidus vars.*, H. *sparsifolius*, Kniphofia *maxima globosa*, K. *multiflora*, K. *R. Wilson Kerr*, Liriope *spicata*, Lobelia *fulgens vars.*, Monardella *macrantha*, Physalis *Alkekengi (fruits)*, P. *Bunyardii (fruits)*, P. *Franchettii (fruits)*, Podophyllum *Emodi (fruits)*, Scabiosa *caucasica and vars.*, Sedum *spectabile and vars.*, Solidago *Virgaurea vars.*, Stokesia *cyanea*, Verbena *venosa*.

HARDY BULBS AND TUBERS.—Colchicum *autumnale*, C. *byzantinum*, C. *Decaisnei*, C. *giganteum*, C. *speciosum vars.*, Crocus *asturicus*, C. *cancellatus*, C. *caspius*, C. *Clusii*, C. *longiflorus*, C. *ochroleucus*, C. *pulchellus*, C. *Salzmannii*, C. *sativus*, C. *speciosus*, C. *zonatus*, Cyclamen *africanum*, C. *cilicicum*, C. *europæum*, C. *neapolitanum*, Galanthus *nivalis Elsæ*, Leucojum *autumnale*, Merendera *bulbocodium*, M. *persica*, Narcissus *serotinus*, Nerine *Bowdeni*, Schizostylis *coccinea and vars.*, Sternbergia *lutea*.

HARDY ROCK PLANTS.—Achillea *tomentosa*, Androsace *lanuginosa Leichtlini*, Ceratostigma *plumbaginoides*, C. *Willmottianum*, Gaultheria *procumbens (fruits)*, Gentiana *Farreri*, G. *Kurroo*, G. *Macaulayi*, G. *sinoornata*, Geum *Borisii*, Iris *lacustris*, Lithospermum *prostratum vars.*, Nertera *depressa (fruits)*, Oxalis *lobata*, Polygonum *vaccinifolium*, Potentilla *mandschurica*, P. *nepalensis minor*, Sisyrinchium *angustifolium convolutum*, Tunica *Saxifraga*, Verbena *chamædryfolia*, Viola *declinata*, V. *florariensis*, V. *gracilis*, Zauschneria *californica*.

HARDY EVERGREEN SHRUBS.—Abelia *grandiflora*, Berberis *Fortunei* (shelter) B. *nepalensis* (shelter), B. *stenophylla autumnalis*, B. *stenophylla semperflorens*, Bigelowia *graveolens*, Buddleia *auriculata*, Calluna *vulgaris and vars.*, Ceanothus *Burkwoodii*, Daboecia *polifolia*, Elæagnus *macrophylla*, E. *pungens*, Erica *carnea Queen Mary*, E. *ciliaris and vars.*, E. *stricta*, E. *Tetralix and vars.*, E. *vagans and vars.*, E. *Watsoni*, Escallonia *macrantha*, E. *pterocladon*, E. *rubra*, E. *viscosa*, escallonia *hybrids*, Hypericum *Moserianum*, H. *galioides*, H. *hircinum*, Olearia *Fosteri* (shelter), Ulex *nanus*, U. *europæus plenus*, Veronica *angustifolia*, V. *speciosa Autumn Glory*.

HARDY DECIDUOUS SHRUBS.—Abelia *Schumannii*, Buddleia *variabilis and vars.*, Calycanthus *occidentalis*, Caryopteris *Mastacanthus*, Ceratostigma *plumbaginoides*, C. *Willmottianum*, Clethra *paniculata*, Cytisus *leucanthus*, C. *nigricans*, Daphne *Mezereum autumnalis*, Desmodium *spicatum*, Disanthus *cercidifolius*, Fremontia *californica* (shelter), Hamamelis *virginica*, Hypericum *Hookerianum*, Hydrangea *paniculata grandiflora*, Indigofera

R

amblyantha, Lavatera *Olbia*, Osmanthus *Aquifolium*, Perowskia *atriplicifolia*, Salix *Bockii*, Spiræa *Margaritæ*, Teucrium *fruticans*, Vitex *Agnuscastus*.

HARDY EVERGREEN TREES.—Arbutus *hybrida*, A. *Unedo*.

HARDY DECIDUOUS TREES.—Alnus *maritima*, A. *nitida*.

HARDY CLIMBING PLANTS.—Clematis *apiifolia*, C. *calycina*, C. *chinensis*, C. *connata*, C. *flammula*, C. *Jackmani* hybrids, C. *Jouiniana*, C. *lanuginosa* hybrids, C. *lasiandra*, C. *paniculata*, C. *Rehderiana*, C. *rubro-marginata*, C. *vitalba*, Jasminum *officinale*, Lonicera *alseuosmoides*, L. *Heckrottii*, Pileostegia *viburnoides*, roses (*climbing hybrid tea and tea, also hybrid musk*).

FRUITING TREES, SHRUBS, AND CLIMBERS.—*Mainly as September, though*

COLCHICUM AUTUMNALE.

birds may strip some varieties. Additional kinds in fruit are as follows: Aucuba *japonica* (*unisexual*), Billardiera *longiflora*, Callicarpa *japonica*, Celastrus *articulatus*, C. *scandens* (*unisexual*), Ilex *Aquifolium and vars.* (*holly*) (*unisexual*), I. *serrata*, Symphoricarpus *racemosus* (*snowberry*), S. *orbiculatus*, Taxus *baccata*.

GREENHOUSE PLANTS.—Abutilons, Bignonia *venusta*, bouvardias, Browallia *speciosa major*, carnations (*perpetual-flowering*), Cassia *corymbosa*, celsias, chrysanthemums, Cobæa *scandens*, Erica *gracilis*, E. *verticillata*, Eupatorium *odoratum*, Humea *elegans*, Luculia *gratissima*, marguerites, Maurandya *Barclayana*, nerines, Oxalis *variabilis*, O. *versicolor*, pelargoniums (*zonal*), Salvia *splendens*, Saintpaulia *ionantha*, streptocarpus, Trachelium *cæruleum*.

OCTOBER: SEASONABLE FLOWERS, ETC.

VEGETABLES IN STORE.—Beetroot, carrots, onions, potatoes, shallots.

VEGETABLES OUTDOORS.—Globe artichokes, broccoli, cabbage (*sown April*), carrots, cauliflowers, celeriac, celery, coleworts (*sown June*), endive, kohlrabi, leeks, lettuce, mushrooms, parsnips, peas, spinach, turnips.

VEGETABLES UNDER GLASS.—French beans, cucumbers, mushrooms, mustard and cress, radishes, tomatoes.

FRUITS OUTDOORS.—Apples : *Allington Pippin (D), Charles Ross (D), Cornish Aromatic (D), Coronation (D), Cox's Pomona (CD), Ecklinville Seedling (C), Egremont Russet (D), Ellison's Orange (D), Emperor Alexander (CD), Exquisite (D), Gascoyne's Scarlet (D), Golden Noble (C), Golden Spire (C), Gravenstein (CD), Herring's Pippin (CD), James Grieve (D), King of the Pippins (D), Lady Sudeley (D), Lord Lambourne (D), McIntosh Red (CD), Mother (American) (D), Peasgood's Nonsuch (CD), Pioneer (D), Rev. W. Wilks (C), Rival (CD), Rosebery (D), Royal Jubilee (C), Schoolmaster (C), St. Edmund's Russet (D), Stirling Castle (C), The Queen (C), Thomas Rivers (C), Wealthy (D), Worcester Pearmain (D).* Figs (*shelter*). Grapes : *Brant, Miller's Burgundy, Royal Muscadine.* Medlars. Peaches : *Dymond, Goshawk, Hale's Early, Peregrine.* Pears : *Beurré Bedford (D), Beurré Diel (D), Beurré Hardy (D), Beurré Superfin (D), Comte de Lamy (D), Conference (D), Durondeau (D), Emile d'Heyst (D), Jersey Gratioli (D), Fondante d'Automne (D), Louise Bonne (D), Maréchal de la Cour (D), Marie Louise (D), Pitmaston Duchess (D), Progress (D), Record (D), Roosevelt (D), Satisfaction (D), Seckel (D), Thompson's (D).* Plums : *Golden Transparent Gage (D), Late Orange (CD), Langley Bullace (C), Merryweather Damson (C), Monarch (CD), President (C), Reine Claude de Bavay Gage (D), Shepherd's Bullace (C), Shropshire Prune Damson (CD), White Bullace (CD).* Quinces. Raspberries (*as September*).

HARDY NUTS.—Cobnuts, filberts, walnuts.

FRUITS UNDER GLASS.—Figs. Grapes : *Alicante, Black Hamburgh, Gros Maroc, Lady Hastings, Muscat Hamburgh.* Peaches : *Gladstone, Golden Eagle, Lady Palmerston, Princess of Wales, Salwey, Sea Eagle, Walburton Admirable.*

NOVEMBER

GENERAL WORK

Tidy up Herbaceous Borders

BY this time most herbaceous perennials will have finished flowering, and the borders may be tidied up for the winter. Cut off all dead or dying stems and leaves, but leave evergreen leaves such as those of kniphofias. Give the ground a dusting of bonemeal if you have not already done this (see October, General Work), and prick over the surface of the border with a fork, but be careful not to disturb roots or to dig up bulbs accidentally. It is really wise to mark the positions of the latter clearly when planting.

Dig all Available Ground

As I have already explained (see October, General Work), the earlier in the autumn ground can be turned over roughly the better. By this time a great deal of the vegetable garden should be free for digging or trenching. The latter, by the by, is simply deep digging to a depth of two or even three spades (almost 3 feet). Very deep trenching can only be practised on rather good soil, but there are few gardens that would not benefit from periodic trenching two spades deep, especially if care is taken to keep the first and second spits (a spit is the depth of a spade) in the same relation one to the other as formerly, and not bring the lower and less fertile soil to the top. Do as much of this work as you can now, and make no attempt to break up the surface as yet. The rougher it is left the greater will be the surface exposed to the beneficial action of wind and frost. Animal manure can be worked in at the same time if required, or alternatively you can apply slow-acting fertilisers or lime,

RIDGING SOIL.

It is an excellent plan to throw the soil into steep ridges in the autumn so that a large surface is exposed to frost and wind.

if not already given (see October, General Work). It is not usually wise to apply manure and lime at the same time, as the latter liberates and wastes ammonia from the manure, but they can be used at a few weeks' interval, one way or the other, without ill effect.

PRUNE DECIDUOUS HEDGES

All deciduous hedges, such as quick (hawthorn), blackthorn, myrobalan plum, sweet briar, beech, and tamarisk, may be pruned during November, and this is a good time to do any hard cutting that may be necessary to keep growth within bounds. The base of a hawthorn or sweet briar hedge sometimes gets bare, but can be kept well furnished with growth by bending down a few long branches and pegging them into position. If the hawthorn branches refuse to bend, half-slit them near the base with a billhook.

GATHER ROSE HEPS

If you have made any special rose crosses and wish to try your hand at seed raising, gather the heps now. Lay them thinly in seed boxes, cover with a little silver sand, and place outdoors in an exposed position for the winter. The more the heps get frozen the better, because this will break them up and prepare the seeds for germination (see March, Second Week). The process is known as stratification, and can be applied to any berries or haws.

PLANT FRUIT AND ORNAMENTAL TREES, SHRUBS, ROSES, ETC.

This is the great month of the year for planting all deciduous trees, shrubs, and climbers, both ornamental and fruiting. The sooner the work can be completed once the leaves have come off the better, but if you have much to do it will almost inevitably be necessary to spread the planting over several weeks, because it is not possible to work either when the ground is frozen or when it is very wet. However, if you cannot finish it all by the first or second week in December, I advise you to postpone the remainder until early February (see February, General Work) rather than to do it when the ground is very cold and wet.

In almost all cases the details of planting are the same. Protect the roots from sun and drying winds until you are quite ready to plant them. Prepare a hole wide enough to accommodate all

261

the roots spread out in a perfectly natural manner and deep enough to permit the uppermost to be covered with a clear 3 or 4 inches of soil. Cut off any broken or bruised root ends, hold the tree or bush in position in the middle of the hole (it is all to the good if you have someone to help you in this), and throw back the soil a little at a time, gently jerking the plant up and down meanwhile, so that the fine particles of soil work down between the roots. When the hole is almost full, tread the soil down really firmly. Then return the rest of the soil, but leave this loose and level on the surface. All standard trees and large bushes should be made secure to strong stakes driven firmly into the soil, while trained fruit trees must also be tied to their supports without delay. There is nothing that will delay rooting so much as constant disturbance by wind.

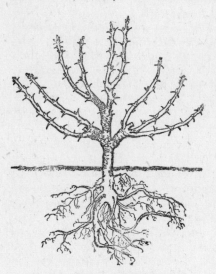

HOW TO PLANT A GOOSEBERRY.

The uppermost roots should be buried an inch or so beneath the surface.

Deciduous climbing plants such as honeysuckles, clematises, Polygonum baldschuanicum, jasmines, and ornamental vines are usually supplied in pots, and this is a great advantage, as it means that one is practically certain to get the roots intact and uninjured. If they are at all dry on arrival, soak them in a bucket of tepid water for a few minutes. Then stand them out to drain for an hour or so, and, when you are ready to plant, crack the pot, remove the fragments carefully, loosen the roots in the pot ball a little and work some of the new soil around them. Be sure to make them really firm in their new surroundings and to tie the shoots up to a support at once.

Bush apples, pears, plums, and cherries should be planted 15 feet apart, but standards of these same trees must be allowed from 25 to 30 feet each. Espalier-trained apples and pears and fan-trained plums, cherries, peaches, nectarines, and apricots must be about 12 feet apart. Cordon apples and pears are planted 2 feet apart, and, if there is more than one row, the rows must be at least 6 feet apart and should run north and south for preference. Bush currants and gooseberries must be at least 4 feet apart each way—it is really wiser to allow blackcurrants 5 feet, as they grow very vigorously. Raspberry canes should be 3 feet apart in rows 6 feet apart, while loganberries, blackberries, and other vigorous bramble fruits need nearly twice that amount of space.

In the case of ornamental trees and shrubs, no hard and fast rules for distance can be given, as they differ greatly in growth, but as a general guide I would suggest that most of the smaller shrubs should be planted 3 feet apart and the bigger kinds 5 to 6 feet apart, and that no trees should be closer than 15 feet. Most climbing plants, including roses, should be at least 6 feet apart. Bush roses must be from 18 inches to 2 feet apart each way, while standards should be at least 4 feet apart.

GENERAL GREENHOUSE MANAGEMENT

During foggy November lack of light and a damp coldness in the atmosphere are two of the principal obstacles that one usually has to overcome in the greenhouse. If the glass is at all dirty, wash it thoroughly, both inside and out. Ventilate very cautiously. Open the top ventilators a little for a few hours during the day when the weather is mild and reasonably clear, but keep them shut if it is very cold or foggy. If you have ample artificial heat at your disposal the problem of ventilation is greatly simplified, for the air within the greenhouse can be warmed, dried, and made to rise steadily through the ventilators even when the atmosphere outside is heavy and cold with moisture.

Keep a sharp look-out for decayed leaves or bracts and remove these at once. Dust the plants with flowers of sulphur to prevent the disease from spreading. Avoid splashing water about. Damping down and syringing will only be required by a few exceptional things, such as tropical foliage plants and winter cucumbers, and as these also require a much higher temperature than the general run of greenhouse plants, they must be grown by themselves. In the mixed greenhouse, where primulas, cinerarias, calceolarias, cyclamens, etc., are growing together with pelargoniums, marguerites, and other stored bedding plants, a day

263

temperature of 55 degs. will serve now, but it should not be allowed to fall below 45 degs. at night.

ATTEND TO PLANTS IN FRAMES

From now on until the early spring plants in frames will require very careful handling. Some, such as rooted viola, pansy, and violet cuttings, sweet pea seedlings, and also violet clumps, are quite hardy and only in need of protection from hard frost or heavy rains, which might disturb the small cuttings and seedlings or prevent the clumps from flowering. These need very free ventilation. Lights may be removed altogether during the day when the weather is mild, but should be placed on the frames again before the sun sets. Cauliflowers, antirrhinums from late summer cuttings and seeds, bedding calceolarias, and pentstemons need just a little more protection, but are almost hardy. They should always be fully exposed on warm, sunny days and ventilated freely whenever there is no frost or very cold wind. Others again, such as pelargoniums, marguerites, and choice fuchsias, are liable to be damaged severely by even a few degrees of frost, and must be well protected with sacks at night. Ventilate the frames on favourable days, but be careful to get the lights back in time to trap sun heat against the night.

In all cases, take advantage of a warm day now and then to have the lights off and examine all plants carefully. Remove and burn any decayed or yellowing leaves. Also stir the surface of the soil with a pointed stick to aerate it.

Water sufficiently to prevent the soil from getting dry, but reduce the amount during frosty weather, especially for the tender plants.

POT SHRUBS FOR THE GREENHOUSE

November is a good month during which to purchase and pot many deciduous shrubs for early flowering in the greenhouse— hydrangeas, for example; also lilacs, brooms, deutzias, and roses. After potting, stand the hydrangeas in a frame and protect from frost, but plunge the others to the pot-rims in a sunny, sheltered place outdoors. Make no attempt to force these shrubs in a high temperature the first winter, but you can bring them into a cool greenhouse in December or January to get flowers a few weeks ahead of the normal season. You can also purchase Indian azaleas in bud now, either in pots or tapped out of them, and these latter have only to be slipped back into pots to be ready for mild forcing.

Cut back Chrysanthemums

As chrysanthemums in the greenhouse finish flowering, cut them back to within 2 or 3 inches of ground level. This will make more room in the house and will also encourage the roots to throw up sucker shoots which will make the ideal cuttings later on (see December, Third Week).

Successional Sowings

The only successional sowings to be made are mustard and cress and radishes, all in a warm greenhouse or frame over a hot-bed. A temperature of 50 to 60 degs. is necessary to ensure germination and quick growth. If it is 10 degs. higher, so much the better.

Protect Broccoli from Frost

The curds of the early broccolis will be forming now, and though they are much hardier than cauliflowers, it is as well to protect them by bending some of the outer leaves over them. Late cauliflowers will certainly need this protection.

Blanch Endive in Frames

Most, if not all, endive plants will be in frames, and you can blanch them as formerly described (see August, General Work), or, if you want a lot at once, by the even simpler process of covering a whole frame so thickly with sacks that all light is excluded.

Prune Fruit Trees

November is the best month for doing any hard pruning of fruit trees and bushes that may be necessary. However, if you have followed out a system of summer-pruning as I have advised (see June, Second Week, and July, First and Third Weeks), there will not be a great deal to do now. Shorten all the laterals (side shoots) of summer-pruned apples, pears, plums, sweet cherries, apricots, gooseberries, and red and white currants to about two, or at most three, dormant growth buds each, unless, in the case of fan-trained trees, there is room to tie in a few at full length.

Leading shoots that are going to extend main branches or lay the foundation of new branches should be shortened by about one-third of their length, while the central leaders of espalier-trained trees are shortened to about 15 inches if another pair of horizontal arms is required, or cut off altogether if the tree already has sufficient arms. In all cases I am referring to the shoots actually formed during the past summer. In estimating the length of any stem that is to be pruned there is no need to take into account any of the old wood formed in previous years. In the case of big trees that were not summer-pruned, this hard winter-pruning is not desirable. Instead content yourself with the removal or shortening of thin, weak, or badly placed stems.

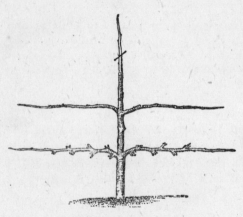

A HORIZONTAL-TRAINED APPLE.

If a further pair of arms is required the vertical shoot must be cut back, as indicated by the black line. The young shoots terminating the existing horizontal branches must in any case be shortened by about one-third.

Peaches, nectarines, and Morello cherries that have been disbudded during the spring and summer (see April, Fourth Week, and July, First Week) are pruned differently. Each old fruiting lateral is cut right out and the new basal lateral retained at its base for the purpose is trained in its place.

Black currants, though not summer-pruned, are now treated in somewhat the same way as these peaches, etc.; that is to say, you must cut out as much as possible of the old growth that has just borne fruit to make way for strong young stems. Many of the best may come right from the base of the bush.

ROOT-PRUNE FRUIT TREES

Sometimes failure to fruit is due to too much vigour (see note on ringing, May, First Week). This can be checked by root-pruning during the period at which the trees are dormant. Dig a trench around the tree and 4 or 5 feet away from it and then work towards it with a fork, unearthing the roots and carefully preserving all those of a fibrous nature but severing any very stout roots that are plunging down into the subsoil. Do not approach nearer than to within about 18 inches of the tree. Then replace the soil again, spreading out and covering the fine roots. Root-pruning can be practised with safety on stone fruits, such as cherries and plums, for which ringing is unsafe.

Ventilate and Prune Trees in Orchard House

All the fruit trees in the orchard house must now be pruned in exactly the same way as those outdoors. No fire heat will be required unless some growth is still unripened (see October, General Work), and ventilation can be really free through both top and side ventilators, the house only being closed completely when the thermometer falls much below freezing point.

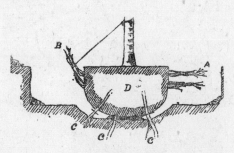

Ventilate Vines according to Growth

ROOT PRUNING.

Valuable fibrous roots (A) should be tied up out of harm's way (B), while the central mass of roots (D) is undermined and any large tap roots (C) are severed.

The latest vines may still be carrying bunches of grapes and will need very careful ventilation and heating. The latter will be used to keep the air dry rather than to maintain a high temperature; 50 degs. will be a sufficient average. Ventilation must be given with the same object. In a damp, stagnant, cold atmosphere berries will crack and mould will appear on them. All fallen leaves must be swept up and removed daily. Vines that have finished fruiting are much easier to manage. They can be ventilated freely and will need no fire heat.

FIRST WEEK

PLACE GLASS OVER ALPINES

Some choice alpines, and especially woolly-leaved plants such as many of the androsaces, suffer badly during the winter from excessive wet, which lodges in their leaves and makes them rot.

Such can be completely protected by covering them now with pieces of glass supported well above the plants on notched sticks or bent pieces of wire. Make no attempt to close in the sides of the shelter. Free circulation of air is essential.

LIFT EARLY-FLOWERING CHRYSANTHEMUMS

Border chrysanthemums are quite hardy in many gardens, but sometimes they rot off during the winter, so to be on the safe side it is advisable to lift a few plants of each variety now and place them close together in a frame or in boxes, which can be stood in a cool greenhouse.

BORDER CHRYSANTHEMUMS FOR PROPAGATION.

The old roots are lifted and placed close together in a frame with a little soil between them. It is the young shoots that grow up from the roots which make the best cuttings.

Simply pack a little light soil between them; that left over from seed trays will do well. Cut off the stems 2 or 3 inches above soil level. No artificial heat will be necessary, and only enough water to keep the soil from drying out. Later on these " stools," as they are called, will furnish plenty of good cuttings (see February, General Work).

Complete Planting of Tulips and Hyacinths

There is still time to plant tulips and hyacinths (see October, Fourth Week), but the sooner the work is completed the better.

Bring Early Bulbs into Greenhouse

Examine the bulbs that were boxed or potted in September and placed in a plunge bed (see September, First Week). A few of the most forward may now be brought into a moderately heated greenhouse, but do not attempt to force them too fast at first. An average day temperature of 60 degs., falling to 50 degs. at night, will be ample to begin with, but may rise to 70 degs. once the flower buds are well formed. Another important point is to make quite certain that the bulbs have made plenty of roots before bringing them into the greenhouse at all. You can tap one or two of the pots out carefully without disturbing them, or alternatively you can learn a lot by examining the drainage holes and slits in the bottoms of the pots and boxes. When the soil begins to get full of roots they will start to grow through these drainage openings.

From this time onwards it is advisable to keep an eye on the plunge bed and either to remove forward boxes and pots of bulbs to the greenhouse, or, if you are not ready for them, to place them in an unheated frame, preferably with a north aspect. Here growth can be retarded for weeks without harm to the bulbs.

Commence to Force Indian Azaleas, etc.

If you want some really early flowers on Indian azaleas, bring the plants into a slightly warmer temperature now—an average of 65 to 70 degs. will do admirably—and syringe them lightly every morning with slightly tepid water. Various other early-flowering shrubs, such as forsythias, ornamental cherries, Viburnum Carlesi, Jasminum primulinum, and even lilac can also be brought into the greenhouse now, but do not subject them to temperatures above 60 degs. unless they are really well established in pots.

Sow Broad Beans

There can be no doubt that the very best way to grow early broad beans is to sow seeds in boxes in February and germinate

269

them in a warm greenhouse (see February, First Week). But if you have no glasshouse it is worth making an outdoor sowing now in a sheltered place. Choose a longpod variety and sow the seeds 4 inches apart in drills 2 inches deep and 18 inches apart for dwarf, or 2½ feet apart for tall kinds.

SECOND WEEK

SOW HARDY CULINARY PEAS

Some people are very successful with culinary peas sown now outdoors where they are to mature. A rather sheltered position and well-drained soil are essentials to success, and you must also use an absolutely hardy variety, such as The Pilot or William the First. Other details of sowing are the same as in the spring (see March, Second Week).

LIFT SEAKALE FOR FORCING

The top growth of seakale should have died down by this time, and the roots will be ready for lifting in preparation for forcing. Dig them up carefully, cut off the side thongs and lay these in bundles in a sheltered position outdoors in readiness for planting out in March (see March, First Week). Then stand the stout central roots, each provided with a crown from which growth will come, against a shady wall or fence and heap ashes or sand around them until only the crowns are visible. They will keep safely like this all the winter, and you can pot up and force a few at a time as you require them. Pot three or four in a 6- or 7-inch pot, using any old potting or seed box compost, bring them into a warm greenhouse, and cover with another empty pot, blocking up the drainage hole in the bottom of this with a piece of slate or turf. The crowns must be in absolute darkness. Water moderately. In a temperature of about 60 degs. growth will be rapid. When the blanched shoots are about 9 inches in length you can cut them. The forced roots are useless and should be thrown away.

START TO FORCE RHUBARB

Rhubarb may also be forced from now onwards throughout the winter. Roots started at once in a temperature of about 70 degs. will give good sticks at Christmas. The method followed differs from that for seakale. Strong roots are lifted and allowed to lie on the ground unprotected for a day or so. If it freezes, so much the better. Growth will be all the quicker for this exposure. Then take the roots into a warm greenhouse, stand them quite close together in deep boxes or on the floor under the stages, pack soil between them and keep them absolutely dark by fixing up a screen of sacking, linoleum, or boards. Water moderately and maintain a temperature of from 55 to 75 degs. A few more roots should be brought in every fortnight or so.

THIRD WEEK

Lift and Store Jerusalem Artichokes, Parsnips, Horse-radish, and Salsify

Jerusalem artichokes will have completed their growth, so cut off all the tops and lift the tubers with a fork. Store the larger tubers in exactly the same way as potatoes (see September, Third Week), and put the smaller tubers on one side in a dry shed or room for planting later on.

Parsnips and horseradish are perfectly hardy, and will not suffer any harm if left in the ground all the winter; indeed, the parsnips are actually improved in flavour by frost, but as it is well-nigh impossible to lift these long roots when the ground is frozen hard, it is as well to dig up a few now and store them in a shed or cellar as a standby. Simply cut off the tops, pile up the roots, and cover them with a little dry sand, ashes, or soil.

At least a portion of the crop of salsify should also be lifted and stored in exactly the same way as the parsnips and horse-radish. If you wish, however, you can leave a portion of the bed undisturbed, so that the roots may produce flowering stems in the spring. These shoots, if cut young, can be boiled and eaten like asparagus. They are very palatable.

FOURTH WEEK

Cut and Store Grapes

There is not much point in trying to keep the bunches of late grapes hanging on the vines any longer, especially if you have a cool, dark, and dry room in which you can store them. Cut each bunch with 9 inches or more of the ripened lateral from which it is hanging, insert the lower end of this into a bottle nearly filled with clean, soft water and containing a few pieces of char-

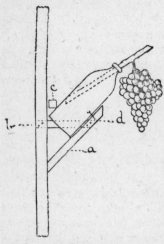

A STORAGE RACK FOR GRAPES.

a, The shelf fixed firmly against a wall or partition. b, Supports at intervals to hold the shelf. c, A piece of quartering running the length of the shelf and holding the bases of the bottles. d, Nails driven in on both sides of each bottle to prevent it from rolling sideways.

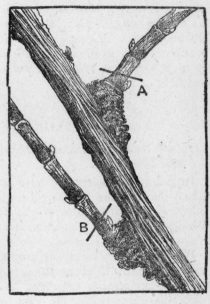

PRUNING A VINE.

Each lateral must be cut back, as at A and B, to within one, or at most two, dormant buds of the main rod or spur.

coal, and then stand the bottle in a rack or on a shelf, tilting it sufficiently to prevent the berries from coming into contact with it, or, for that matter, with anything else.

PRUNE EARLY AND MAINCROP VINES

By this time the leaves should have fallen from early and main-crop vines, and the sooner most of them are pruned the better. Outdoor vines may also be pruned. In all cases of present pruning the method is the same. Cut back every lateral (side) growth to within one, or at most two, dormant growth buds of the main rod or spur. Then rub or pull all loose shreds of bark

272

1. Rough digging vacant ground in the autumn. 2. Cutting back dead growth on herbaceous perennials. 3. Celery fully earthed up and protected from frost with dried straw. 4. A vine ready for pruning. The white lines indicate where the laterals should be cut off. 5. Planting a vine. The roots must be spread out to their full extent.

1. A tent-like shelter of twigs and straw built over a gunnera root to protect the crowns from frost. 2. Protection for alpines against excessive rain. 3. A wattle hurdle placed in front of a tender evergreen shrub and stuffed with dry bracken. 4. Gladioli and dahlias stored beneath greenhouse staging. 5. A good arrangement of greenhouse and frames. Note the corrugated-iron boiler shelter. 6. Forcing rhubarb beneath the greenhouse staging.

from the main rods and paint the latter thoroughly with Gishurst compound. Be particularly careful to work this in to all rough, gnarled places round the spur, where insects may be hiding. After pruning and cleaning, cut the ties holding the main rod and lower it on long pieces of cord so that it hangs more or less parallel

Cleaning a Vine.

Usually most of the old, loose bark can be rubbed off by hand, but a blunt kitchen knife can be used on tough pieces, providing the live bark is not injured.

with the floor. This will discourage sap from rushing up to the top when the vine is restarted and will ensure an even "break" all over.

FLOWERS, VEGETABLES, AND FRUITS IN SEASON DURING NOVEMBER

Hardy Herbaceous Plants.—Aster *grandiflorus*, Funkia *lancifolia tardiflora*, Helianthus *orgyalis*, H. *sparsifolius*, Helleborus *niger altifolius*, Iris *unguicularis* (*stylosa*), Kniphofia *maxima globosa*, K. R. Wilson Kerr,

s

Liriope *spicata*, Monardella *macrantha*, physalis *in variety (fruits)*, Podophyllum *Emodi (fruits)*, Pulmonaria *angustifolia azurea*, P. *saccharata*, Viola *florariensis*.

HARDY BULBS AND TUBERS.—Colchicum *byzantium cilicicum*, C. *Decaisnei*, C. *hydrophyllum*, Crocus *asturicus*, C. *Boryi and vars.*, C. *cancellatus and vars.*, C. *caspius*, C. *Clusii*, C. *hadriaticus and vars.*, C. *hyemalis and vars.*, C. *Medius*, C. *ochroleucus*, C. *pulchellus*, C. *Salzmannii*, C. *speciosus*, Cyclamen *africanum*, C. *neapolitanum*, Galanthus *cilicicus*, G. *nivalis vars.* (*snowdrops*), Merendera *bulbocodium*, M. *persica*, Narcissus *serotinus*, Schizostylis *coccinea and vars.*, Sternbergia *lutea*.

IRIS UNGUICULARIS.

ROCK PLANTS.—Gentiana *Farreri*, G. *gentilis*, G. *intermedia*, G. *Kurroo*, G. *Macaulayi*, G. *ornata*, G. *sino-ornata*, Primula *Juliana vars.*

HARDY EVERGREEN SHRUBS.—Berberis *Fortunei*, B. *nepalensis (shelter)*, Buddleia *auriculata*, Erica *carnea vars.*, E. *ciliaris*, E. *Maweana*, E. *darleyensis*, E. *stricta*, Elæagnus *macrophylla*, E. *pungens*, Fatsia *japonica*, Hypericum *Moserianum*, Olearia *Fosteri (shelter)*, Veronica *angustifolia*, V. *speciosa Autumn Glory*, Viburnum *Tinus*.

HARDY DECIDUOUS SHRUBS.—Chimonanthus *fragrans*, Colletia *armata*, Cratægus *monogyna præcox*, Daphne *Mezereum autumnalis*, Lonicera *Standishii*, Viburnum *fragrans*.

HARDY EVERGREEN TREES.—Arbutus *hybrida*, A. *Unedo*.

HARDY DECIDUOUS TREES.—Prunus *subhirtella autumnalis*.

274

NOVEMBER: SEASONABLE FLOWERS, ETC.

HARDY CLIMBING PLANTS.—Clematis *calycina*, C. *cirrhosa*, Jasminum *nudiflorum*, Lardizabala *biternata* (*shelter*).

FRUITING TREES, SHRUBS, AND CLIMBERS.—*Mainly as October, but most pyrus fruits will have fallen.*

GREENHOUSE PLANTS.—Abutilons, begonias (*Gloire de Lorraine and Optima types*), Bignonia *venusta*, Boronia *heterophylla*, B. *megastigma*, bouvardias, Browallia *speciosa major*, carnations (*perpetual-flowering*), chrysanthemums, Crassula *lactea*, cyclamen, Erica *gracilis*, Eriostemon *buxifolia*, Libonia *floribunda*, Oxalis *versicolor*, pelargoniums (*zonal*), Primula *kewensis*, Saintpaulia *ionantha*, Salvia *splendens*, Sparmannia *africana*, Trachelium *cæruleum*.

FLOWERS IN FRAMES.—Violets.

VEGETABLES IN STORE.—Beetroot, carrots, onions, parsnips, potatoes, shallots, turnips.

VEGETABLES OUTDOORS.—Jerusalem artichokes, broccoli, Brussels sprouts, cabbage (*sown April*), celeriac, celery, coleworts (*sown June*), endive, kohlrabi, leeks, lettuce (*shelter*), parsnips, savoys, spinach, turnips.

VEGETABLES UNDER GLASS.—French beans, cucumbers, endive, lettuce, mushrooms, mustard and cress, radishes, tomatoes.

FRUITS IN STORE.—Apples: *Allington Pippin* (D), *Beauty of Kent* (C), *Barnack Orange* (D), *Bismarck* (C), *Blenheim Orange* (D), *Bramley's Seedling* (C), *Charles Ross* (D), *Cornish Aromatic* (D), *Coronation* (D), *Cox's Orange Pippin* (D), *Cox's Pomona* (CD), *Cutler Grieve* (D), *Egremont Russet* (D), *Emperor Alexander* (CD), *Gascoyne's Scarlet* (D), *Golden Noble* (C), *Gravenstein* (CD), *Herring's Pippin* (CD), *Imperial* (D), *Joy Bells* (D), *King of the Pippins* (D), *Lane's Prince Albert* (C), *Lord Derby* (C), *Lord Lambourne* (D), *Margil* (D), *McIntosh Red* (CD), *Mother* (*American*) (D), *Norfolk Royal* (D), *Peasgood's Nonsuch* (CD), *Pioneer* (D), *Rev. W. Wilks* (C), *Ribston Pippin* (D), *Rival* (CD), *Roundway Magnum Bonum* (D), *Royal Jubilee* (C), *Schoolmaster* (C), *The Queen* (C), *Thomas Rivers* (C), *Triumph* (D), *Warner's King* (C), *Wealthy* (D), *Wellington* (C). Medlars. Pears: *Bellissime d'Hiver* (C), *Beurre Diel* (D), *Beurre Superfin* (D), *Charles Ernest* (D), *Conference* (D), *Doyenne du Comice* (D), *Durondeau* (D), *Emile d'Heyst* (D), *Forelle* (*Trout Pear*) (D), *Maréchal de la Cour* (D), *Marie Louise* (D), *Pitmaston Duchess* (D), *Record* (D), *Thompson's* (D), *Victor* (D), *Wonderful* (D). Plums: *Langley Bullace* (C), *Shropshire Prune Damson* (CD). Quinces.

FRUITS UNDER GLASS.—Grapes: *Alicante, Appley Towers, Canon Hall Muscat, Gros Colmar, Gros Guillaume, Lady Downe's, Lady Hastings, Lady Hutt, Mrs. Pearson, Mrs. Pince, Muscat of Alexandria, Prince of Wales.*

NUTS IN STORE.—Cobnuts, filberts, walnuts.

DECEMBER

GENERAL WORK

Continue to Dig Vacant Ground

DIGGING and trenching can be continued throughout the month as opportunity offers, but it is not wise to do this work when there is much snow on the ground, nor when it is frozen, or very wet.

Sterilise Infected Soil

This is a task which can be done at any time of the year, but as it is essential that the soil should have no plants growing in it, and, also, in all cases of chemical sterilisation, that it should remain unused for a month or so after treatment, December is often the most convenient month for the work. The purpose of sterilisation is to rid the soil of all harmful organisms, including insect pests and the spores of fungi, which cause diseases. There is no point in treating soil that is in good order, but if diseases or pests have been rampant, sterilisation may be well repaid.

Chemical sterilisation is commonly carried out with either formaldehyde or cresylic acid. Formaldehyde of 40 per cent. purity (the common commercial strength) is diluted with 49 times its own bulk of water and the soil is then soaked thoroughly with it. Soil can be treated in situ, but a more effective method is to spread it out on a hard floor, soak it, and then immediately draw it into a heap and cover with sacks to trap the fumes. You must not use the soil until it has lost all smell of the chemical.

Precisely similar methods are adopted with cresylic acid. This you can purchase in various strengths, but that known as " pale straw-coloured carbolic acid " is most suitable. Dilute it with 39 times its own bulk of water.

Another method of sterilising soil is by heat. If dry heat is used, as in an oven, great care must be taken not to char the soil and so destroy all the humus that it contains. This danger can be avoided by wetting the soil thoroughly and placing in a fairly airtight oven so that the steam is trapped. Several useful baking apparatuses of small size and embodying this principle are manufactured. Alternatively, steam instead of dry heat may be

276

used to heat the soil. This is really the ideal method, but the apparatus required is more costly and difficult to handle.

When sterilising soil by heat its temperature must be raised to 200 degs. Fahrenheit and maintained at that for about 30 minutes. The soil, unlike that chemically treated, can be used for any purpose as soon as it has cooled, but as the treatment

STERILISING SOIL.

The soil has been spread out and is being soaked with a dilute solution of formaldehyde or cresylic acid.

TRAPPING THE FUMES.

After treatment with the chemical the soil is drawn into a heap and covered with sacks or a tarpaulin.

results in a reduction of fertility for a while, it is advisable to counteract this by adding suitable chemicals (see pages 24 and 62).

You should note that soil fumigation is a rather different matter from sterilisation, as it is directed solely at insect pests—*e.g.*, wireworms, leatherjackets, millepedes, etc., and has no effect upon diseases. Flaked naphthalene is commonly used for the purpose, and is dug into any vacant ground at the rate of 4 ounces per square yard. There are also a number of proprietary soil fumigants, many of them embodying naphthalene

277

in some form or other, which must be used strictly in accordance with manufacturers' instructions.

COMMENCE TO PROPAGATE CARNATIONS

Perpetual-flowering carnation cuttings may be taken from now until the end of March. They are best prepared from side shoots produced a little way up the flowering stems. Avoid those right at the base and right at the top. Shoots about 3 inches in length are ideal and can be obtained by pulling gently away and down from the plant. The heel or small strip of skin that comes away from the old stem should be trimmed off close to the base of the cutting, which is then ready for insertion. Alternative methods are to cut the shoot just below a joint and not pull it away at the heel, or to pull it upwards so that it slips out of the joint. This last method is known as taking a piping. These cuttings are ready for insertion without further fuss. They should be inserted nearly an inch deep in either pure silver sand or a mixture of good loam and silver sand in about equal parts. They root more quickly and reliably in the pure sand, but need considerably more attention as to watering, which is a nuisance if one has to be away from home most of the day. Carnation cuttings are rooted in a greenhouse maintained at a temperature of about 50 degs., but it is an advantage to keep them close, either in a propagating box or under a bell-glass, and to warm the soil to about 60 degs.

CONTINUE TO CUT BACK CHRYSANTHEMUMS

Throughout the month continue to cut back the later chrysanthemums as soon as they finish flowering (see November, General Work).

STOP SWEET PEAS

Autumn-sown sweet peas (see September, Second Week) should be pinched at some time during the winter. It does not matter when it is done, so long as it is before the plants have made shoots more than 3 inches in length. Stopping in this case means that the top of each seedling is pinched out.

BRING MORE BULBS INTO THE GREENHOUSE

Bring in further batches of bulbs to the greenhouse from plunge bed and frame to ensure a succession of flowers later on (see November, First Week).

Continue to Force Seakale and Rhubarb

At intervals of about a fortnight bring in further roots of rhubarb and seakale and force them in the greenhouse (see November, Second Week).

Continue to Protect Broccoli

From time to time during the month you must continue to bend down leaves over the curds of broccoli as they form (see November, General Work).

Successional Sowings

These are exactly the same as last month—mustard and cress and radishes—all in a warm greenhouse or a frame placed on a hotbed.

Continue to Prune Fruit Trees

Throughout the month you can proceed with the pruning of fruit trees and bushes of all kinds (see November, General Work). It is a mistaken notion that fruit trees must not be pruned when the weather is frosty.

Ventilate Vinery and Orchard House Freely

There is really nothing of importance to add to my November notes on the management of these houses. Free ventilation should be the rule right up to the time at which vines and fruit trees are restarted into growth. If the weather is very cold, close up the houses in sufficient time in the afternoon to keep off the worst frost, but a few degrees of frost will do no harm at all.

FIRST WEEK

Protect Tender Plants, Christmas Roses, and Celery

Very little damage is done by early autumn frosts to such slightly tender plants and shrubs as gunneras, eremuri, escallonias, evergreen ceanothuses, tricuspidarias, etc., but as the winter sets in with greater rigour it is advisable to provide some protection for these if they happen to be growing in rather exposed places. Wall shrubs and climbers about which you are at all nervous can be protected efficiently and without danger by hanging sacking in front of them or fixing wattle hurdles close up to them and then stuffing any intervening space with straw or bracken. In no case must the plant be entirely shut off from air. Whatever form of protection you use, always leave the top open so that foul air and moisture may escape.

In the case of slightly tender herbaceous plants, the crowns of which may be injured by frost, the best method of protection is to place a piece of fine-mesh galvanised wire-netting over each, humped in the form of a tunnel, heap dry leaves, straw, or bracken on this, and cover with another piece of netting pegged down at the corners.

Christmas roses (hellebores) are not in the least tender, but they will be forming their flower stems now and the blooms will benefit from a little protection to keep off heavy rain and mud splashes. Cover them with spare lights supported on bricks at the four corners, or with cloches of one type or another.

Late celery may be injured by very hard frosts or heavy rain, so it is good policy to cover the ridges at about this time with a little dry straw or bracken, held in position with some wire-netting pegged down to the soil, and also to dig a shallow trench on each side of the ridge to run off surplus surface water.

Prune Clematis Jackmani

Clematises of the Jackmani and nearly allied Viticellæ classes may be pruned. It is not absolutely essential to do the work at once, so long as it is completed before the end of February, but in the interests of tidiness the sooner it is completed the better. There are two methods of pruning. One is to cut all growth back to within about 1 foot of the ground every year, so keeping the plants fairly small, and the other to allow a framework of main vines to form and then prune each side growth back to one joint.

SECOND WEEK

Make a Mushroom Bed for Succession

This is a very good time to make a mushroom bed in an out-house, frame, or other covered place, because the bed will start to crop in February and provide a succession to that made in September (see September, First Week). The details are exactly the same as before.

THIRD WEEK

Commence to Take Chrysanthemum Cuttings

Some growers start taking cuttings of chrysanthemums considerably earlier than this, but I do not think that the amateur gains anything by being in too much of a hurry. You should

PROPAGATING CHRYSANTHEMUMS.

Some of the cuttings are being rooted in a propagating frame, while others have been inserted in a shallow bed of sandy soil actually made up on the greenhouse staging. On the extreme right are some rooted cuttings that have been potted singly.

start on those varieties that are to be grown for second crown buds, and particularly on November incurves and singles.

The best shoots to select are those that come up through the soil direct from the roots. These should be severed just below soil level when they are a couple of inches or so in length. They are

281

prepared by slipping off the lower leaves with a very sharp knife and trimming off the base cleanly just below a joint; then insert them about ½ inch deep in sandy soil. It does not matter much whether they are in boxes, pots, or directly in a bed made up on the staging in the greenhouse so long as there is ample provision for drainage. The cuttings cannot be rooted out of doors at this time of the year. It is possible to manage them in a well-constructed frame, but it is much easier in a greenhouse with just a little artificial heat to keep out frost. Some growers keep the cuttings close in a frame within the greenhouse, while others prefer to have them open on the staging. Both schemes work well, but in the latter case rather more watering is necessary, and it is advisable to syringe every morning with slightly tepid water.

FOURTH WEEK

Remove Christmas Plants to Glasshouse

The sooner pot plants used in the house for decorations during the Christmas festivities can be returned to the greenhouse the better. They do not like the over-dry atmosphere and ever-changing temperature of living-rooms at all, and quickly deteriorate as a result. Palms, aspidistras, and dracænas will benefit from a thorough sponging down with tepid water into which a few drops of milk have been stirred. After this they should be kept in a rather warm atmosphere for a few days and syringed daily with clear water. Flowering plants such as cyclamens, primulas, cinerarias, and heaths should be given as light a place as possible on the staging in a temperature of 55 to 60 degs., and be watered very carefully, all excesses one way or the other being avoided. Remove any withered or mouldy leaves. Berried solanums should also be given plenty of light and a rather higher temperature.

FLOWERS, VEGETABLES, AND FRUITS IN SEASON DURING DECEMBER

Hardy Herbaceous Plants.—Adonis *amurensis*, Aster *grandiflorus*, Helleborus *niger and vars.*, Iris *unguicularis* (*stylosa*), Liriope *spicata*, Monardella *macrantha*, Petasites *fragrans*.

Hardy Bulbs and Tubers.—Colchicum *byzantinum cilicicum*, C.

Decaisnei, C. *hydrophyllum*, C. *libanoticum*, Crocus *alatavicus*, C. *Boryi* and vars., C. *caspius*, C. *hadriaticus*, C. *hyemalis*, C. *Imperati*, C. *medius*, C. *ochroleucus*, C. *pulchellus*, C. *Salzmannii*, Cyclamen *coum*, Galanthus *cilicus*, G. *nivalis* vars., Merendera *bulbocodium*, M. *persica*, Narcissus *serotina*, Sternbergia *lutea angustifolia*.

HARDY EVERGREEN SHRUBS.—Arctostaphylos *tomentosa*, Azara *integrifolia* (*shelter*), Berberis *japonica hyemalis*, Buddleia *auriculata* (*shelter*), Erica *carnea* vars., E. *darleyensis*, Fatsia *japonica*, Lonicera *fragrantissima*, Olearia *Fosteri* (*shelter*), Rhododendron *Lee's Scarlet*, Viburnum *Tinus and* vars.

HARDY DECIDUOUS SHRUBS.—Chimonanthus *fragrans*, Daphne *Mezereum*

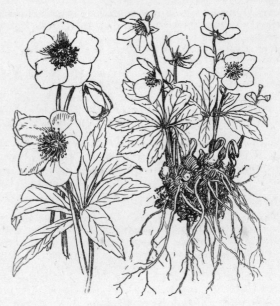

HELLEBORUS NIGER.

autumnalis, Hamamelis *mollis*, Lonicera *Standishii*, Rhododendron *mucronulatum*, Viburnum *fragrans*.

HARDY EVERGREEN TREES.—Arbutus *Unedo*, Eucalyptus *Gunnii*.

HARDY DECIDUOUS TREES.—Cratægus *monogyna præcox*, Prunus *subhirtella autumnalis*.

HARDY CLIMBING PLANTS.—Clematis *calycina*, C. *cirrhosa*, Jasminum *nudiflorum*, Lardizabala *biternata* (*shelter*).

FRUITING TREES, SHRUBS, AND CLIMBERS.—Aucuba *japonica*, Berberis *Hookeri*, Celastrus *articulatus*, C. *scandens*, Cotoneaster *frigida*, C. *horizontalis*, C. *microphylla*, C. *rotundifolia*, Cratægus *Carrierei*, C. *cordata*, C. *Crus-galli*, C. *spathulata*, Hippophæ *rhamnoides*, Ilex *Aquifolium* (holly),

283

Pyracantha *angustifolia*, P. *coccinea*, P. *Gibbsii*, P. *Rogersiana*, Rosa *Fargesi*, R. *Moyesi*, Taxus *baccata*. *Some of the other varieties mentioned in October may continue, but these are particularly reliable. Much depends upon birds.*

GREENHOUSE PLANTS.—Abutilons, begonias (*Gloire de Lorraine and Optima types*), Bignonia *venusta*, bouvardias, Browallia *speciosa major*, camellias, carnations (*perpetual-flowering*), chrysanthemums, cinerarias, Correa *cardinalis*, cyclamen, Erica *gracilis and vars.*, E. *hyemalis*, Primula *kewensis*, P. *obconica*, P. *sinensis and vars.*, Saintpaulia *ionantha*.

FLOWERS IN FRAMES.—Anemone *coronaria vars.*, violets.

VEGETABLES IN STORE.—Jerusalem artichokes, beetroot, carrots, onions, parsnips, potatoes, turnips, shallots.

VEGETABLES OUTDOORS.—Jerusalem artichokes, broccoli, Brussels sprouts, celeriac, celery, coleworts (*sown July*), endive, kales, leeks, lettuce (*shelter*), parsnips, savoys, spinach, turnips.

VEGETABLES UNDER GLASS.—Cucumbers, endive, lettuce, mushrooms, mustard and cress, radishes, rhubarb, seakale.

FRUITS IN STORE.—Apples : *Adams' Pearmain (D), Allington Pippin (D), Annie Elizabeth (C), Barnack Beauty (CD), Barnack Orange (D), Baumann's Red Winter Reinette (CD), Beauty of Kent (C), Belle de Boskoop (CD), Bismarck (C), Blenheim Orange (D), Bramley's Seedling (C), Christmas Pearmain (D), Claygate Pearmain (D), Coronation (D), Cornish Aromatic (D), Cornish Gilliflower (D), Court Pendu Plat (D), Cox's Orange Pippin (D), Cutler Grieve (D), Gascoyne's Scarlet (D), Golden Noble (C), Gravenstein (CD), Houblon (D), Imperial (D), Joy Bells (D), King of Tompkins County (D), Lane's Prince Albert (C), Laxton's Pearmain (D), Lord Derby (C), Lord Lambourne (D), Madresfield Court (D), Margil (D), Monarch (C), Newton Wonder (C), Norfolk Royal (D), Orleans Reinette (D), Ribston Pippin (D), Rival (CD), Rosemary Russet (D), Roundway Magnum Bonum (D), Royal Jubilee (C), Royalty (D), Saltcote Pippin (D), Schoolmaster (C), Superb (D), The Queen (C), Thomas Rivers (C), Triumph (D), Wellington (C), William Crump (D), Wyken Pippin (D)*. Pears : *Admiral Gervais (D), Bellissime d'Hiver (C), Beurre Six (D), Blickling (D), Catillac (C), Charles Ernest (D), Forelle (D), Glou Morceau (D), Le Lectier (D), Nouvelle Fulvie (D), Santa Claus (D), Vicar of Winkfield (C), Winter Nelis (D)*.

FRUITS UNDER GLASS.—Grapes (*as November*).

INDEX

INDEX

INDEX